Commercial Paper and Payment Law

DOUGLAS J. WHALEY

Moritz College of Law
The Ohio State University

Eighteenth Edition

Gilbert Law Summaries is a trademark registered in the U.S. Patent and Trademark Office

© 2006 by Barbri, a Thomson business
© 2013 LEG, Inc. d/b/a West Academic Publishing
© 2021 LEG, Inc. d/b/a West Academic
    444 Cedar Street, Suite 700
    St. Paul, MN 55101
    1-877-888-1330

West, West Academic Publishing, and West Academic are trademarks of West Publishing Corporation, used under license.

Printed in the United States of America

ISBN: 978-1-68467-872-3

Note to the Reader

The author and the editors of this Summary would much appreciate any feedback that readers can give us. If there are errors in the text or matters that are confusing and should be made clearer, etc., please send such comments or suggestions to support@westacademic.com.

Summary of Contents

Capsule Summary

I. INTRODUCTION TO COMMERCIAL PAPER

A. PURPOSES OF COMMERCIAL PAPER

1. The Credit Function

Some forms of commercial paper are used to obtain present credit that is to be repaid in the future (*e.g.*, promissory notes).

2. The Payment Function

Other paper (*e.g.*, check, draft) is used in lieu of money to pay obligations.

B. HISTORICAL DEVELOPMENT OF COMMERCIAL PAPER

1. The Law Merchant

"Law merchant" refers to the law as it is understood by merchants and traders. Originating prior to 1600, it is still an important source of authority in construing business practices ("usage of trade"). It has been incorporated into the U.C.C. and other statutes.

2. Statute of Anne (1704)

Prior to the Statute, English courts would enforce bills of exchange (drafts), but not promissory notes. The Statute gave promissory notes the same enforcement as that afforded bills of exchange and thus was the foundation of modern law regarding negotiable instruments.

3. Subsequent Statutes

a. Uniform Negotiable Instruments Law (1895)

N.I.L., modeled on the English Bill of Exchange Act of 1878, developed uniform rules for commercial paper and was adopted by every state.

b. Bank Collection Code (1929)

This Code was a similar model act, regarding bank collection procedures, but it was adopted by only 19 states.

4. Uniform Commercial Code

Begun in 1942, the U.C.C. was designed to replace most of the existing statutes governing commercial transactions. The U.C.C. has been adopted by all states except Louisiana, but even Louisiana has adopted Articles 3 and 4, which govern negotiable instruments. To account for advancements in electronic banking and to clear up problems with the original versions, Articles 3 and 4 were rewritten in 1990 and revised in 2002, though not many states have so far adopted this newer version.

C. TYPES OF COMMERCIAL PAPER

1. Notes

A promissory note is a written promise by a *maker* to pay money to a *payee*.

a. "Promise"

A "promise" is an *undertaking to pay* and thus must be more than a mere acknowledgment of a debt (*e.g.*, an I.O.U. is *not* a note).

b. **Certificates of Deposit**

A CD is a note, signed by a bank acknowledging receipt of money coupled with a duty to repay the debt. Courts disagree as to whether Article 3 (commercial paper) or Article 8 (securities) governs.

2. **Drafts** (Bills of Exchange)

A draft is an instrument in which the *drawer* (person who creates the instrument) orders a designated *drawee* to pay money to a third person (*payee*). Drafts (also called bills of exchange) must identify the drawee with reasonable certainty.

a. **Checks**

If the draft names a *bank as the drawee* (payor) and is payable *on demand*, it is called a check.

b. **Requirement of an "Order" to Pay**

More than mere authorization or a request to pay is necessary. The drawer must *order* the drawee to pay.

D. LAW PROTECTS HOLDERS IN DUE COURSE

1. **"Holder in Due Course"**

If the requirements for "negotiability" and "negotiation" are met, and if a bona fide purchaser pays value for the instrument, without notice of claims or defenses to it, that purchaser becomes a holder in due course ("HDC").

2. **Special Status of HDC**

An HDC is *immune from most defenses* of prior parties who are liable on the instrument; *i.e.*, prior parties must pay the HDC. Non-HDCs take an instrument subject to *all* valid claims and defenses.

II. NEGOTIABILITY

A. SIGNIFICANCE OF "NEGOTIABILITY"

If an instrument is not negotiable, it is a mere contract (subject to the claims and defenses of prior parties), and HDC status is impossible.

B. REQUIREMENTS FOR NEGOTIABILITY

To be negotiable, an instrument must meet the following requirements:

1. **Written Instrument**

A negotiable instrument must be in writing; however, the writing need *not* be on paper.

2. **Signature of Maker or Drawer**

Any mark or symbol made by the maker or drawer with the *intent to authenticate* the writing is sufficient.

a. **Signature by Agent or with Assumed or Trade Name**

A signature by an authorized agent will bind the maker or drawer, as will a signature under an assumed or trade name.

b. **Unauthorized or Forged Signatures**

Unauthorized signatures will not bind the purported maker, absent ratification or estoppel, but *will* bind the actual signer.

c. **Burden of Establishing Signatures**

In most cases, a rebuttable presumption exists that the signature is valid. A defendant must specifically plead invalidity, whereupon the plaintiff must prove that the signature is valid. The defendant must then produce evidence of forgery, etc., or the plaintiff will recover.

d. **Location of Signature**

The signature may be placed *any place* on the instrument as long as it is intended to authenticate the writing.

3. **Unconditional Promise or Order to Pay**

A promissory note must contain an unconditional promise and a draft must contain an unconditional order. The purchaser must be able to determine the terms and conditions from the four corners of the instrument.

a. **Implied Conditions**

Implied or constructive conditions *are* permissible. However, *express* conditions make an instrument nonnegotiable.

b. **Reference to Other Agreements**

Mere reference to a separate agreement between the same parties (*e.g.,* "this note arises out of a contract between A and B") does *not* impair negotiability.

c. **Descriptions of Consideration**

A description of collateral or of other transactions connected with the instrument is not a condition; therefore, negotiability is *not* destroyed.

d. **Incorporation of Separate Document**

Mere reference to or description of separate documents is permissible but their *incorporation destroys negotiability*. However, "as per" or "in accordance with" language is allowable, as are separate terms for prepayment or acceleration. Reference to another document is also permissible concerning rights to collateral.

e. **Statement of Security**

A *description* (but not incorporation) of the collateral and security agreement does *not* affect negotiability.

4. **Fixed Amount of Money**

a. **What Constitutes "Money"**

Money is "the medium of exchange authorized or adopted by a domestic *or foreign* government as part of its currency."

b. **What Constitutes a "Fixed Amount"**

Absolute certainty as to the sum due at all times is not required. However, at any particular time, the amount due must be ascertainable by *mathematical computation*. Interest rates can be fixed, variable, or based on an outside source, such as a particular bank's prime rate or the local judgment rate.

5. **Specified Time of Payment**

The face of the instrument must show when (or upon what events) the obligation is due.

a. **Demand Instruments**

An instrument is payable "on demand" if so expressed, or *if no time for payment* is stated.

b. **Time Instruments**

An instrument *payable at a definite time* in the future is a time instrument.

(1) **Date Left Off**

If the date is left off an instrument and maturity depends on a date being stated, the instrument is not enforceable *until the date is filled in* by someone with authority.

(2) **Acceleration Clauses**

Either the maker *or* the holder may be given the unconditional right to accelerate the maturity date. However, the holder must have a *good faith belief* that the prospect of payment is impaired in order to accelerate "at will."

(3) **Extension Clauses**

Extension of the maturity date at the *option of the holder* is valid. However, extension at the *option of the maker* or upon the *happening of an event* is permissible only if the new maturity date is stated in the instrument.

c. **Impact of Dates**

Undated instruments are payable at any time, on demand, while antedated or postdated instruments are payable on or after the date stated.

6. **Words of Negotiability**

An instrument must be payable either *"to bearer"* (bearer instrument) or *"to order of"* a specified payee (order instrument).

a. **Effect of Omitting Words of Negotiability**

If an instrument is not payable to order or bearer, it is *nonnegotiable*. However, Article 3 of the U.C.C. still governs the rights and liabilities of the involved parties, but no one can be an HDC. (*Note:* Words of negotiability are *not* required for checks).

7. **"No Other Promise" Requirement**

With the exception of *promises affecting security* (*e.g.*, regarding confession of judgments or maintenance of collateral, waiving laws benefiting bound parties, and the like), the instrument may not contain any other undertaking or instruction by the person promising or demanding payment to do any act in addition to the payment of money.

C. **AMBIGUITIES IN INSTRUMENTS**

1. **Rules of Construction**

a. **Words vs. Figures**

A sum denoted by *words controls* over a sum expressed in figures.

b. **Handwriting vs. Typing or Printing**

Where there are ambiguities, *handwritten provisions prevail* over typed or printed terms. Typed terms prevail over printed terms.

2. Descriptions of Payee

An instrument made payable to an agent is treated as being payable to the *principal*. If it is payable to an entity (*e.g.*, partnership), it is considered payable to the current *representatives* thereof.

3. Omission of Interest Rate

If an instrument is payable "with interest," but no rate is stated, the state's statutory "judgment rate" is applied.

III. NEGOTIATION

A. DEFINITION OF KEY TERMS

1. "Negotiation"

"Negotiation" is the process by which an instrument is transferred by a person other than the issuer to another who qualifies as a "holder."

2. "Holder"

"Holder" means that the person in current possession is either the original payee or has taken the instrument thereafter pursuant to a valid negotiation.

3. "Issue"

An "issue" is the *first* delivery of an instrument by the maker or drawer to a holder or remitter (*i.e.*, a person who makes payment using an instrument).

4. "Transfer"

A "transfer" is a delivery by a person other than the issuer for the purpose of giving one the right to enforce the instrument.

5. "Person Entitled to Enforce"

Article 3 gives a person rights to enforce an instrument only if the person qualifies as a "person entitled to enforce the instrument," which includes the holder and certain other persons. Anyone in possession of bearer paper qualifies as its holder. Order paper must be indorsed and transferred before another may become a holder of it.

B. NEGOTIATION PROCESS

1. Bearer Instruments

Bearer paper is negotiated simply by *delivery* because possession qualifies a transferee as a holder.

2. Order Instruments

Delivery of an order instrument to the *named payee* is sufficient for negotiation. Further negotiation requires a *valid indorsement* and *delivery* to the transferee. Unauthorized indorsements of required signatures (*i.e.*, of the payee or special indorsees) prevent negotiation and subsequent transferees do not become holders.

a. Multiple Payees

An instrument made payable to multiple payees whose names are connected by an "and" is payable *jointly* and *all* payees must indorse. If the names are connected by "or" or "and/or," the instrument is payable alternatively and an indorsement by *one* of the payees is a negotiation.

b. **Location of Indorsement**

An indorsement must be written on the instrument (usually on the reverse side) or on an allonge (*i.e.*, a separate paper firmly attached to the instrument).

c. **Effect of Delivery Without Indorsement**

Transfer of an instrument without the necessary indorsement does not constitute a negotiation, and the transferee does not become a holder (except where a bank takes a check for collection).

(1) Indorsement Later Obtained

If an indorsement is later obtained, the transferee becomes a holder.

d. **Indorsement of Partial Interests**

An indorsement must convey the *entire instrument*; if it attempts to convey less than the whole, it is not a negotiation.

3. **Special or Blank Indorsements**

a. **Special Indorsements**

If the payee of order paper names a *new* payee when indorsing, there is a "special" indorsement. Any further negotiation requires the valid indorsement of the new payee.

(1) Forgery of Special Indorsee's Name

In such cases, no one can be a holder following the forgery because the indorsement was not valid.

(2) Words of Negotiability not Required

Words such as "pay to the order of" are *not* required in an indorsement.

b. **Blank Indorsements**

If the payee of an order instrument indorses and does not name a new payee, the instrument is converted to *bearer* paper. However, it can be converted back into order paper by writing a new payee above the last indorsement.

c. **Multiple Indorsements**

If the instrument has been indorsed several times, the *last valid indorsement controls* what is necessary for further negotiation.

4. **Other Types of Indorsements**

a. **Qualified Indorsements**

Adding the words "without recourse" is a qualified indorsement that limits indorser liability.

b. **Restrictive Indorsements**

Any other language added to an indorsement creates a restrictive indorsement (*e.g.*, "for deposit only").

c. **Anomalous Indorsement**

This is an indorsement by a person who is not a holder (*e.g.*, a surety).

5. **Common Problems with Indorsements**

   a. **Wrong or Misspelled Name**

   If an instrument is payable to a holder but the holder's name is not accurately reflected in the instrument (*e.g.*, a misspelling or a nickname is reflected), the payee may indorse in that name, in payee's own name, or in both names. However, a payor may require that both names be signed.

   b. **Ambiguities**

   Any ambiguity concerning the capacity in which a signature is made is usually resolved in favor of an indorsement; parol evidence to show otherwise is *not* admissible.

   (1) **Exception—"Usage of Trade"**

   Courts may note that a signature in the lower right hand corner of a promissory note, by "usage of trade," is a *maker's* signature rather than an indorser's name.

IV. HOLDERS IN DUE COURSE

A. CODE REQUIREMENTS FOR DUE COURSE HOLDING

An HDC is a *holder* who takes the instrument *for value*, in *good faith*, and *without notice* that it is overdue or has been dishonored or of claims or defenses against it.

1. **Holder**

   To be a holder, the transferee must have *possession pursuant to a valid negotiation*, free of forgeries of the names of the payee(s) and any special indorsees.

2. **Purchase for Value**

   A holder takes for "value" when taking in return for consideration, a lien, security, or a negotiable instrument.

   a. **Executory Promise Not "Value"**

   A promise to give value *in the future* is *not* enough for HDC status. *But note:* A holder can be a partial HDC if only part of the consideration is executory.

   b. **Antecedent Debt**

   The holder takes for value when taking the instrument as security for, or in payment of an antecedent debt.

   c. **Lien (Security Interest) on Instrument**

   To qualify as value, a lien on the instrument must be acquired *by agreement* (rather than by legal process).

   d. **Special Rules Where Holder Is a Bank**

   Merely crediting a depositor's account is *not* value. However, the bank becomes an HDC of a deposited instrument to the extent that it permits withdrawals against that instrument. A collecting bank gives value any time it has a *security interest* in the collected item.

   e. **Special Cases Where Purchaser Mere Successor to Prior Holder**

   In a few situations, a holder, even though having *paid* for an instrument, merely succeeds to the transferor's rights: by purchasing it at a *judicial sale*; by acquiring it in taking over an *estate*; or by purchasing it as part of a *bulk transaction*.

f. Federal Regulatory Agencies

Federal law gives holder status to federal regulatory agencies (*e.g.*, the FDIC) who take possession of negotiable instruments when they take over a failed financial institution.

3. Purchase in Good Faith

The purchaser must have demonstrated *"honesty in fact"* in her actions. This is a purely subjective test. There also is an objective test: The purchaser must observe *reasonable commercial standards of fair dealing*.

4. Without Notice

A holder must purchase an instrument without knowledge or reason to know that it is *overdue*, *dishonored*, or of any *defense* or *claim* against it. Whether a holder has notice is measured by the reasonable person (objective) test.

a. Without Notice That It Is Overdue

Notice that an instrument is overdue exists if the purchaser had knowledge (or reason to know) of *default* or *acceleration*, or took a demand instrument *after demand* was made or beyond a reasonable time after the instrument's issue. But notice of a default in payment of *interest* is not notice.

(1) Demand Instruments

Checks are overdue 90 days after their date. Other instruments are overdue after an "unreasonably long" time has passed.

b. Without Notice That It Has Been Dishonored

Notice that an instrument has been dishonored exists if the purchaser had knowledge (or reason to know) that the instrument was returned after presentment *without payment or acceptance* within the allotted time.

c. Without Notice of Defenses and Claims

(1) Time When Notice Received

Effective notice must be received by the purchaser in such a manner and time as to allow a *reasonable opportunity* to act upon it. The purchaser's good faith and notice are determined as of the time the purchaser acquires and gives *value* for the instrument as a holder.

(2) Imputed Notice—"Red Lights" Doctrine

Notice is imputed to the purchaser where the instrument bears "apparent evidence of forgery or alteration or is . . . otherwise so irregular or incomplete as to call into question its authenticity" (the "red lights" doctrine).

(3) Notice—"Closed Eyes" Doctrine

Although good faith does not require due care, a purchaser cannot ignore obvious problems ("closed eyes" doctrine).

(a) Limitation—"Close Connection" Doctrine

Many courts impute notice if the purchaser was closely connected to the transaction creating the instrument (*e.g.*, preparation of instrument, agency, continuous dealings with seller). Federal and state *consumer protection statutes* have adopted this doctrine.

(4) Notice of Breach of Fiduciary Duty

A transferee may not qualify as an HDC if the transferee takes the instrument from a fiduciary with knowledge that that fiduciary has breached his fiduciary duty (*e.g.*, used the instrument as security for a personal loan or to pay a personal debt).

(a) Claim of Represented Person

A transferee who has taken an instrument with notice of breach of a fiduciary duty must surrender the instrument or its proceeds to the person represented by the fiduciary.

(5) Waiver of Defenses by Contract

Contractual waiver of defenses clauses are permissible but are limited by the "good faith" and "without notice" requirements, and also by consumer protection statutes.

(6) Other Factors Affecting "Good Faith" and "Notice"

(a) Purchase at a Discount

The fact that an instrument was purchased at a discount does *not*, by itself, indicate a lack of good faith. However, HDC status may be denied where there is a very large discount coupled with other *suspicious circumstances*.

(b) Constructive Notice

The filing or recording of a document does *not* constitute notice. There must be *actual* notice.

(c) "Forgotten" Notice

The holder who has received notice may still be an HDC if the holder has forgotten the earlier information. Generally, this occurs only when the time lapse was long *and* the holder's good faith is obvious.

5. Time at Which HDC Status Determined

HDC status is determined at the later of when the instrument is *negotiated* to the holder and/or when the holder gives *value*.

B. PAYEES AS HOLDERS IN DUE COURSE

1. In Practice

Although the U.C.C. provides that a payee may be an HDC, generally a payee is so involved in the transaction that the payee will have notice of claims or defenses against the instrument.

2. U.C.C. Provisions

U.C.C. section 3–302 lists seven situations where it may be possible for a payee to qualify as an HDC.

C. SUCCESSORS TO HOLDERS IN DUE COURSE

In certain circumstances, a transferee can acquire the *rights* of an HDC without actually qualifying as an HDC.

1. Shelter Rule

A basic rule of commercial law is that a transferee acquires *whatever rights the transferor had*. The transferee takes "shelter" in the transferor's status.

a. **Exceptions**

HDC rights are *not* transferred under the shelter rule where the holder was a *party to fraud or illegality* affecting the instrument ("washing through").

2. **HDC Rights and Remote Transferees**

All subsequent transferees from an HDC acquire the same HDC rights, *unless* those rights are cut off by a transferee who is disqualified from HDC status by a shelter rule exception.

D. **BURDEN OF PROOF AS TO HOLDING IN DUE COURSE**

1. **Burden of Establishing Defenses**

There exists a *presumption* that every holder is entitled to recover once he establishes the validity of the signatures and can *produce the instrument*. An HDC needs to prove HDC status only when a defendant establishes a defense that would be negated by HDC status. A few persons other than a holder may also have a right to enforce, *e.g.*, former holder of lost or destroyed instrument.

2. **Burden of Establishing Due Course Holding**

After it is shown a defense exists, a holder must prove HDC status by a preponderance of the total evidence or defeat the defense on the merits.

E. **STATUTORY EROSION OF HDC DOCTRINE**

1. **Background**

The original purpose of the HDC rule was to insulate lenders from disputes between the immediate parties to an instrument. However, this doctrine has given rise to dissatisfaction in consumer credit transactions where innocent customers were being victimized by unscrupulous sellers and lenders.

2. **State Consumer Protection Statutes**

Many states have enacted statutes that restrict the HDC rule where its application would allow unfairness in consumer financing transactions.

3. **Federal Regulation**

The lack of uniformity in state regulation in this area has led to federal regulation of unfair or deceptive trade practices in or affecting interstate commerce (FTC regulations).

V. **CLAIMS AND DEFENSES ON NEGOTIABLE INSTRUMENTS**

A. **INTRODUCTION**

1. **HDC vs. Non-HDC**

The legal effects arising from a transfer to an HDC differ substantially from those arising out of transfers to a non-HDC. An HDC may take free of claims and defenses whereas other transferees may be forced to litigate the claims and defenses of other parties.

2. **Basic Definitions**

a. **"Claim"**

A claim to a negotiable instrument is an *affirmative* cause of action for recovery on the instrument based on superior ownership rights of the claimant.

b. **"Defense"**

A defense is a ground for *refusing to pay* on an instrument. The few defenses good against an HDC are *real* defenses; personal defenses *cannot* be asserted against an HDC.

c. Claim in Recoupment

A claim in recoupment is the right of someone who owes a debt to subtract from the amount due damages arising from the *same* transaction for which the instrument was given. A claim in recoupment may be asserted against any non-HDC, but may be asserted against an HDC only if the claim is against the HDC.

B. REAL DEFENSES

Unlike personal defenses, real defenses are assertable against *both* HDC and non-HDC transferees, and are as follows.

1. Infancy

Infancy is a real defense if it would be a defense under *state contract law*; otherwise, it is merely a personal defense.

2. Incapacity to Contract

Incapacity to contract that renders a contract *void* (from its inception) under state law constitutes a real defense. However, a personal defense arises if the contract is only voidable.

3. Illegality

Illegality in the underlying transaction renders the obligation *void* and is a real defense; illegality is a personal defense if the obligation is merely voidable.

4. Duress

Duress (where one party acts involuntarily) can be either a real or personal defense, depending on the degree of duress.

5. Fraud in the Factum (Real Fraud)

Real fraud is a defense against an HDC and occurs where fraud has induced an obligor to sign an instrument with neither knowledge nor reasonable opportunity to learn of the instrument's character or essential terms.

a. Requirement of Excusable Ignorance

Real fraud is *not* assertable if the defendant failed to take reasonable steps to ascertain the nature of the transaction.

6. Discharge in Insolvency Proceedings

Insolvency includes an assignment for the benefit of creditors and any proceeding to liquidate or rehabilitate the estate of the involved person (*e.g.*, bankruptcy).

7. Discharge Known to HDC

Except for discharges in insolvency, discharge (*e.g.*, release) is a real defense only if the HDC had notice of the discharge when becoming an HDC. Mere public filing or recording does not constitute notice.

a. Cancellation of Liability

A holder may cancel the liability of a prior party by striking out that party's signature. Consideration is *not* necessary for a valid cancellation.

b. Agreement Not to Sue

An agreement that discharges liability on a simple contract will also discharge liability on a negotiable instrument and is assertable as a real defense if the HDC has notice.

c. Discharge Usually a Personal Defense

Unless an HDC *knows* of the discharge or the discharge is apparent from the face of the instrument (*e.g.*, line drawn through a name), it is a personal defense.

d. Caution—Certain Discharging Events Prevent HDC Status

Certain discharging events (*e.g.*, delay in presentment, *infra*) also give **notice** of problems with the instrument and will prevent "due course" holding.

8. Suretyship as a Real Defense

If an HDC *knew* prior to acquiring an instrument that some of the prior parties were sureties (accommodation parties), the HDC takes subject to the suretyship defenses (*infra*).

9. Alteration of Instrument

A change in the terms of an instrument (*e.g.*, thief alters amount) *may* be a partial real defense (*infra*).

10. Forgery

No subsequent taker can be an HDC if a **name necessary to proper negotiation** (*i.e.*, payee or any special indorsee) is forged. Forgery of any other name (maker, drawer, etc.) does *not* affect HDC status, but the person whose name was forged has a real defense absent ratification or estoppel.

C. CLAIMS AGAINST NEGOTIABLE INSTRUMENTS

1. Non-HDC Subject to Valid Claims

Unless a transferee is an HDC or has HDC rights under the "shelter" rule, the instrument is taken subject to all valid claims.

2. What Constitutes a Valid Claim

A claim is an affirmative right to a negotiable instrument because of *superior ownership*.

D. PERSONAL DEFENSES

1. Definition

Personal defenses are assertable only against non-HDCs. Such defenses consist of all defenses, including contract, other than real defenses.

2. Common Examples of Personal Defenses

a. Consideration and Negotiable Instruments

Although a negotiable instrument must be supported by sufficient consideration, consideration technically is not a prerequisite to negotiability. However, its absence may be a *partial or complete* defense against a non-HDC. Defendant has the burden of proof.

b. Claims or Defenses of Another ("Jus Tertii")

Usually, a party must rely on her *own* defenses and cannot use the claims and defenses of third parties unless the third party joins the suit.

(1) Exceptions

There are two exceptions to this rule: theft and violation of a restrictive indorsement. In both these situations, the person making payment is exposed to the possibility of *double* payment if unable to raise third-party rights.

VI. LIABILITY OF THE PARTIES

A. INTRODUCTION

When a dispute arises involving commercial paper, one must determine whether the instrument is technically *negotiable* and thus within the scope of Article 3. Also, one must determine whether a party is an HDC and the manner in which relevant *claims or defenses* are thereby affected.

B. SUITS ON THE UNDERLYING OBLIGATION—THE MERGER RULE

The obligation underlying the issuance of an instrument is *merged* into that instrument and is not available as a cause of action *unless the parties have agreed otherwise*.

1. Suspension of Underlying Obligation

If a negotiable instrument is accepted as a conditional payment for the underlying obligation, that obligation cannot support a cause of action until the instrument is *presented for payment and dishonored*.

a. Partial Payment

If the instrument is only partial payment, the obligation is suspended "pro tanto" (*i.e.*, by that much).

b. Choices Available to Holder upon Dishonor

If the instrument is dishonored, the holder may sue on the instrument, on the underlying obligation, or both, but only *one* recovery is permitted.

c. Discharge of Instrument

If liability on the instrument is discharged in any way, the obligation is also discharged (because of merger).

2. Cancellation of Underlying Obligation

The obligation is canceled when the party primarily liable on the instrument is a *bank* (*e.g.*, cashier's or certified check), as long as the person who owed the obligation is not liable *on* the instrument.

C. CONTRACT SUITS—SUITS "ON THE INSTRUMENT"

1. Commercial Paper "Contracts"—in General

Under Article 3, merely by signing a negotiable instrument, a person assumes certain obligations.

a. Procedural Rights

Some parties who may be liable on an instrument because their names appear on it are entitled to the procedural rights of presentment or notice of dishonor (*see infra*).

2. "Obligation" of a Maker

The maker's obligation is a promise to pay the note according to its terms at the time of signature. A maker generally has no procedural rights (except in limited circumstances).

a. Incomplete Instruments

If a maker signs a note with blanks or spaces, the maker is bound by the *subsequently filled-in* terms.

b. Co-Makers

If two or more persons sign as co-makers, they are *jointly and severally liable*. A co-maker who pays the full amount has a right of *contribution* from the other co-makers.

3. "Obligation" of an Indorser

An indorser becomes a type of surety for all prior parties and promises to pay any later holder. This promise is *conditioned* on the indorser *first* being accorded the procedural rights of *presentment and notice of dishonor*.

a. Indorsement "Without Recourse"

An indorser may avoid the above obligation by adding "without recourse" to the signature. This is a *qualified* indorsement and transfers the instrument without incurring liability.

b. Indorsement of Bearer Instruments

Bearer paper does not need an indorsement to be negotiable; however, a transferee may insist on an unqualified indorsement in order to acquire the transferor's indorser's liability.

c. Multiple Indorsers

The common law presumes that when one person indorses after another, the later indorser can recover in full from the prior indorser, but the U.C.C. changes this rule between joint payees, two or more anomalous indorsers, and co-makers. Such parties are liable *to each other* only for their *proportionate share*.

(1) Reacquisition and Cancellation

If a *prior indorser* reacquires an instrument, he may cancel indorsements made between the time he formerly held the instrument and the present, thus discharging those indorsers from liability to *any subsequent holder*, including HDCs. *Intervening indorsers* are *automatically* discharged from liability to the reacquirer upon reacquisition.

4. "Obligation" of a Surety

A surety's obligations are construed strictly in favor of the surety. In addition to U.C.C. rights, a surety has state and common law rights.

a. Common Law Rights

Under the common law, a surety has the rights of *exoneration, subrogation, reimbursement,* and *contribution*.

b. U.C.C rights

(1) In General

(a) Terminology

A surety is an *"accommodation"* party; a principal is the *"accommodated"* party. A surety who adds words of guarantee to the signature is a surety and a *guarantor*.

(b) Obligation of Accommodation Party

Accommodation makers and accommodation indorsers incur the same obligation as makers or indorsers, respectively, and thus have the same rights as makers or indorsers *plus* special surety rights.

(c) Proof of Surety Status

Oral proof of the accommodation nature of a surety's signature is permissible, except as to an HDC without notice of surety status. If an indorsement appears *outside the usual chain of title* (called an *anomalous indorsement*), every subsequent taker is presumed to know that it was a surety's signature.

(2) Surety Not Liable to Principal

A surety is not liable to the accommodated party, regardless of the order of the signatures.

(3) Tender of Payment Rule

If a *surety (or indorser)* tenders payment at maturity and is refused, the surety is still liable for the full amount but is *not* liable for any subsequent amounts (interest, etc.). If tender is made by the *principal*, the surety (or indorser) is *completely discharged*.

(4) Impairment of Collateral

If holder "impairs" the collateral for an instrument by failing to take reasonable care, nonconsenting sureties are discharged up to the amount of the impairment. *Failure to perfect a security interest* is an impairment.

(5) Agreements Between Creditor and Principal

When a holder fails to collect payment at maturity, a surety is *not* discharged. However, where a holder and principal *agree* to extend or suspend the time of payment, a nonconsenting surety is discharged to the extent of the *harm* caused by the extension.

(a) Agreements Not to Sue

A holder's agreement not to sue the principal does *not discharge* nonconsenting sureties.

(b) Agreements to Modify the Terms

Such agreements discharge nonconsenting sureties up to the amount of harm caused by the modification.

(c) Consent by Surety

If the surety consents to an extension (suspension agreement), the surety is not discharged. Consent may be *implied* from the circumstances or *express* in the terms of the original instrument.

(d) New Notes

If a new note is issued, a surety is discharged to the extent of the harm caused.

(6) Obligation of Guarantor of Collection

If a surety adds words to the signature *guaranteeing collection*, the holder must first attempt all steps necessary to obtain payment from the master or acceptor or show that such attempts would be useless. If a surety signs merely as a "guarantor," without clearly indicating that a guaranty of collection is intended, the surety is liable in the capacity in which the surety signed and cannot require the holder to first attempt to collect from the maker or acceptor.

c. **Notice to Cosigner**

Under the federal Credit Practices Rule regarding consumer credit, a cosigner (*i.e.*, a surety) must be warned of liability by a separate instrument prior to becoming obligated.

5. **"Obligation" of a Drawer**

A drawer's obligation is similar to that of an indorser. A drawer can *eliminate* liability by adding *"without recourse"* to her signature.

6. **Presentment and Notice of Dishonor—Technical Procedural Rights**

a. **Presentment**

Presentment is a demand for payment or acceptance made by the *holder* of an instrument to the *maker* (promissory notes) or the *drawee* (drafts).

(1) **Rights of Presentee (Maker or Drawee)**

When presentment is made, a maker or drawee may demand: (i) exhibition of the instrument; (ii) identification; (iii) evidence of presenter's authority; (iv) reasonable time and place; (v) a receipt; and (vi) surrender of the instrument. Failure to comply with these demands allows the presentee to refuse to pay without dishonor.

b. **Dishonor**

Dishonor occurs when a maker or drawee returns an instrument after presentment without paying or accepting within the allowed time.

(1) **Time Allowed for Decision Regarding Checks and Drafts**

If a check or draft is presented *across the counter*, it must be paid or returned that day. If it is presented through *bank collection channels*, the drawee bank has until its *midnight deadline*—midnight of the banking day following the banking day of receipt (deferred posting).

(a) **"Banking Day"**

A "banking day" is that part of the day in which a bank is open to the public for carrying on *nearly all* banking functions. However, a bank may establish a cutoff hour and treat items received after that time as received on the *next* banking day.

c. **Notice of Dishonor**

A notice of dishonor may be given to anyone liable on the instrument, and it operates for the benefit of *all* parties with rights on the instrument against the notified party. Notice may be oral and given in any reasonable manner.

(1) **Time for Giving Notice**

A *bank* must give notice before its midnight deadline (*supra*); nonbanks have 30 days in which to give notice of dishonor.

d. **Protest**

A protest is a certificate stating that a dishonor has occurred. It must identify the instrument and be sealed by a U.S. consul, notary, or some other authorized person.

(1) **When Used**

Protest is never required, but it is used because it is presumptive evidence of dishonor and notice.

e. **Necessity for Presentment and Notice of Dishonor**

   (1) Indorser's Liability

   Presentment and notice of dishonor are necessary (unless excused) to bind indorsers. An indorser incurs no liability if these requirements are not properly accomplished.

   (2) Drawer's Liability

   Generally, a drawer is not entitled to notice of dishonor. But if presentment of a check occurs more than 30 days after the date of the check and the *drawee* becomes insolvent during the delay, the drawer has no liability upon assignment of rights against the drawee to the holder.

   (a) Stale Checks

   A noncertified check presented more than six months after its date is "stale," and payment is subject to a *good faith* limitation.

f. **Situations Excusing Technical Procedures**

   (1) Delay in Compliance Excused

   The U.C.C. excuses delay in compliance with the technical procedures whenever such delay is caused by circumstances beyond the party's (bank's and other's) control, and *reasonable diligence* is used to comply after the problem ceases (banks must use reasonable diligence to avoid the problem).

   (2) Compliance Excused Completely

   Compliance is completely excused by *waiver* (written or implied), *unavailability of a primary party, impossibility,* or *"futility"* (anticipatory repudiation, prior dishonor, countermanded payment).

7. **"Obligation" of a Drawee or Acceptor**

   A drawee has *no* U.C.C. contractual liability merely by being named as such by a drawer.

   a. **Signature Rule**

   No person is liable on an instrument unless her signature appears thereon. A drawee's name on an instrument (*e.g.,* your bank's name on your checks) is *not a signature*.

   b. **"No Assignment" Rule**

   The issuance of a check or draft does *not* create an immediate assignment of the drawer's funds in the possession of the drawee (if the rule were otherwise, the holder could sue the drawee under regular contract rules).

   c. **Liability Outside U.C.C.**

   However, a drawee may be liable to the payee in *tort* (*e.g.,* negligence, fraud) or in *contract* (*i.e.,* special agreements with drawer).

   d. **Obligation of the Acceptor**

   An acceptor is a drawee who by signing an instrument agrees to honor it.

   (1) Purpose of Acceptance

   Once an instrument contains the obligation of the acceptor, it has greater commercial worth and is more easily sold. Therefore, parties frequently make a *presentment for acceptance* (*e.g.,* have the bank certify a personal check) with a subsequent presentment for payment.

(2) Characteristics of Acceptor's Obligation

The acceptor has the same liability as a maker (primary)—*i.e.*, acceptor promises to pay the instrument according to its terms at the time of acceptance. When sued on the obligation, an acceptor may raise all available defenses (***exception for certified checks***).

(3) Acceptance Varying Draft

Acceptance conditioned on alteration of the draft's terms can be treated as a dishonor. If the presenter agrees to the drawee's conditional acceptance, all prior nonconsenting parties are discharged. *Note:* ***Domiciling*** (*i.e.*, naming a place for presentment for payment) the draft is ***not*** a change in terms.

(4) Check Certification

If a bank certifies a check, it is ***primarily liable*** as an acceptor and the drawer may not stop payment. Certification discharges the drawer and indorsers, no matter who procures certification.

8. Liability of an Agent

A negotiable instrument may be signed by an agent on behalf of the principal. An agent's authority is determined by the common law rules of agency (no formalities required).

a. Unauthorized Signatures

An unauthorized signature does not bind the person whose name was signed, but does bind the actual signer. A principal can ***ratify*** an unauthorized signature, thereby becoming liable on the instrument. However, the actual signer is still liable to the person whose name was forged.

b. Personal Liability of Agent

An ambiguous signature binds the agent as an ***indorser***. To escape liability against all persons, an agent must (i) name the principal ***and*** (ii) indicate that the agent's signature is made only in a representative capacity. If an agent fails to comply with one of the requirements, no liability accrues as long as an HDC does not hold the instrument. Further, no liability is imposed on an agent who signed a check without noting representative status ***if*** the principal's name is printed on the check.

c. Unidentified Principal

If an agent signs an instrument with authority from and on behalf of a principal, the principal is liable on the instrument even if the principal is not named in the instrument.

D. WARRANTY SUITS

1. Introduction

Warranty suits involving a negotiable instrument arise ***off*** the instrument and are based on ***property rights***. Intentions of the parties are not relevant. Moreover, plaintiff need not be a "holder," as in contract suits (*supra*).

2. Stages in Life of a Negotiable Instrument

Separate warranties exist at different stages in the life of an instrument (*i.e.*, issuance, transfer, and presentment).

3. No Warranties on Issuance

No implied warranties are created by the issuance of a negotiable instrument.

4. **Warranties on Transfer**

Any movement of an instrument *other than* an issuance or presentment is a transfer. The transfer warranties are as follows:

a. **Person Entitled to Enforce Instrument**

This warranty means that the transferor has taken the instrument pursuant to a valid negotiation.

b. **Valid Signatures**

This warranty guarantees that *all* signatures are authentic and authorized. It applies even to bearer paper.

c. **No Alterations**

This warrants against any change in the terms of the instrument.

d. **No Defenses Good Against Transferor**

The transferor warrants that there are no legal defenses or claims in recoupment good against the transferor.

e. **No Knowledge of Insolvency Proceedings**

The transferor warrants that he has *no knowledge* of any insolvency proceeding by or against the party from whom payment is expected. This is *not* a warranty that no such proceedings exist.

f. **Warranties Depend on Consideration**

Warranties are dependent on receipt of *consideration*, and run to an immediate transferee.

g. **Parties to Whom Warranties Extend**

The U.C.C. is unclear concerning whether *later* transferees may sue for breach of warranty: Article 3 permits suit if the transferor *indorses* the instrument; Article 4 protects all *collecting banks* (regardless of indorsement).

5. **Warranties on Presentment**

The warranties made on presentment for acceptance or payment are *narrower* than transfer warranties, due to the *Price v. Neal* doctrine.

a. **Doctrine of *Price v. Neal***

As between an innocent holder and drawee, the *drawee* must bear the loss. Once *final payment* has occurred, this doctrine provides that the drawee (or maker of a promissory note) cannot undo the transaction and recover money paid unless a presentment warranty was breached or the payee was not acting in good faith.

b. **Same Presentment Warranties in Articles 3 and 4**

Articles 3 and 4 include the same presentment warranties as listed below.

(1) **Person Entitled to Enforce Instrument**

Again, this is a warranty of valid negotiation; a warranty that no payee's or special indorsee's signature is forged. No presentment warranty is breached where a drawer's or maker's signature is forged.

(2) **No Alterations**

This warranty—that there are no alterations—is not given to makers of notes or acceptors of drafts.

(3) No Knowledge That Drawer/Maker's Signature Unauthorized

This is **not** a warranty that the signature is genuine; it merely warrants **no knowledge** of unauthorized signature.

(4) Persons Who Make Presentment Warranties

Warranties are made by anyone who **transfers** the instrument or receives payment or acceptance. Thus, the payor can sue anyone in the chain.

6. Notice Requirement

Notice of breach of warranty of transfer or on presentment must be given to the warrantor **within 30 days** after the claimant has reason to know of the breach. Failure to give notice discharges the warrantor to the extent of the discharge.

7. Statute of Limitations

The limitations period for warranty claims is **three years** after accrual of a cause of action.

8. Damages for Breach of Warranty

The U.C.C. allows recovery for breaches of its warranties, not to exceed the amount of the instrument plus expenses and lost interest.

9. Remotely Created Consumer Items

To address problems with remotely created consumer items—checks drawn on a consumer account, created by the payee and not bearing the handwritten signature of the drawer (preauthorized drafts or telechecks)—the 2002 revision of Articles 3 and 4 created new transfer and presentment warranties that the purported drawer of the check really did authorize the issuance of the check. If the drawer did not do so, these warranties allow banks to **pass the liability back** to the telemarketers or their own banks.

E. CONVERSION

1. Definition

At common law, conversion is the unauthorized assumption of ownership rights over the personal property of another. Good faith is no defense to conversion.

2. Common Law Preserved

The U.C.C. preserves the common law of conversion so that any wrongful taking of a negotiable instrument would be conversion.

3. Restrictive Indorsements

The U.C.C. severely restricts lawsuits that may be brought for violation of a restrictive indorsement. **Restrictions on transfers** do **not** prohibit further transfers. Similarly, **conditional indorsements** bind the original parties only, not later parties. **"For Deposit Only"** indorsements mean that the depositary bank must be the next indorser; otherwise conversion has occurred. Only the **first bank** to handle the instrument is liable; later banks are excused from conversion liability.

4. Forged or Missing Indorsements

A transfer constitutes a conversion **whenever** there is a forgery of a necessary indorsement or a necessary indorsement is missing. Note that a payee cannot sue in conversion unless the payee received **delivery** of the instrument directly or through an agent or co-payee.

5. **Damages in Conversion Suits**

Under the original Article 3, in a suit for conversion against a *drawee*, there is a *conclusive presumption* that the damages are equal to the face amount of the instrument. Under the Revision, the presumption is not conclusive and damages are limited to the plaintiff's interest.

VII. BANK DEPOSITS AND COLLECTIONS

A. INTRODUCTION

Article 4 modifies Article 3 where negotiable instruments (especially checks) enter the bank collection process. In cases of conflict, *Article 4 controls*. The basic parts of Article 4 are the rules concerning the relationship between banks and customers, and the rules governing check collection processes among banks.

B. RELATIONSHIP BETWEEN BANKS AND DEPOSITORS

1. **Wrongful Dishonor**

When an item is properly payable from the drawer's account but the bank wrongfully refuses to honor it, the drawer, and *only* the drawer, may sue.

   a. **Damages for Wrongful Dishonor**

   Damages must be *proximately caused* by the wrongful dishonor (but may include consequential damages for arrest and prosecution). Injured drawers must prove actual damages to recover. Noncompensatory damages are only awarded for outrageous conduct by the bank.

2. **Death or Incompetence of Customer**

Collection or payment by a bank prior to knowledge of customer's death or incompetency is *valid*. Upon *actual* knowledge of the event, a bank may elect to pay or certify checks for 10 days following a death unless an interested party stops payment. Most banks will freeze an account because of state tax laws.

3. **Requirement That Item Be "Properly Payable"**

If an item is not "properly payable," the bank usually must recredit the customer's account if a timely complaint is made.

   a. **Overdrafts**

   If payment of an item would overdraw a customer's account, the bank has the option to pay or not pay.

   b. **Altered and Completed Items**

   An altered item (*e.g.*, the amount changed) may be charged to the customer's account only as to its *original* terms. If the customer's negligence led to alteration, the bank has the option of paying as altered. Where a customer leaves blanks that are later *completed*, the item may be charged as drawn.

   c. **Contract of Deposit**

   A contract of deposit (between customer and bank) cannot waive bank liability for bad faith or failure to exercise ordinary care, nor can it disclaim the provisions of Article 4.

   d. **Proper Presenter**

   A bank may charge its customer's account only if it pays a "person entitled to enforce the instrument" (usually a "holder")—*e.g.*, a person to whom the instrument has been negotiated.

e. **Postdated Checks**

A postdated check may be paid *unless* the customer gives the bank *notice* of the postdating.

f. **Stop Payment Orders**

Items subject to a "stop payment" order are not "properly payable." Exceptions are bank obligations (*e.g.*, cashier's or certified checks), which remain "properly payable."

(1) **Requirements**

A customer must give *oral or written notice*, which *reasonably identifies* the item, in time to allow a bank *reasonable opportunity* to act. A *customer* must prove that the *loss* occurred and the amount of the loss.

g. **Right of Subrogation**

If a bank pays an item not "properly payable," the bank is subrogated to ("steps into the shoes of") any person connected with the item to the extent necessary to prevent *unjust enrichment*.

4. **Right of Setoff for Bank**

A bank can set off a customer's debts to the bank against a *general* checking or savings account, *without notice*. However, *no setoff* is permitted for *credit card* debts or after *final payment* has been made.

5. **Customer's Duty to Examine Bank Statements**

A customer's failure to use reasonable and prompt care in examining bank statements can validate improper payment by his bank.

C. **BANK COLLECTION PROCEDURES**

1. **Deposit Availability Under Federal Law**

The Expedited Funds Availability Act regulates how quickly a customer can draw against funds she has deposited in her account.

a. **Government and Bank Checks**

Funds from such checks must be made available on the *next business day*. The same time period applies to checks drawn on the same bank in which deposited, cashier's checks, certified checks, teller's checks, or similar bank-generated checks, and to wire transfers.

b. **The $100 Availability Rule**

For checks other than those above, the customer may withdraw $100 on the business day following the business day of deposit.

c. **Local Checks**

Local checks are those drawn on banks in the same geographical area served by the Federal Reserve check processing center. Such funds must be available for *withdrawal by check* (payable to a third party) no later than two business days after deposit. A customer can withdraw $100 *cash* after one business day and $400 more by 5 p.m. on the second business day after deposit.

d. Nonlocal Checks

For nonlocal checks, funds must be available for *withdrawal by check* no later than five business days after deposit. On that same day, a customer may withdraw $400 *cash* before 5 p.m., and the rest of the cash at the opening of the next business day.

e. ATM Deposits

The above rules apply to deposits made at an Automatic Teller Machine ("ATM") owned or controlled by the depositary bank, except items requiring next-day availability are given an extra day. Deposits made at "nonproprietary ATMs" must be available no later than two business days for local checks and five business days for nonlocal checks.

f. Safeguard Exceptions

Congress has established some safeguards for banks in specific areas, *e.g.*, new accounts, large checks, repeated overdrafts, emergency conditions.

g. Civil Liability

Banks that fail to follow these statutory rules are subject to actual and punitive damages in suits by injured customers.

2. Deposit Availability Under the U.C.C.

Article 4 of the U.C.C. regulates fund availability in cases where the federal act has failed to do so (*e.g.*, check deposited in first 30 days after account opened).

a. Money

If cash is deposited, the customer may draw against it on the *next banking day*.

b. Checks

If a check is deposited, the length of time depends on the collection process.

(1) Where Depositary Bank Is Also Payor Bank

If the check drawer and the payee have accounts in the same bank, the payee may withdraw against the check at the opening of the *second* banking day after the day of deposit (unless check is dishonored). *Note:* Federal regulations (*supra*) may require next business day availability.

(2) All Other Situations—"Final Settlement" Rule

A depositary bank must be allowed sufficient time for a check to go to the payor bank and (if dishonored) to come back, before allowing its depositor to withdraw against the check. If payor bank does not dishonor the check by its *midnight deadline* (*supra*), *final payment* occurs.

(a) "Final Settlement"

At the moment of final payment, bookkeeping entries (concerning the check) of all collecting banks firm up and become "final settlements." Dishonor is no longer possible, and after a reasonable time, the item is considered paid and withdrawal allowed.

(3) Right of "Charge Back"

Prior to final settlement, a depositary bank (or any collecting bank) that learns payment will not be made on a check may "charge back" (reverse) any provisional settlement given its customer on the item. "Charge back" is permitted even if the customer has been allowed to draw against the check; customer *must repay* the money.

(a) Failure to Use Ordinary Care

Failure by a collecting bank to use ordinary care makes that bank liable for the amount of the item, but the bank is not liable for *consequential* damages unless it acted in *bad faith*. However, negligence does *not* destroy a bank's right of charge back.

(b) Effect of Final Settlement

The right of a depositary bank to charge back an uncollected check expires at the moment of final settlement.

3. Final Payment

Final payment occurs at the moment the payor bank becomes *accountable* for the amount. The basic rules for determining this precise moment are as follows:

a. Payment in Cash

Once a payor bank hands over money, final payment occurs and no dishonor is possible.

b. Settlement

Final payment occurs when a bank settles an item and has no right to revoke the settlement.

c. Failure to Revoke Provisional Settlement

Final payment automatically occurs if the payor bank does not revoke a provisional settlement by its *midnight deadline*. Federal regulations permit banks to miss the midnight deadline in two limited exceptions involving transportation.

d. Legal Effect of "Final Payment"

Upon final payment (or certification) under any of the above methods, the bank is accountable for the item; the bank *cannot avoid payment* by applying the "four legals." The bank must pay except where there has been *bad faith by the presenter* or a *breach of presentment warranties*.

4. Check Encoding

When a check is deposited for collection, it is magnetically encoded with special *"magnetic ink character recognition"* symbols so that it can be read by automatic check processing machinery. There is a *warranty* that the check has been properly encoded.

5. Check Retention

In check truncation systems, the depositary bank copies the check, destroys it, and passes on through the bank collection process a *description* of the check. There is a *warranty* that the check truncation agreement terms have been complied with.

6. Check Collection in the 21st Century

Banks have a right (not duty) under Check 21 to create *images* of checks and pass them on to receiving banks as electronic computer files. If the receiving bank does not accept images, the *truncating bank* (*i.e.,* bank that preserves the original check) or any bank that is passing the image can create a paper version of the check from the image (a *substitute check*). The bank that prints out the substitute check (*reconverting bank*) must add all of the necessary *indorsements*.

a. Legal Equivalence of Substitute Checks

Substitute checks are legally the same as the original as long as they include certain *mandatory language*. Thus, no one can refuse a substitute check, and the customer does not have a right to get the original back.

b. Warranties Under Check 21

Every party passing on an image/substitute check warrants that the check meets all of the requirements for legal equivalence and that there is no other substitute check floating around.

c. Expedited Recredit of Consumer Accounts

Subject to Check 21's *safeguard exceptions*, if a *consumer* disputes the validity of the charge to her account, the consumer may be entitled to an expedited recredit.

d. Lawsuits

Lawsuits under Check 21 may be brought up to *one year* after the transaction. If damages for a *warranty* breach are sought, banks may be held liable on a comparative negligence theory for the amount of the loss. If the claim is for *indemnity*, the measure of damages is the loss *up to the amount of the substitute check*.

VIII. FORGERY OR ALTERATION OF NEGOTIABLE INSTRUMENTS

A. COMMON LAW PRINCIPLES

Two basic common law rules may still affect the outcome of forgery suits:

1. Payment to Agent

Delivery to an *authorized* agent transfers risk to the payee and discharges the deliverer.

2. "No Damages" Defense

If, despite a forgery or alteration, the proper person received the proceeds, there has been no damage and usually no lawsuit may ensue.

B. VALIDATION OF FORGERY OR ALTERATION

A person whose signature is forged is *estopped* from raising the forgery issue in the following circumstances.

1. Impostor Rule

Carelessness of a drawer or maker in issuing an instrument may be effective to *pass good title* to later transferees.

a. Issuance to an Imposter

Issuance to an imposter will validate a forgery. An imposter need not communicate face to face with the drawer, nor is the *identity of the actual forger* relevant.

b. Issuance to Fictitious Payee or Payee Not Intended to Have Interest in Instrument

In this situation, a resulting forgery of the payee's name is *effective*. Validation also applies when an agent or employee furnishes the payee's name. An employer also is liable for all employee forgeries if the employee is entrusted with responsibility for the instrument.

c. **Effect of Negligence by Subsequent Parties**

The U.C.C. uses *comparative negligence* to allocate loss where subsequent parties neglect to use ordinary care in dealing with the forged instrument.

2. **Negligence Rule**

If a person fails to exercise ordinary care (*e.g.*, failure to guard signing device, leaving blanks, etc.) and that failure substantially contributes to an alteration or forgery, the person is precluded from asserting the alteration or forgery against a person who in good faith pays the instrument or takes it for value or for collection.

a. **Effect of Subsequent Negligence**

If more than one party was negligent, they must share liability according to their comparative negligence.

3. **Bank Statement Rule**

A customer has a duty to examine bank statements and canceled items for forgery or alteration. If the customer does not report a problem to the bank within a reasonable time, the customer is precluded from claiming that the item was not "properly payable" if such a delay caused the bank *further loss*.

a. **No Further Loss**

Where the bank has *only* its original loss from the improper payment, the customer *may* assert the forgery or alteration.

b. **"Repeated Offender" Rule**

When a customer does not report a problem within 30 days, the customer is estopped from demanding recredit on any other items forged or altered during the delay by the same wrongdoer and subsequently paid by the bank.

c. **Result Where Bank Is Also Negligent**

If a bank is negligent in paying an item (*e.g.*, obvious forgery), the above rules *do not apply*. The U.C.C. applies comparative negligence when both parties are negligent. However, if the bank did not pay in *good faith*, the customer wins even if the customer failed to report the statement's inaccuracies.

d. **Burden of Proof**

Each party has the burden of establishing lack of care by the other party. No matter who was negligent, all customer complaints must be made within *one year* after the statement was made available to the customer. If the customer timely complains and the bank fails to take appropriate action, the customer has *three years* to file suit.

e. **Banks Must Assert Section 4–406 Defenses**

A bank *must* raise *any* applicable defense (under the bank statement rule or some other rule, like the imposter rule) against its customer or lose its rights against prior parties (breach of warranty suits, etc.).

C. ALTERATION

1. **"Alteration" Defined**

An alteration occurs where a change in the terms of a negotiable instrument alters the instrument's *contract* in any way.

2. Fraudulent Alteration

If a *fraudulent* alteration occurs, all prior nonnegligent parties are discharged from liability on the instrument and on the underlying obligation (due to the merger rule).

a. Effect of Negligence

If the alteration was caused by the negligence of a party, that party is *not* discharged but is liable on the instrument as *altered*.

b. Discharge Is Personal Defense

Because discharge is a personal defense, the discharged parties are still liable as to the *original terms* if the instrument is transferred to an HDC.

c. Rights of Drawee Bank

A drawee or payor bank may charge an altered item against the drawer's account according to its *original terms*.

d. Incomplete Instruments

Where the alteration involves an unauthorized completion of an incomplete instrument, an HDC and a drawee/payor bank may enforce the item as it is *completed*.

e. Alteration of Certified Check

The U.C.C. makes the acceptor of a certified check liable to an HDC for the *altered amount* unless the certification states the amount certified.

D. LOST, DESTROYED, OR STOLEN INSTRUMENTS

1. General Rule

When an instrument is lost, destroyed, or stolen, its true owner may still sue upon it but first must prove ownership and explain the nonproduction of it.

2. Lost Cashier's, Teller's, or Certified Checks

Article 3 provides a special procedure when such checks are lost, but not all states have adopted these rules. The customer who lost the cashier's, teller's, or certified check must fill out a declaration of loss form. If the check is presented within 90 days after issuance or acceptance, the bank will pay the presenter; otherwise the bank will pay the customer who filled out the form.

IX. ELECTRONIC BANKING

A. ARTICLE 4A—FUNDS TRANSFERS

Most wire transfers in this country are carried out through the Federal Reserve Banks (the *Fedwire* system).

1. Scope of Article 4A

Article 4A governs fund transfers in which payment orders are given to move money from one bank account to another.

a. Terminology

(1) "Payment Order"

This is a direct, unconditional instruction—orally, electronically, or in writing—by a *"sender"* to a receiving bank to pay a fixed or determinable amount to a "beneficiary." The first sender is an *"originator."*

    (2) **"Beneficiary"**

    The *final recipient* of a payment order is the beneficiary.

    (3) **Bank Terminology**

    The first bank in the transfer process is the "originator's bank" and the last one is the "beneficiary's bank"; any other banks are "intermediary banks." The bank receiving a payment order is a "receiving bank."

b. Consumer Transaction Excluded

The Electronic Fund Transfers Act governs transfers into and out of consumer accounts; Article 4A is inapplicable.

2. Acceptance and Rejection of Payment Orders

Once a bank has *accepted* a payment order, it *must* pay the funds to the recipient of the order.

a. Acceptance

"Acceptance" is defined according to whether the bank making the acceptance is the beneficiary's bank.

(1) Acceptance by Other than Beneficiary's Bank

A receiving bank that is not the beneficiary's bank accepts a payment order when it *executes* it, *i.e.*, becomes a sender and passes it on to the next bank.

(2) Acceptance by Beneficiary's Bank

A beneficiary's bank accepts a payment order when it:

    (i) *Pays the beneficiary* or credits the beneficiary's account;

    (ii) *Notifies* the beneficiary that the funds are *available for withdrawal*;

    (iii) *Receives full payment from the sender*; or

    (iv) *Fails to reject* the payment order before expiration of requisite time periods.

    (a) **Payment Date**

    If the payment order states a payment date, acceptance cannot occur before that date, and credits to accounts before that date are subject to charge back and cancellation.

b. Rejection of Payment Orders

A receiving bank's announced intention not to accept a payment order must be contained within *notice* (given orally, electronically, or in writing) to the sender. A bank cannot reverse its decision to accept or reject.

c. Acceptance Not Required by U.C.C.

A receiving bank is not required to accept a payment order (absent a contract obligation to do so). If it proceeds to pay the funds before receiving them from the sender, the credit risk rests with the bank, not the beneficiary.

d. Effect of Acceptance

Once a payment order is accepted, the beneficiary must be paid by the beneficiary's bank by the *next business day*, unless a later payment date is stated in the order (*see supra*).

(1) Notice to Beneficiary

Upon acceptance, the beneficiary's bank must notify (by reasonable means) the beneficiary of the funds' availability before midnight of its next funds-transfer business day following the payment date.

(2) Damages for Failure to Pay

If a beneficiary's bank, after acceptance, fails to pay the beneficiary upon demand, it is liable for *all damages* of which it had *notice* at the time of refusal. Liability for consequential damages is excused if the bank proves it had *reasonable doubt* of the beneficiary's right to payment.

(3) Sender's Duty to Pay

A sender has a legal duty to pay once a receiving bank accepts. However, a sender may *cancel or amend* a payment order by reasonable notice given before the receiving bank accepts.

(a) Bank Failure

If the sender or a receiving bank becomes insolvent after acceptance, the payment order is still effective. The loss falls upon the person who chose the insolvent bank. Note that if the beneficiary agreed to a funds transfer, acceptance by the beneficiary's bank *discharges the underlying obligation*, even if the beneficiary's bank becomes insolvent.

3. Misdescription of Beneficiary

A beneficiary is usually described by name and account number. When a misdescription results in unidentifiability, the payment order cannot be accepted.

a. Wrong Account Number

Banks are permitted to ignore names and deal only with account numbers. A beneficiary's bank is not liable for putting money in a wrong account if it received a payment order with the wrong number. Generally, whoever made the mistake (with some exception) bears the loss.

4. Erroneous Payment Orders

If a transmission error occurs (*e.g.*, wrong amount), the party making the mistake bears the loss and the responsibility of recovering the funds in a restitution action against the wrongful holder.

5. Criminal Fraud and Security Procedures

If a bank's failure to follow its security procedures results in a loss, the bank bears the loss. If a fraudulent transfer occurs despite security procedures, the party whose security procedure was breached must bear the loss.

B. CONSUMER TRANSFERS—ELECTRONIC FUND TRANSFERS ACT

A federal statute, the Electronic Fund Transfers Act ("EFTA") (not Article 4A) governs transactions involving consumer transfers of funds into or from the consumer's bank account.

1. Definitions

Transactions covered by EFTA include the use of a *debit card*, usually in an *automated teller machine*, and other electronic fund transfers ("EFTs") (*e.g.*, computer authorization to credit or debit a consumer account).

2. **Documentation**

A bank must inform an EFT customer of certain rights and procedures and must issue bank statements.

3. **Issuance of Debit Cards or Other Access Devices**

Banks are allowed to mail unsolicited debit cards as long as the consumer must take some action before the card becomes validated.

4. **Preauthorized Transfers**

A consumer and bank may agree to automatic transfers into or out of an account. Banks must have procedures enabling the consumer to learn whether transfer has occurred. Consumers may *stop payment* of a preauthorized transfer by giving notice to the bank up to three business days before the scheduled transfer date.

5. **Error Resolution**

   a. **Reporting Requirements**

   A consumer must give the bank oral or written notice of supposed errors *within 60 days* after the bank sent a statement to the consumer.

   b. **Bank's Duties**

   A bank must promptly investigate, in good faith, an alleged error, notify the consumer of its findings, and recredit the account if necessary. A bank has *10 business days* to investigate without recrediting the account. If, after recrediting an account, the bank finds *no error*, it must give the consumer five business days' notice before withdrawing the money and send a written explanation.

6. **Unauthorized EFTs**

An unauthorized EFT is one not authorized by a consumer and from which the consumer receives no benefit. Involuntary transactions are considered to be unauthorized EFTs. The consumer is liable for all uses of a debit card the consumer gave another person to use until notice of a withdrawal of authority is given to the institution.

   a. **Consumer Liability for Unauthorized EFTs**

   A consumer is liable for only *$50 worth* of unauthorized EFTs (less if the bank is notified before $50 is withdrawn), unless the consumer *fails to report a missing card* to the financial institution within two business days; the consumer is then liable for *$500 maximum* for amounts withdrawn after the two-day period.

   (1) **Failure to Report Bank Statement Problems**

   If a consumer does not report a statement problem to the institution within 60 days of the sending of the statement, the consumer has *unlimited liability* (*in addition* to the above-stated liability) for unauthorized transfers occurring after the 60-day period and until the bank is so notified.

   (2) **Negligence of Consumer**

   Consumer negligence does not alter the above rules or increase consumer liability.

7. **Civil Liability of Bank**

Failure to follow federal rules subjects a financial institution to *actual damages and punitive damages* between $100 and $1,000 (different for class actions), plus costs and attorneys' fees. Attorneys' fees are recoverable from a consumer for a baseless action.

Suits may be brought in state or federal court within one year of the alleged violation. No amount in controversy is required for jurisdiction.

Approach to Exams

This Summary deals with the rights and liabilities of parties to commercial paper. "Commercial paper" is the term applied to the negotiable instruments most widely employed in everyday business practice—checks, drafts, promissory notes, and certificates of deposit.

Problems involving the rights and liabilities of parties to negotiable instruments usually can be analyzed by the following approach:

1. **Negotiability**

    First of all, does the instrument meet formal requirements of negotiable paper? Unless it does, a holder has no greater rights than the assignee of an ordinary contract. Furthermore, if the instrument is not negotiable, Article 3 of the Uniform Commercial code may not apply.

2. **Negotiation**

    If the instrument is negotiable, has there been such a *transfer* as to constitute a valid "negotiation" thereof-to vest in the transferee both *possession and title to* the instrument?

    a. If there has not been a valid negotiation, what rights (if any) does the transferee of the instrument have?

3. **Holder in Due Course**

    Has the instrument been negotiated to a holder in due course ("HDC")? If so, does the other party to the dispute have a *real* or a *personal* defense?

4. **Liability of the Parties**

    Consider the liability of each party to the instrument upon its issuance and following each transfer or negotiation thereof:

    a. The obligation *on the instrument* itself:

        (1) Primary party (*maker*).

        (2) Secondary parties (*drawer, indorser*).

            (a) Have the necessary steps been taken to fix their liability? What is the effect of failure or delay?

    b. *Implied warranty* liability of every transferor.

    c. *Conversion* liability in tort for failing to return the instrument, paying on a forged or missing instrument, or paying in violation of a restrictive indorsement.

    d. Can liability be passed on to some other party? Under what theory?

5. **Defenses**

    Depending on which parties are sought to be held liable, what defenses exist and what defenses can be asserted?

    a. Has the instrument come into the hands of a HDC? If so, what is the effect?

    b. Has any party otherwise entitled to assert defense acted in such a way so as to be *estopped* to assert the defense?

Commercial Paper and Payment Law

Eighteenth Edition

Chapter One
Introduction to Commercial Paper

CONTENTS	PAGE

Chapter Approach

This chapter discusses the purposes of commercial paper and the historical background of the law in this area. While you are not likely to be tested on this introductory material, the law of commercial paper is best understood in light of these purposes and the important historical developments that culminated in Articles 3 and 4 of the Uniform Commercial Code.

This chapter also introduces you to the first issue to consider in any commercial paper problem—whether the instrument involved qualifies for coverage under Article 3. Is it a negotiable instrument or merely a contract in the process of being assigned? If it is not negotiable, it will not fall under the "holder in due course" ("HDC") rule. This extraordinary rule provides that a negotiable instrument that reaches the hands of a HDC (*i.e.*, a bona fide purchaser who is unconnected with the underlying transaction and who knows of no problems with the instrument) arrives free of most defenses. Thus, the HDC gets paid even though in a lawsuit between the original parties, payment would never be ordered because defenses exist. The policy here is to promote the free alienability of commercial paper by inspiring confidence in the purchaser that payment will be forthcoming in all but the rarest of circumstances. It has the unfortunate side effect of denying injured parties the ability to assert their legitimate defenses, and the tension between these conflicting polices has caused the courts much angst through the last two centuries.

A. Purposes of Commercial Paper

1. The Credit Function

Some forms of commercial paper are used primarily to obtain credit now, to be repaid out of future income. Examples of such paper include promissory notes, certificates of deposit, and investment securities (*i.e.*, stocks and bonds, which are covered by Article 8 of the Uniform Commercial Code ("U.C.C.") and are therefore excluded from Article 3 [*see* U.C.C. § 3–102(a)]).

a. Note

Creditors willing to extend credit in return for this type of instrument frequently demand security for the debt, in the form of *collateral* in which the creditor has a security interest (*see* Secured Transactions Summary) or a *surety* (*see* discussion of suretyship p. 79).

2. The Payment Function

On the other hand, some types of commercial paper are used primarily as a means of paying obligations in lieu of money, which may be too awkward (or dangerous) to transfer directly. Checks, drafts, bills of exchange, and trade acceptances are examples of commercial paper used as payment.

B. Historical Development of Commercial Paper

1. The Law Merchant

The term "law merchant" (still in use today) refers to the law as it is understood by merchants and traders, and is an important source of authority in construing the various business devices used in commerce. The Uniform Commercial Code adopts it specifically in §§ 1–103(b) and through the adoption of "usage of trade" [§§ 1–303(c)] as a method of contract interpretation.

2. Uniform Commercial Code

In 1942, the National Conference of Commissioners on Uniform State Laws and the American Law Institute began drafting the Uniform Commercial Code. The U.C.C. was designed to replace many of the existing uniform acts governing commercial transactions.

a. Basic Law on Commercial Paper

After going through many drafts to reach its present form, the U.C.C. has been adopted by every state except Louisiana (which did not adopt Article 2 of the Code on the law of Sales, but did adopt the other Articles, including the ones considered in this Summary). The chief provisions in the U.C.C. covered in a course on Commercial Paper (sometimes called "Payment Law") are Article 3 on "Commercial Paper" (an updated version of the Negotiable Instruments LAW) and U.C.C. Article 4 on "Bank Deposits and Collections" (an updated version of the Bank Collection Code).

b. The 1990 Revision of Articles 3 and 4

Articles 3 and 4 of the Uniform Commercial Code were rewritten from the 1960 original and the revised version was sent to the states for adoption in1990. These changes (hereafter the "Revision") clear up many of the problems with the original versions and permit banks to move from a paper-based system to electronic banking. The Revision was adopted in all jurisdictions except New York. This Summary will be devoted to the rules of the Revision, which the exception noted next.

c. The 2002 Revision of Articles 3 and 4

These articles were given minor revisions in 2002, and this version has so far been adopted in Arkansas, the District of Columbus, Indiana, Kentucky, Minnesota, Mississippi, New Mexico, Nevada, Oklahoma, South Carolina, and Texas (Massachusetts was considering its enactment as this Summary went to press). This Summary therefore continues to refer to the *1990 revision* unless otherwise noted, but the chief changes proposed by the 2002 revision will be highlighted as they arise.

C. Types of Commercial Paper

1. Notes

A promissory note—frequently referred to simply as a "note"—is a written promise to pay money to a designated party (the "payee") by the *maker* of the promise. [U.C.C. § 3–104(e)]

a. "Promise" Defined

A "promise" is an ***undertaking to pay,*** and therefore must be more than a mere acknowledgment of an obligation. [U.C.C. § 3–103(a)(9)]

 Example:

> PROMISSORY NOTE
>
> I, Max Maker, promise to pay to the order of Peter Payee One hundred dollars ($100).
>
> *Max Maker*

Compare: An "I.O.U." is not a promise to pay, but merely recognition that a debt exists. Hence, a simple "I.O.U." does not constitute a promissory note. [U.C.C. § 3–103, Off. Com. 3; **Jacob v. Harrison**, 2002 WL 31840890 (Del. Super. 2002)]

b. Bank's Note—Certificates of Deposit

If a note is signed by a bank (*i.e.*, if the bank is the ***maker*** of the note) and the note acknowledges the receipt of money coupled with an obligation to repay it, it is called a certificate of deposit, or "CD." [U.C.C. § 3–104(j); **Southview Corp. v. Kleberg First National Bank**, 512 S.W.2d 817 (Tex. 1974)]

(1) U.C.C. Article 8 May Apply

U.C.C. Article 8 ("Investment Securities") governs stocks, bonds, and other commercial "specialities" that are transferred as investment paper on recognized markets. Some courts have held that "CDs" qualify as Article 8 securities and are therefore ***excluded*** from the provisions of U.C.C. Article 3. [*See* **Victory National Bank v. Oklahoma State Bank**, 520 P.2d 675 (Okla. 1973); U.C.C. §§ 8–102, 3–102(a)]

2. Drafts

A draft is an instrument in which the ***drawer*** (the person who creates the instrument) orders a designated "drawee" to pay money to a third person, called the "payee." Drafts (which may also be referred to as "bills of exchange") must identify the drawee with "reasonable certainty" so that the payee knows where to present the instrument for payment. [U.C.C. §§ 3–104(e), 3–103(a)(6)]

 Example:

> To: Dan Duke   January 1, 2022
> P.O. Box 37
> Denver, Colorado
>
>   Pay to the order of _____Pam Payee_____ $5,000
>
>   Five thousand and 00/100----------dollars
>
>   *Debbie Dante*

	DEFINITION	PARTIES
NOTE	Instrument in which a party *promises to pay* money to a designated party	*Maker* = person promising to pay *Payee* = person designated to receive money
DRAFT	Instrument in which a party *orders another party* (often a bank) *to pay* money *to a third party*	*Drawer* = creator of instrument ordering payment *Drawee* = party (often a bank) ordered to pay the money *Payee* = person designated to receive money

a. What Constitutes a "Check"

If a draft names a *bank* as the drawee *and* is payable on demand (*see* p. 15), it is called a "check." [U.C.C. § 3–104(f)]

(1) Note

In U.C.C. Article 4 ("Bank Deposits and Collections"), the drawee bank is called a *"payor bank."* [U.C.C. § 4–105(3)]

(2) Traveler's Checks

Traveler's checks are defined in § 3–104(i) as drafts payable on demand (*see* p. 15), drawn on a bank, designated as "traveler's checks" (or using similar language), and requiring a countersignature by the person whose specimen signature is already signed to the check.

(3) Cashier's Checks

The Code defines cashier's checks as drafts drawn by a bank *on itself* (so that the drawer and the drawee are the same). [U.C.C. § 3–104(g)] The person who buys such a check intending to transfer it to another to pay a debt is called the *remitter* (*see* p. 26). [U.C.C. § 3–103(a)(11)]

(4) Teller's Checks

The Code defines teller's checks as drafts drawn by a bank *on another bank.* [U.C.C. § 3–104(h)] The person who buys such a check intending to transfer it to another to pay a debt is also called the *remitter* (*see* p. 26). [U.C.C. § 3–103(a)(11)]

b. Requirement of an "Order" to Pay

The drawer of a draft must "order" the drawee to pay. This requires more than mere authorization to pay or a request that the drawee pay, but the use of polite, "precatory" language (*e.g.*, "please pay," "kindly pay") is still sufficient to qualify the instrument as a "draft." [U.C.C. § 3–103(a)(6)]

To determine whether the instrument is a note or a draft, pay particular attention to the parties involved with the instrument. Remember, in the beginning there are only two parties on a note (a *maker* promises to pay a *payee*) and there are three parties on a draft (a *drawer* orders a *drawee* to pay a *payee*).

D. Law Protects Holders in Due Course

1. "Holder in Due Course" Defined

If: (i) an instrument meets the technical requirements of "negotiability" (*see* p. 9), (ii) it is transferred so that a "negotiation" occurs, and (iii) a bona fide purchaser pays value for the instrument without notice of claims or defenses to it, that purchaser becomes a "holder in due course" ("HDC"). (*See* discussion of HDC p. 38)

2. Special Status of HDC

The HDC may sue prior parties who are liable on the instrument but (with a few exceptions) those parties *have no defenses* against the HDC. In other words, prior parties must simply pay the holder in due course.

a. Rationale

The justification for protecting HDCs in this fashion is that it promotes the commercial viability of negotiable instruments. Institutions that purchase negotiable paper as HDCs need not worry about whether the paper will be paid at maturity, because it circulates very much like money.

b. Non-HDCs

If the transferee of the instrument does *not* qualify as a HDC, the transferee is merely the assignee of a contract, and (like all assignees) takes the instrument *subject to all valid claims and defenses* to it; Restatement (2d) of Contracts § 336.

Chapter Two
Negotiability

CONTENTS	PAGE

Chapter Approach

This chapter examines the concept of negotiability, the technical *form* that the instrument must meet to qualify as a negotiable instrument subject to Article 3 of the Uniform Commercial Code. If the instrument's form fails to meet the necessary requirements, Article 3 applies only by analogy, and the concept of holding in due course does not come into play.

To be negotiable, an instrument must:

(i)   Be in *writing;*

(ii) Be *signed* by the maker or drawer;

(iii) Contain an *unconditional promise or order* to pay a *fixed amount of money,* on *demand* or at a *definite time;*

(iv) Contain *"words of negotiability";* and

(v)   Be free from *unauthorized promises.*

Remember these requirements. In your exam question, if any party is claiming to be a HDC, your first step will be to examine the instrument carefully, checking *for all of the elements of negotiability.* If the instrument is not technically negotiable, no one can be a HDC, and thus all defenses may be asserted by parties to the instrument.

A. Significance of "Negotiability"

1. Introduction

The extensive protection afforded to buyers of commercial paper (HDCs and others) applies *only* when the instrument in question *is "negotiable"* under the terms of the U.C.C. [U.C.C. § 3–104(a)]

2. Nonnegotiable Instrument Is Merely a Contract

If an instrument is found not to be negotiable, it only has the status of a contract that has been assigned. Because the assignee of a contract merely acquires the rights of the assignor, the purchaser of a nonnegotiable instrument takes the paper *subject to the claims and defenses of prior parties.* [U.C.C. § 3–306] (*See* p. 67, *and see* Contracts Summary.)

3. No HDC Status if Instrument Not Negotiable

It follows that one *cannot* be a holder in due course of a *nonnegotiable instrument.* [**Geiger Finance Co. v. Graham**, 182 S.E.2d 521 (Ga. 1971)]

B. Requirements for Negotiability

1. Definition of Negotiability

"Negotiability" refers to the *form* of an instrument. To be "negotiable" under the terms of U.C.C. § 3–104(a), an instrument must: (i) be in *writing;* (ii) be *signed* by the maker or drawer; (iii) contain an *unconditional promise or order* to pay a *fixed amount of money, on demand or at a definite time;* (iv) contain *"words of negotiability";* and (v) be *free from other promises* or the like, except as permitted by Article 3.

2. Written Instrument

A negotiable instrument *cannot be oral.* The writing requirement is found in the definition of "order" (necessary for a draft) and "promise" (necessary for a promissory note). [U.C.C. § 3–103(a)(6), (9)]

a. But Note—Paper Not Essential

However, the writing need not be on paper, and writings on objects other than paper are sometimes encountered. For example, the I.R.S. is faced from time to time with checks from irate taxpayers written on the backs of shirts!

3. Signature of Maker or Drawer

Any mark or symbol placed on the instrument (or already there and subsequently "adopted") by the maker or drawer *with the intent* to authenticate the writing constitutes a "signature." [U.C.C. § 1–201(b)(37), Off. Com. 37—initials or thumbprint would qualify] Thus, a full formal signature is *not* required if the requisite intent to authenticate was present. Illiterate people sometimes sign their names with an "X" and that is a valid signature since it is a mark made with intent to authenticate.

a. Signature by Agent

The name of the maker or drawer may be placed on an instrument by an authorized agent. [U.C.C. § 3–402(a)] Liability of the agent in this situation is discussed p. 97.

b. Trade Name or Assumed Name Sufficient

The maker or drawer is bound even if he/she signs with an assumed name or a trade name. [U.C.C. § 3–401(b)]

e.g. **Example:** Alice Wonderland is the sole proprietor of Carroll Book Store and signs all of the store's checks "Carroll Book Store." Wonderland is nevertheless bound on the checks just as if she had signed her own name.

c. Unauthorized or Forged Signatures

The U.C.C. defines an "unauthorized" signature as one made without authority. This definition includes a forgery or a pretense of agency. [U.C.C. § 1–201(b)(41)]

(1) Liability

The person whose name is signed under these circumstances is not liable on the instrument unless he/she *ratifies* the signature (*e.g.*, adopts the unauthorized signature as his/her own) or is *precluded* (estopped) from denying it. [U.C.C. § 3–403(a); *and see* discussion p. 97] However, the *unauthorized signer* (*e.g.*, the forger or purported agent) *is personally liable* just as if the forger had signed the forger's own name. [U.C.C. § 3–403(a), Off. Com. 2]

e.g. **Example:** Chester Cat steals a check from Alice Wonderland and forges her name as the drawer. Chester is viewed as having signed his own name as drawer, while Alice is not liable on the check.

d. Burden of Establishing Signatures

(1) Where Defendant's Pleadings Do Not Raise Issue

Unless specifically denied in the pleadings, each signature on an instrument is *deemed admitted.* [U.C.C. § 3–308(a)]

(2) Where Defendant Raises Issue in Pleading

If the defendant-obligor raises an issue in the pleadings as to the validity of any signature, the burden is on the *plaintiff* (as the party claiming under the signature) to prove that the signature is genuine. [**Esposito v. Fascione**, 299 A.2d 165 (R.I. 1973)]

(a) Presumption of Validity

However, the plaintiff is aided by a rebuttable presumption that all signatures are genuine or authorized. [U.C.C. § 3–308(a)]

(b) Effect

The defendant must then produce evidence of forgery, etc., or the plaintiff-holder will be entitled to recover. [**Virginia National Bank v. Holt**, 219 S.E.2d 881 (Va. 1975)]

(c) Exception

The rebuttable presumption of validity does not apply where the purported signer has died or become incompetent. In such cases, the plaintiff must prove genuineness, and there is no presumption to aid the plaintiff's case. [U.C.C. § 3–308(a)]

e. Location of Signature

The signature need not appear at the bottom of the instrument. It may be placed in the letterhead, the body of the writing, or any other location thereon, as long as it is meant to authenticate the instrument. [U.C.C. § 1–201, Off. Com. 37]

4. Unconditional Promise or Order to Pay

A promissory note must contain an "unconditional promise"—and a draft must contain an "unconditional order"—to be negotiable. (The meanings of "promise" and "order" are discussed p. 4, p. 5.)

a. Rationale

Requiring that the operative terms of a negotiable instrument be unconditional helps to promote its marketability, because subsequent purchasers will be able to determine the applicable terms and conditions from the four corners of the instrument. A purchaser could not evaluate the worth of an instrument if the liability of its maker or drawer were conditioned upon some extraneous matter or anything other than a pure promise to pay money

b. Implied Conditions

Implied or constructive conditions in the instrument do *not* destroy negotiability.

Example: A promissory note stating that it is given as a down payment on a contract to rent an apartment is not conditional merely because of the possibility that the building might burn down.

(1) Distinguish—Express Conditions

A promissory note that is *expressly* conditioned on some event (*e.g.*, "I promise to pay only if the apartment I am renting is not destroyed") violates the requirement of an unconditional promise and is nonnegotiable.

c. Reference to Other Agreements

A separate agreement executed between the immediate parties (*i.e.*, the maker or drawer and the payee) as part of the same transaction is effective in regulating *their* rights, but it *will not bind a later HDC.* [U.C.C. § 3–117; **Demaio v. Theriot**, 343 So. 2d 1143 (La. 1977)] Mere reference in the instrument to such other agreements or documents does not impair negotiability. [U.C.C. § 3–106(a)]

Example: A promissory note stating that "this note arises out of a contract signed this date" is negotiable, as is a draft stating that it is "drawn under a letter of credit." [*See* U.C.C. § 3–106(a)]

d. Descriptions of Consideration or Other Transactions

A description of collateral or of other transactions connected with the instrument does not, by itself, make the instrument conditional as to the matters described. The negotiability of the instrument is therefore unaffected by such recitals.

Example: A promissory note describing in detail the contract that gave rise to the note (including all of the contract terms) is negotiable as long as the promissory note is not made *subject to* the contract (*see* below). [U.C.C. § 3–106(a), Off. Com. 1]

e. Incorporation of Separate Agreement or Document in Instrument

While mere reference to or description of agreements or other writings does not affect negotiability, an *incorporation* of those other matters into an instrument makes the instrument *nonnegotiable* because later purchasers cannot determine the applicable terms from the four corners of the instrument. [U.C.C. § 3–106(a); see **DZ Bank AG Deutche Zentral-Genossenschaftsbank v. McCranie**, 720 F. App'x 576, 584 (11th Cir. 2018)]

Example: A promissory note stating "this instrument is subject to the terms of a separate contract" makes the note nonnegotiable. [**Verner v. White**, 108 So. 369 (Ala. 1926)] Similarly, reference in a note to the fact that "the terms of the mortgage are made part hereof" would destroy negotiability. [**Holly Hill Acres, Ltd. v. Charter Bank**, 314 So. 2d 209 (Fla. 1975)]

(1) Distinguish—"as per" or "in Accordance with"

An instrument that states that it is executed or matures "in accordance with" another contract, or "as per" another contract, is negotiable. These two phrases constitute a mere reference to other matters, rather than an incorporation of such matters.

(2) Exception—Terms Concerning Prepayment or Acceleration

Article 3 permits an instrument to incorporate the terms of another writing to govern the rights of the parties regarding **prepayment of the instrument or acceleration of the maturity date** and for a statement of rights with respect to any collateral. [U.C.C. § 3–106(b)]

 Example: A note that states "see the mortgage for rights on prepayment, which terms shall govern this note" is **negotiable.**

 Compare: A note that states "see the mortgage, which terms shall govern the rights of the parties to this note" is **nonnegotiable.**

(a) Rationale

Prepayment or acceleration of the debt means that the person holding the instrument will be paid *early,* which benefits the holder. Thus there is no harm in making the holder examine other instruments to see when this benefit will happen.

f. Statement of Security

A statement in an instrument that the underlying obligation is **secured**—and describing, but not incorporating, the collateral and security agreement—does not affect negotiability. [U.C.C. § 3–106(b); **Best Fertilizers of Arizona, Inc. v. Burns**, 571 P.2d 675 (Ariz. App. 1977)]

	LANGUAGE	EXAMPLE
CONDITIONAL (NONNEGOTIABLE)	***Express*** condition	"I promise to pay $10,000 ***if*** Owner conveys Whiteacre to me."
	Subject to (or ***governed by***) another writing	"This note is ***subject to*** the contract signed by the parties on June 1."
	Rights ***stated in*** another writing	"The rights of the parties with respect to this note are ***stated in*** the contract signed by the parties on June 1."
UNCONDITIONAL (NEGOTIABLE)	***Implied*** condition	"I promise to pay $10,000 ***for*** Whiteacre."
	Reference to another writing	"This note is executed ***in accordance with*** the contract signed by the parties on June 1."
	Description of ***consideration***	"In ***consideration*** of Owner's promise to convey Whiteacre to me, I promise to pay."
	Rights regarding ***prepayment or acceleration***	"The rights of the parties to this note ***regarding prepayment and acceleration*** are governed by the contract signed by the parties on June 1."
	Statement of ***security***	"This note is ***secured*** by a security interest in collateral described in a security agreement dated June 1."

5. Fixed Amount of Money

a. What Constitutes "Money"

The U.C.C. adopts a formal definition of "money" as a "medium of exchange authorized or adopted by a domestic ***or foreign*** government as part of its currency." [U.C.C. § 1–201(b)(24)]

e.g. **Example—payment in foreign currency:** A promise to pay "1,000 Japanese yen" is negotiable, and this is true regardless of the fact that the instrument was executed in the United States and the parties had no substantial contact with Japan. This is one method of protecting a note or draft against the effects of inflation and the rise and fall of the United States dollar.

(1) Note

Even though the amount owing is stated in foreign currency, the instrument is deemed payable in an equivalent number of dollars at the due date, unless the instrument *expressly* requires *payment* in the foreign currency. [U.C.C. § 3–107]

(2) But Note

If the instrument states that it is payable *only* in a foreign currency, it is payable only in that currency. Such a provision will not impair the negotiability of the instrument. [U.C.C. § 3–107]

EXAM TIP ◣GILBERT

Keep in mind that the payment must be in *money.* Thus, although requiring foreign currency payment does not destroy negotiability, requiring payment in something *other than money* (even as an alternative, *e.g.,* "$500 or my diamond bracelet") makes an instrument *nonnegotiable.*

---

b. What Constitutes a "Fixed Amount"

Absolute certainty as to the sum due at all times is not required. It is sufficient if, as of any particular time, the amount due on the instrument may be *mathematically computed.* The fixed amount may include "interest or other charges." [U.C.C. § 3–104(a)]

(1) Must Interest Rate Be "Stated"?

Under the original version of Article 3, a note payable with interest at "the prime rate" or the "bank rate" was *not* negotiable. The rate of interest could not be determined *from the face* of the note, thus rendering the sum uncertain. [**A. Alport & Son, Inc. v. Hotel Evans, Inc.**, 65 Misc. 2d 374 (1970)] The Revision permits fixed and variable interest rates, and implies the judgment rate when the interest rate cannot be ascertained from the description. [U.C.C. § 3–112]

(a) Variable Interest Rate

A variable interest rate is a rate tied to the "prime rate" or some other ascertainable standard (*e.g.,* "3% over prime, adjusted each six months based on then prevailing bank rates in New York City").

(b) Judgment Rate

If a note merely states that it is payable "with interest," but does not state the interest rate, the note is still negotiable. The state judgment rate (determined by a special statute) will be implied (*see* p. 23). [U.C.C. § 3–112(b)]

Under exam pressures, don't forget that "fixed amount of money" doesn't necessarily mean that the amount is spelled out in the instrument. Rather, "fixed amount":

- Can be a **set amount** or one that **can be mathematically calculated** at any time;

- Allows for a **fixed or variable interest rate**;

- Allows for just a statement "with interest" but **giving no rate** (state **judgment rate** will be used).

6. Specified Time of Payment

Unless it can be determined from the face of the instrument when, or at least upon what events, the obligation will become due, the instrument is not negotiable. Without time certainty, the value of the instrument is so speculative that it cannot be accorded the protection of a negotiable instrument. Accordingly, the U.C.C. requires that a negotiable instrument be payable either **on demand** or **at a definite time.** [U.C.C. § 3–104(a)]

a. Demand Instruments

An instrument is payable "on demand" if it is expressly made so payable, if words of similar import are used ("at sight," "upon presentation"), or **if no time for payment** is stated. [U.C.C. § 3–108(a)] An instrument payable "on demand" means just what it sounds like—the holder of the instrument can present it for payment whenever the presenter desires.

(1) No Maturity Date

Thus, where there is no maturity date on the instrument, the law construes it as being payable on demand, and parol evidence to the contrary is inadmissible. [**Cohan v. Flanders**, 315 F. Supp. 1046 (S.D. Ga. 1970)]

b. Time Instruments

An instrument payable at a definite time in the future is referred to as a "time instrument." [U.C.C. § 3–108(b)]

(1) Definite Time

An instrument is payable at a definite time if it is payable: (i) on a **fixed date;** (ii) on **or before a fixed date;** (iii) at a time **readily ascertainable** when the instrument is issued; or (iv) after elapse of a specified **period after sight.** [U.C.C. § 3–108(b)] But remember, an instrument stating that it is "payable at sight" is a **demand** instrument. [U.C.C. § 3–108(a)]

 Example: An instrument dated January 10, 2022, is payable at a definite time if it states that it is payable:

- "On February 10, 2022" (or any date in the future);

- "On or before February 10, 2022" (or any date in the future);

- "60 days after date" (or any period more or less than 60 days); or

- "60 days after sight" (or any period more or less than 60 days).

(2) Date Left Off

If the date is left off the instrument and its maturity depends on a date being stated (*e.g.*, "payable 60 days after _____"), the instrument is not enforceable *until the date is filled in* by someone with *authority* to do so. [U.C.C. § 3–115]

(a) Note

If the date is inserted by someone without authority, the rules on alteration apply. [U.C.C. § 3–115(c); *see* p. 144]

(3) Acceleration Clauses

Under the U.C.C., acceleration clauses—*i.e.*, clauses that make the instrument payable *earlier* than its stated maturity date—have *no effect* on negotiability. [U.C.C. § 3–108(b)] Either the maker *or* the holder may be given the unconditional right to accelerate the maturity date of the instrument.

Example: If Maker promises to pay to the order of Payee "on or before March 15," Maker has a right to pay before the due date. If Maker promises to pay to the order of Payee "on March 15, or sooner if holder chooses to accelerate," Payee has a right to demand payment from Maker before the due date.

(a) Rationale

The actual time for payment is not more indefinite than it is when dealing with an instrument payable "on demand," and a demand instrument is clearly negotiable (*see* above). In addition, because acceleration means early payment, the holder of the instrument, who will receive the early payment, has no reason to object.

(b) Good Faith Limitation on Holder's Right to Accelerate

Where the holder is given the right to accelerate "at will," this is construed to mean that the holder has the power to do so only if the holder *"in good faith believes that the prospect of payment is impaired."* However, good faith in this situation is presumed. [U.C.C. § 1–208]

(4) Extension Clauses

An extension clause makes an instrument payable *later* than the stated maturity date. Whether an extension clause violates the "definite time" required for negotiability depends on the terms of the clause.

(a) Extension at Option of Holder

The "holder" is the current possessor of an instrument with title thereto. (*See* p. 26) If extension is at the *option of the holder*, the instrument is deemed "payable at a definite time" (and hence negotiable) even if no new maturity date is stated. [U.C.C. § 3–108(b)(iii)]

1) Rationale

At the maturity of any instrument, the person entitled to receive payment can delay a demand for payment. If the maker or drawer wants to stop interest from running, he/she may do so by following the procedure authorized under U.C.C. § 3–603(c). (*See* p. 81)

(b) Extension at Option of Maker or Drawer, or Extension Automatically on Happening of Event

Farmers frequently wish to execute instruments payable "in six months, but extended another six months if my crop fails," or "extended six months at my option." Such extension clauses are valid *only* if a new maturity date on extension is stated in the instrument. [U.C.C. § 3–108(b)(iv)]

1) Rationale

Without a new maturity date in the extension clause, subsequent holders of the instrument would not know when it would be paid. Such uncertainty prevents negotiability because the instrument is not payable either on demand or at a definite time.

c. Impact of Dates on Negotiability

The negotiability of an instrument is *not* affected by the fact that it is undated, antedated, or postdated. Undated instruments are payable on demand (meaning at any time), while antedated or postdated instruments are payable on or after the date stated. [U.C.C. § 3–113]

7. Words of Negotiability

The basic definition of "negotiability" in U.C.C. § 3–104(a)(2) requires that the instrument be *payable either "to order" or "to bearer."* If an instrument states either "pay to bearer" or "pay to the order of [name of payee]," it is said to contain "words of negotiability." An instrument payable to bearer names no specific payee and can be transferred without indorsement, just like cash. On the other hand, order paper names a specific payee ("pay to the order of _____") and requires the payee's indorsement for further negotiation. (*See* pp. 27–28) An instrument stating simply "Pay to J. Doe" is generally nonnegotiable because it contains *neither* order nor bearer language. [**Hall v. Westmoreland, Hall & Bryan**, 182 S.E.2d 539 (Ga. 1971); *but see* p. 18]

a. What Constitutes an "Order" Instrument

An instrument is payable to order when it is drawn "payable to the order of an identified person." [U.C.C. § 3–109(b)]

(1) *It may be drawn payable to the order of the maker or drawer* (*i.e.*, the obligor herself), *the drawee, or a payee* who is not the maker, drawer, or drawee.

(2) *It may also be drawn payable to several payees,* jointly or severally ("to the order of Ben and Jerry, or either of them"). [U.C.C. § 3–110(d)]

(3) *It may be drawn payable to the order of a partnership* or other unincorporated association, or to the order of an *estate, trust, or fund,* in which case it is payable to the order of the *representative* of such entity (*e.g.,* a check drawn to the "Community Chest" may be cashed by its representative). [U.C.C. § 3–110(c)(2)]

(4) *Or it may be drawn to a public office or officeholder* ("to the order of the County Tax Collector" or "to the order of John Jones, Tax Collector"), in which case it is payable to the *incumbent* holder of the office. [U.C.C. § 3–110(c)(2)(iv)]

b. What Constitutes a "Bearer" Instrument

An instrument is payable to bearer only if it is drawn payable: (i) to *bearer,* (ii) to a *specified person or bearer* (*i.e.,* "pay to John Doe or bearer"), or (iii) to *"cash,"* the order of "cash," or any *other indication that does not purport to designate a specific payee.* [U.C.C. § 3–109(a)]

 Example: A check "Pay to the order of Happy Birthday" creates bearer paper. [U.C.C. § 3–109(a)(3)]

(1) Bearer Language Controls

If an instrument is made payable both to order and to bearer (*e.g.,* "pay to the order of John Jones and bearer"), the *bearer* language controls. [U.C.C. § 3–109, Off. Com. 2]

c. Effect of Omitting Words of Negotiability

If an instrument is not made payable to order or bearer, it is nonnegotiable.

 Example:

> On March 1, 2022, I promise to pay <u>Pat Payee</u> $1,000
> One thousand and 00/100---------dollars.
>
> Murray Maker

The above instrument is nonnegotiable because it does not contain the "magic words" of negotiability. It is not payable to the *order* of anyone, nor is it payable to bearer since it names a payee. Failure to use either order or bearer language (the "words of negotiability") is a common drafting error in the creation of promissory notes. (though sometimes this is done deliberately where the drafter does not want the possibility of a HDC in his/her future).

(1) Exception—Checks

Words of negotiability are not required for checks, and holder in due course status is not affected by their absence on checks. Thus, a check that says "Pay to Mary Doe" would be negotiable, and later takers might qualify as holders in due course of such a check. There is no similar rule for promissory notes or non-check drafts, so such instruments are not governed by Article 3, except by analogy. [U.C.C. § 3–104(c), Off. Com. 2]

8. "No Other Promise" Requirement

With certain exceptions to be noted below, the instrument must "not state any other undertaking or instruction by the person promising or demanding payment to do any act in addition to the payment of money." [U.C.C. § 3–104(a)(3)] This is meant to keep the document free of clutter so that the negotiable instrument may be a "courier without luggage." [**Overton v. Tyler**, 3 Pa. 346 (1846)]

Example: A promise to pay $500 **and deliver** a quantity of goods makes the instrument nonnegotiable. Likewise, wording in an instrument giving the holder the **election** of requiring some act to be done **in lieu** of payment of money destroys the negotiability of the instrument; *i.e.,* a promise to pay $500 **or** to deliver goods, whichever is requested, is nonnegotiable.

a. Distinguish—Promises Affecting Security

However, certain promises pertaining to the security or enforcement of the obligation are "expressly authorized" by Article 3 [U.C.C. § 3–104(a)(3)] and hence do not affect negotiability:

(1) Confession of Judgment

A "confession of judgment" is a clause in a contract or note that allows the other party to file a lawsuit and then automatically win because the signer agrees that judgement should be entered in favor of the plaintiff. A provision authorizing the holder to enter a confession of judgment against the promisor if the note is not paid when due is permissible; *i.e.,* it will not destroy the negotiability of the instrument. [U.C.C. § 3–104(a)(3)(ii)]

(a) Consumer Protection—Credit Practices Rule

Note that both the Federal Trade Commission and the Federal Reserve Board have adopted a regulation called the Credit Practices Rule, which *prohibits* the use of a confession of judgment clause in any extension of credit to *consumers.* [16 C.F.R. § 444; 12 C.F.R. § 227]

(2) Maintain or Deposit Additional Collateral

Provisions requiring the promisor to maintain or protect collateral deposited as security for the loan, or to *deposit additional collateral* on demand of the holder, are also permissible. [U.C.C. § 3–104(a)(3)(i)]

(a) Good Faith Limitation

Wherever the payee or holder is given the right to require the obligor to deposit additional security, the U.C.C. reads in a limitation that the payee or holder must "in good faith believe that the prospect of payment or performance is impaired." [U.C.C. § 1–309]

(b) Statement of Security Interest

The instrument may state that collateral has been given as security for repayment of the obligation, and the Code further authorizes a clause providing that upon default the holder may foreclose on the collateral. [U.C.C. § 3–104(a)(3)]

1) Security Agreement in Instrument

The U.C.C. clearly permits the instrument to contain "an undertaking or power to give . . . collateral to secure payment," and this would apparently permit the coupling of an Article 9 security interest with an Article 3 promissory note. [U.C.C. § 3–104(a)(3)(i)]

b. Waiver of Laws

The U.C.C. authorizes clauses in a negotiable instrument that purport to *waive* the benefit of certain laws. Thus, waivers of rights to presentment and notice of dishonor (*see* p. 93), homestead exemptions, trial by jury, etc., do *not* destroy negotiability. [U.C.C. § 3–104(a)(3)(iii)]

(1) Validity of Waiver

Note that § 3–104(3)(a)(iii) does not make waiver provisions *valid* as a matter of Jaw. It merely indicates that such clauses do not violate the "courier without luggage" requirement. The legal effect of waiver clauses must be determined by other law.

EXAM TIP

Remember that only three undertakings or instructions are authorized by the U.C.C.: (i) an authorization or power given to the holder to *confess judgment* against the promisor; (ii) an undertaking or power to *give, maintain, or protect collateral*; and (iii) a *waiver of the benefit of a law* that protects the obligor. Any other undertaking or instruction will *destroy negotiability*.

---

c. "Payment in Full" Clauses

Debtors who pay disputed debts by check frequently add a clause stating that by cashing the check the creditor/payee acknowledges it as "payment in full" for the entire amount owed. Under the 1962 version of Article 3, the addition of such a clause did not destroy the negotiability of the check, and the payee who cashed such a check had no further rights against the drawer (assuming that the check was tendered in good faith on a disputed debt), unless the payee returned the money within 90 days or the drawer sent it to the wrong place. This was true even if the payee crossed off the "payment in full language" or cashed the check "under protest." [U.C.C. § 3–311] The 1990 Revised version of Article 3 drops any discussion of the effect of "payment in full" language on negotiability. However, it is likely that a court would hold that such language does destroy negotiability since it clearly adds conditions to the instrument's terms.

9. Illustrations

a. Negotiable Note

```
Max Maker Markets, Inc.                              No. 123
Market Street
Erehwon, NY

On demand⁽ᵛ⁾ the undersigned promises to
pay⁽ᶦᶦᶦ⁾ Bearer ⁽ᵛᶦ⁾            $1,200
Twelve Hundred and 00/100----------------dollars ⁽ᶦᵛ⁾

                              Max Maker Markets, Inc.

                              By Max Maker, Pres.⁽ᶦᶦ⁾
```

The above is a negotiable note because it (i) is in writing, (ii) is signed by the maker (Max Maker Markets), (iii) contains an unconditional promise to pay ("the undersigned promises to pay"), (iv) a fixed amount of money ($1,200), (v) on demand (no payment date is stated), (vi) to bearer, and (vii) contains no unauthorized undertaking or instruction.

b. Negotiable Draft

```
To: Dan Duke                            January 1, 2022
P.O. Box 37
Denver, Colorado

       Pay⁽ᶦᶦᶦ⁾ to the order⁽ᵛᶦ⁾ of      Pam Payee      $5,000

       Five thousand and 00/100---------dollars⁽ᶦᵛ⁾

                              Debbie Dante⁽ᶦᶦ⁾
```

The above is a negotiable draft because it (i) is in writing, (ii) is signed by the maker (Debbie Dante), (iii) contains an unconditional order to pay ("To: Dan Duke . . . Pay"), (iv) a fixed amount of money ($5,000), (v) on demand (because no time is stated for payment it is considered payable on demand), (vi) to order ("the order of Pam Payee"), and (vii) contains no unauthorized undertaking or instruction.

TO DETERMINE WHETHER AN INSTRUMENT IS NEGOTIABLE, BE SURE THAT IT HAS ALL OF THE FOLLOWING CHARACTERISTICS:

- ☑ In *writing*
- ☑ *Signed* by the maker or drawer
- ☑ *Unconditional* (does not state a condition for payment and is not subject to or governed by another writing)
- ☑ *Promise* (note) *or order* (draft) to pay
- ☑ A *fixed amount of money* (with or without interest)
- ☑ *On demand* or at a *definite time*
- ☑ Contains *"words of negotiability"* (payable to order or bearer)
- ☑ Contains *no unauthorized promise or undertaking*

C. Ambiguities in Instruments

1. Introduction

The U.C.C. provides a set of presumptions to guide the courts in determining negotiability where the instrument is ambiguous as to terms, parties, or legal consequences. Such presumptions are obviously important in assessing (or drafting) an instrument.

2. Rules of Construction

Express provision is made in the U.C.C. for certain types of ambiguity. Where the language of the instrument is ambiguous or there are omissions therein, the following U.C.C. rules of construction apply:

a. Words vs. Figures

Where the sum payable is expressed in words and also in figures, and there is a discrepancy between the two, the sum denoted by the *words* is the sum payable; however, if the words are ambiguous or uncertain, the figures control. [U.C.C. § 3–114]

Example: "Pay five hundred dollars ($5,000)" is construed as an order to pay $500.

Compare: But, "Pay sixt dollars ($6.00)" is construed as an order to pay $6.00.

b. Handwriting vs. Typing or Printing

Where there is a conflict between handwritten and typed or printed provisions of the instrument, the *handwritten* provisions prevail. Typed terms in turn prevail over printed ones. [U.C.C. § 3–114]

3. Descriptions of Payee

a. Agent as Payee

If an instrument is made payable to someone described as an agent (*e.g.,* "Pay to the order of Jane Roe, Agent"), the instrument is construed as if it were payable to the ***principal***—although the agent may still negotiate the instrument as a "holder." [U.C.C. § 3–110(c)(2)(ii)]

b. Fiduciary as Payee

A fiduciary is a person who has a legal relationship of trust with someone else, for example taking case of that person's assets or holding them in trust. An instrument payable in a fiduciary capacity (*e.g.,* "Pay to the order of Richard Doe, trustee") is deemed payable to the fiduciary. [U.C.C. § 3–110(c)(2)(i)]

c. Partnerships, Officeholders, Unincorporated Associations, Estates, Trusts, or Funds as Payees

Instruments payable to such entities are considered payable to the current representatives of the entity in question. [U.C.C. § 3–110(c)(2); *and see* p. 17]

4. Omission of Interest Rate

Every state has a statutory rate of interest which is added to the damages awarded in a lawsuit so that judgment bears interest until paid in full. This rate of interest is referred to as the "judgment rate." The U.C.C. will apply the judgment rate of interest with respect to negotiable instruments in the following circumstances:

a. "With Interest"—No Rate Specified

A provision in a negotiable instrument stating that the maker or drawer agrees to pay an amount "with interest" but not specifying the rate is construed as calling for the judgment rate. [U.C.C. § 3–112(b)]

(1) Note

Interest accrues on the amount specified from the date of the instrument or, if undated, from the date on which it was first issued to the payee. [U.C.C. § 3–112(a)]

b. Interest Not Provided for

If the instrument does not provide for interest, none is payable, although most states have statutes providing a judgment rate of interest for liquidated debts that have accrued. [U.C.C. § 3–112]

Chapter Three
Negotiation

CONTENTS	PAGE

Chapter Approach

This chapter examines the concept of negotiation. Negotiation is the process by which an instrument is transferred from one person to another. If a negotiable instrument is not properly negotiated, no subsequent holder of the instrument can qualify as a HDC and thus take free of personal defenses.

If an examination question involves someone claiming to be a holder, you must determine whether the instrument was properly negotiated. To do this you must determine whether the instrument is *bearer paper* or *order paper.* Bearer paper is properly negotiated by delivery alone. Order paper requires necessary signatures as well as delivery.

Also, be sure not to confuse negotiability with negotiation. Negotiability refers to the *form* of the instrument; negotiation is *the transfer process.*

A. Definition of Key Terms

1. "Negotiation"

"Negotiation" is the *process* by which an instrument is transferred by a person other than the issuer to a subsequent party who qualifies as a "holder." [U.C.C. § 3–201(a)]

2. "Holder"

"Holder" is a technical term, meaning that the person in current *possession* is either the original payee or has taken the instrument thereafter pursuant to a valid *negotiation.*

3. "Issue"

An "issue" is the *first* delivery of an instrument by the maker or drawer to a holder or a remitter (*see* below). [U.C.C. § 3–105(a)]

 Example: Don Drawer writes a check naming Paula Payee as payee and signs it as the drawer. The check is "issued" as soon as Don gives it to Paula.

a. Remitter

A "remitter" is a person who makes payment using an instrument created by someone else. The most common example is a bank cashier's check drawn up at the request of a customer and sent to a creditor. In this situation, the bank is the drawer, the creditor is the payee, and the bank's customer is the remitter. The bank would "issue" the check by delivering it to the remitter for transmittal to the creditor/payee.

(1) Note

The remitter is not a "holder" because the remitter does not have *title* to the check. (*See* definition of "title," below.)

4. "Transfer"

The term "transfer" is defined as delivery by a person other than the issuer "for the purpose of giving to the person receiving delivery the right to enforce the instrument." [U.C.C. § 3–203]

5. "Person Entitled to Enforce the Instrument"

The original 1962 version of Article 3 spoke of certain persons as having "good title," a phrase that was left undefined. In the 1990 Revision, the concept of "good title" was dropped, and in its place a party is given rights only if that party qualifies as a *"person entitled to enforce the instrument."* [U.C.C. § 3–301] § 3–301 describes the "person entitled to enforce the instrument" as the holder (as well as certain other entities, such as the prior holder of a now-destroyed instrument). A "person entitled to enforce the instrument" is sometimes called a "PETE" (from the initials).

a. Bearer Paper

Anyone in *possession* of a bearer instrument is a holder thereof; *i.e.,* for bearer instruments, possession makes the holder entitled to enforce the instrument.

b. Order Paper

In the case of an instrument payable to the order of a named payee ("order paper"), the *named payee* becomes a holder upon acquiring possession of the instrument. Before a subsequent transferee can acquire title, however, the payee must *indorse* (sign his/her name to) the instrument and surrender possession to the transferee.

B. Negotiation Process

1. Bearer Instruments

A negotiable instrument created as bearer paper or subsequently converted into bearer paper (*see* p. 32) is negotiated *simply by delivering* the instrument. Once the transferee has possession, the transferee technically qualifies as a "holder." [U.C.C. § 1–201(21)]

Example: Dan Drawer writes a check payable to "Cash," which makes the check a bearer instrument. Any person coming into possession of the instrument is therefore a "holder," because he will have the requisite possession. (*See* p. 26)

2. Order Instruments

An instrument that is payable to the order of a specific payee is negotiated by *delivery* of the instrument *to that payee.* As noted previously, any further negotiation requires that the payee *indorse* the instrument *and deliver it* to the transferee. [U.C.C. § 3–205]

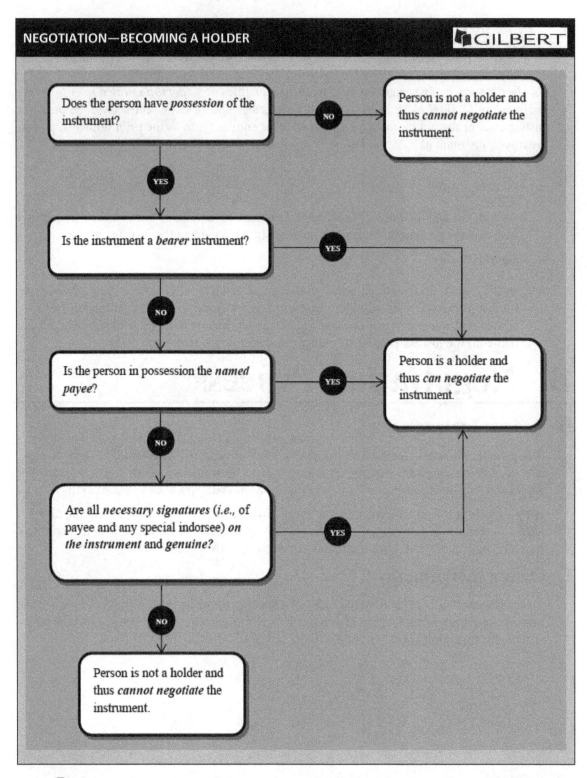

e.g.   **Example:** Dan Drawer writes a check payable to the order of Paula Payee. Upon receiving the check, Paula qualifies as a "holder." If Paula subsequently wishes to negotiate the check, she must indorse it and deliver possession to her transferee, who will then also qualify as a "holder."

a. Payee's Indorsement Must Be Valid

A person will not be entitled to enforce an order instrument unless the payee's indorsement is **authorized** and **valid.** Forging the payee's name prevents further negotiation, and no subsequent possessors of the instrument can qualify as "holders," nor a "person entitled to enforce the instrument." (*Note:* In certain situations, however, an unauthorized signature can be made "effective" under the principles of ratification or estoppel. *See* p. 99, p. 137)

Example: Dan Drawer writes a check payable to the order of Paula Payee. Before indorsement by Paula, the check is stolen from her by Terry Thief, who signs "Paula Payee" on the back and deposits the check in his account at Forgers National Bank for collection from Big Bucks Bank (the "drawee bank"). The check is still the property of Paula Payee. No one taking the check after the forgery (not Terry, Forgers National, or subsequent innocent transferees) can qualify as a "holder" or a "person entitled to enforce the instrument."

(1) Rationale

The order instrument is payable to whomever the payee *orders* payment, and when there is a forgery, there is no such valid order. Until she really orders payment to someone, only the payee has title to the instrument. The forger's pretense that the payee ordered payment to bearer by her apparent blank indorsement has no effect.

(2) Note

Technically, the forgery of the payee's name is treated as if the forger had foolishly signed his *own* name. [U.C.C. § 3–403(a); *and see* p. 9] Thus, the forger will be liable on the instrument, but because the valid signature of the payee is missing, the instrument has not been validly negotiated.

b. Multiple Payees

An instrument may be made payable to more than one payee. If their names on the payee line are connected by an "and," the instrument is payable to them *jointly* and any subsequent negotiation is effective only if *all* indorse the instrument. However, if the names are connected by "or" or "and/or," the instrument is payable to the payees alternatively, and the valid indorsement of any *one* of them is sufficient to pass title to a subsequent transferee. [U.C.C. § 3–110(d)]

Example: A check payable to the order of "George *and* Martha Washington" requires that *both* payees indorse the check in order to negotiate it further. If only one signs, the subsequent transferee would not qualify as a "holder" because a necessary indorsement is missing.

Compare: On the other hand, a check payable to "George *or* Martha Washington," or a check to "George *and/or* Martha Washington" can be negotiated by the indorsement of *either* payee—and that single signature is sufficient to transfer the instrument.

(1) Where Unclear

If it is not clear whether the instrument is payable jointly or in the alternative, the latter is presumed. [U.C.C. § 3–110(d)]

EXAM TIP   🔲GILBERT

Keep in mind that for order instruments the right to enforce the instrument will pass only if *all necessary signatures* of all payees and special indorsees (*see* p. 32) are on the instrument. Therefore, in questions involving order instruments, always check the indorsements carefully to make sure that all necessary ones are there.

---

c. Location of Indorsement

An indorsement must be written on the instrument. Typically, the indorsement is placed on the reverse side of the instrument, but it may also properly be placed on the front or on an *allonge.* [U.C.C. § 3–204(a)]

(1) Allonges

An "allonge" is a separate piece of paper "affixed" to an instrument and upon which an indorsement is written. [U.C.C. § 3–204(a)] The common law required that an allonge be glued to the original instrument, but under the U.C.C. the courts have held that an allonge may be stapled to the instrument. [*See* **Lamson v. Commercial Credit Corp.**, 531 P.2d 966 (Colo. 1975); One court has also blessed the use of an Acco fastener; **Federal Home Loan Mortg. Corp. v. Madison**, 2011 WL 2690617 (D. Ariz. 2011); another has held a paper clip is okay, **Olive Portfolio Alpha, LLC v. 116 West Hubbard Street, LLC**, 75 N.E.3d 381 (Ill. App. 2017)]

d. Effect of Transferring an Order Instrument Without Indorsement

The delivery of an order instrument without indorsement (or with one of several indorsements missing) may be effective to transfer *possession,* but it is *not* effective to constitute a valid *negotiation.*

(1) Rights of Transferee Without Indorsement

Unless and until obtaining the indorsement, the transferee of the instrument does *not* have the status of a "holder," and certainly cannot qualify as a HDC, discussed *infra.* Therefore, the transferee *cannot negotiate* the instrument. However, the transferee is not entirely without rights:

(a) Suit to Compel Indorsement

If the transferee paid *value* for the instrument, the transferee has "the specifically enforceable right to have the unqualified indorsement" of the transferor. [U.C.C. § 3–203(c)] What this means, however, is that the transferee would have to sue in equity for a decree ordering the transferor to indorse.

(b) Suit to Enforce Instrument

Similarly, if the instrument is due, the transferee can bring suit to enforce it even though it lacks an indorsement, but the transferee would have to prove ownership rights in the instrument (*i.e.,* that the transferee was entitled to the missing indorsement). The transferee would qualify as a "person entitled to enforce the instrument." [U.C.C. § 3–301]

1) Note

Lacking the status of "holder," the transferee will also have to bear the burden of proving the *validity* of the instrument itself (*i.e.,* due execution and negotiation, etc.). [**Northside Building & Investment Co. v. Finance Co. of America,** 166 S.E.2d 608 (Ga. 1969)] A "holder," on the other hand, is prima facie entitled to recover on the instrument; *i.e.,* once the signatures are established, the burden is always on the defendant-obligor to prove some defense. [U.C.C. § 3–308; *and see* p. 55]

(2) Different Rules for Banks

Traditional concepts governing negotiable instruments give way to the rules governing bank collections under Article 4 of the U.C.C. A depositary bank that takes an unindorsed check *for collection* becomes a holder without the necessity of any indorsement at all. As long as the depositary bank's customer was a holder at the time of deposit, the depositary bank becomes a holder whether or not the customer indorses the check, and, by initiating collection on the check, the depositary bank warrants to later parties that the check was paid" to the customer or deposited into the customer's account. In effect this is a warranty that the money got to the right place, and puts the risk that it did not on the depositary bank. [U.C.C. § 4–205]

Example: Dan Drawer writes a check payable jointly to the order of Terry Thief and Paula Payee. Careless National Bank allows Terry to deposit the check in his individual account without either his indorsement nor that of Paula, and forwards it for collection. Section 4–204 clears up the missing indorsement of Terry, the bank's own customer, but not that of Paula, who is not its customer. Careless National is liable to Paula for conversion of her interest in the check. It makes no difference that Careless National was acting in good faith.

(3) When Indorsement Later Obtained

Upon obtaining the transferor's indorsement, holder status is thereupon vested in the transferee, who now becomes a person entitled to enforce the instrument.

(a) HDC Status

The transferee may qualify as a HDC if the other requirements for due course holding are met. (*See* p. 38)

1) But Note

For the purpose of determining whether the transferee had "notice" of any adverse claim or defense to the instrument (an essential element for due course holding), the transferee's knowledge is measured *at the time the transferee obtains the missing indorsement.* [U.C.C. § 3–203(c)] This means that if the transferee finds out about some defense or claim in the interval between the time of paying for and obtaining possession of the instrument and the time the missing indorsement is obtained, the transferee cannot qualify as a HDC. (*See* p. 51)

EXAM TIP   GILBERT

If your exam question involves the transfer of an order instrument without a valid indorsement, pay attention to the party who is the *transferee.* If the transferee is a *bank* taking the unindorsed instrument for collection, the bank becomes a holder even without the indorsement. However, if the transferee is *not a bank,* a valid indorsement is necessary to attain the status of a holder.

---

e. Indorsement of Partial Interests Not a "Negotiation"

If a transferor purports to transfer only part of an instrument, no negotiation occurs. [U.C.C. § 3–203(d)] An indorsement that attempts to convey less than the complete amount of the instrument is not a negotiation and the transferee does not qualify as a "holder." The rationale is that a cause of action on a negotiable instrument cannot be split up.

e.g. **Example:** Dan Drawer draws a check payable to the order of Paula Payee, who indorses it: "Pay George Washington two-thirds and Martha Washington one-third, /s/ Paula Payee." Neither George nor Martha qualifies as a holder.

cf. **Compare:** If Paula writes "pay George and Martha Washington, /s/Paula Payee," a negotiation has occurred; *i.e.,* this indorsement transfers the entire interest to George and Martha as tenants in common of the whole amount, and they both become holders.

3. Special or Blank Indorsements

a. Special Indorsements

If the payee of order paper names a **new** payee when indorsing the instrument, there is a "special" indorsement, and any further negotiation of the paper requires the valid (authorized) indorsement of the new payee. Only the new payee (referred to as the "special indorsee") can now qualify as a holder. Naming a new payee when the original payee indorses thus preserves the "order" character of the instrument (so that negotiation requires *indorsements* as well as possession). [U.C.C. § 3–205(a)]

e.g. **Example:** Dan Drawer draws a check payable to the order of Paula Payee and gives it to her, which makes Paula a "holder." Paula wishes to negotiate the check to her mother, Flora Flowers, so she indorses it "Pay to Flora Flowers, /s/ Paula Payee." This special indorsement means that Flora alone (upon obtaining possession) is the only possible "holder" of the check. No one after Flora can qualify as a "holder" without Flora's valid indorsement, which is necessary to a valid negotiation.

(1) Forgery of Special Indorsee's Name

Because the special indorsee's name must be validly indorsed on the instrument for further negotiation, no one can be a "holder" following the forgery of the special indorsee's name. Legally, it is treated the same as a forgery of the payee's name. (*See* p. 28)

(2) Words of Negotiability Not Required

Words of negotiability (*e.g.,* "pay to the order of . . .") are not required in an indorsement; thus the lack thereof does **not** affect the negotiability of the instrument.

e.g. **Example:** A special indorsement reading "pay to John Smith" is as freely negotiable as one indorsed "pay to the order of John Smith."

b. Blank Indorsements

If the payee of an order instrument simply signs the back of the instrument without naming a new payee, a "blank indorsement" occurs and the instrument is converted into **bearer** paper, which can be negotiated without further indorsements. [U.C.C. § 3–205(b)]

e.g. **Example:** Dan Drawer writes a check to the order of Paula Payee, who signs the check on the back (a "blank indorsement"). The check is blown out the window and recovered by Frank Forger, who takes the check to Gullible Grocery and indorses it as "Mark Money" (the town's wealthiest citizen) in payment for groceries. Gullible is a "holder" because the instrument was bearer paper at the time of Frank's forgery and could have been negotiated by delivery alone. Forgery of names **not** necessary to a valid negotiation will not keep later takers from becoming "holders" or "persons entitled to the instrument." [U.C.C. § 3–301]

 Compare: If, in the previous example, Paula had written "Pay to Mark Money, /s/ Paula Payee," there would have been a *special* indorsement, and the check would have remained order paper. A forgery of Money's name would *not* be a valid *negotiation.* Thus, Gullible or other subsequent transferees could not qualify as "holders."

c. **Conversion of Blank Indorsements to Special Indorsements**

Bearer paper is often considered too negotiable because it must be guarded like cash. Thus, a holder of bearer paper may convert it into order paper by writing in the name of a new payee above the last indorsement.

Example: Dan Drawer gives Paula Payee a check payable to her order, which Paula indorses in blank and mails to her mother, Flora Flowers. Flora can convert this bearer instrument back into order paper by writing "Pay to Flora Flowers" above Paula's indorsement. The check can then be negotiated only with Flora's valid indorsement.

d. **Multiple Indorsements—Last Valid Indorsement Controls**

If the instrument has been indorsed several times, some specially and some in blank, the *last valid indorsement controls* what is necessary for further negotiation.

Example: Harry has in his possession a check that was drawn payable "to the order of Paula Payee." The back of the instrument is as follows:

> Pay John Smith
> */s/ Paula Payee*
> */s/ John Smith*
> Pay Peggy Lee
> */s/ Fred Farmer*
> */s/ Delta Dawn*

Harry cannot qualify as a holder of the check. As originally drawn, the check was order paper ("paper to the order of Paula Payee"). When Paula indorsed, she named a specific payee (John Smith) and so the paper remained order paper (requiring Smith's signature for negotiation). Smith signed in blank (he did not name a new special indorsee) and so the check was converted to bearer paper and could be negotiated by delivery alone. At some point, the paper was negotiated to Fred Farmer, who changed the check back into order paper by naming a new special indorsee (Peggy Lee). Thus, further negotiation required Peggy Lee's indorsement plus delivery. The check apparently was delivered to Delta Dawn, but there was no indorsement by Peggy Lee. Delta Dawn signed in blank and the paper was delivered to Harry. Unfortunately, Harry does not qualify as a holder because the check was not properly negotiated, because Peggy Lee did not indorse.

EXAM TIP GILBERT

If the instrument has been indorsed several times, some in blank and some specially, the *last valid indorsement controls* what is necessary for further negotiation.

---

4. Other Types of Indorsements

a. Qualified Indorsements

An indorsement that adds the words *"without recourse"* is a "qualified" indorsement. The effect is to limit the legal liability otherwise imposed on indorsers by U.C.C. § 3–415. (*See* discussion p. 78)

b. Restrictive Indorsements

Any other language added to an indorsement creates a "restrictive" indorsement. Examples include *conditions* ("pay Flora Flowers only if she has paid her daughter all the money still owing under her father's will"), *trust indorsements* ("pay John Doe in trust for Jane Doe"), and indorsements restricting further negotiation to the *check collection system* ("for deposit only," "pay any bank," etc.). (The legal effect of restrictive indorsements is discussed p. 108)

c. Anomalous Indorsements

An "anomalous" indorsement is one made "by a person who is not a holder of the instrument." [U.C.C. § 3–205(d)] Thus, a person who adds his name to an instrument to become a surety thereon is making an anomalous indorsement (for the rules of suretyship connected with such indorsement, *see* p. 81).

Example: When Albert borrowed $5,000 from Big Bank, the bank made him get a co-signer, so Albert had his mother, Mae, indorse the promissory note on the back as an indorser. The promissory note was then signed by Albert as maker and given to Big Bank, the payee. Big Bank sold the promissory note to Gouge Finance Company, indorsing "Big Bank" under Mae's signature on the back of the note. Gouge Finance Company is on notice that Mae has signed for accommodation because she has made an *anomalous* indorsement; she was not a "holder" at the time she indorsed, and her name has nothing to do with the negotiation of the instrument; therefore she must have signed for accommodation, and Gouge must give her whatever rights flow from that status.

TYPES OF INDORSEMENTS	◤GILBERT
SPECIAL	Names a *particular person* as indorsee; the indorsee must sign in order for the instrument to be further negotiated.
BLANK	Does *not name a particular person* as indorsee; creates bearer paper, which may be negotiated by delivery alone.
QUALIFIED	Contains the words *"without recourse,"* which limit the legal liability otherwise imposed on indorsers.
RESTRICTIVE	Any other language that *limits payment* (*e.g.,* conditions, trust indorsements, and restrictions on the check collection system).
ANOMALOUS	Made by a person who is *not a holder* of the instrument, usually for suretyship purposes.

5. Common Problems with Indorsements

In addition to the situations discussed above, the following problems are often encountered with indorsements:

a. Wrong Name or Misspelled Name

If an instrument is payable to a holder but the instrument does not reflect the person's true name (*e.g.,* because of a misspelling, use of a nickname, etc.), indorsement will be effective if it is made in the name as stated, in the holder's true name, or in both names. In any case, a person paying or taking the instrument for value or collection may demand that indorsement be made in both names. [U.C.C. § 3–204(d)]

Example: When Dan Drawer makes a check to Paula Payee, he spells her name "Paula Payie." Paula may negotiate the check by signing *any* version of her name, but her transferee (*e.g.,* her bank) can require Paula to indorse the check in a form acceptable to the transferee.

b. Ambiguities

Any ambiguity concerning the capacity in which a signature is made is resolved in favor of an indorsement. [U.C.C. § 3–204(a)]

Example: A promissory note contains the language "Ann promises to pay," but is signed "Ann" and "Bob." Bob would be deemed to have signed as an indorser (and hence would be only secondarily liable on the instrument; *see* p. 78).

(1) Parol Evidence Inadmissible

Parol evidence is *not admissible* to show that Bob (above) intended to sign in any other capacity (*e.g.,* as maker or guarantor). Any signature on an instrument that has no obvious contrary meaning is *conclusively presumed* to be an indorsement, and gives rise to indorser liability. [U.C.C. §§ 3–204(a), 3–117]

(2) Exception—"Usage of Trade"

However, courts may take judicial notice of the fact that a signature placed in the lower right hand corner of a promissory note is meant by "usage of trade" [U.C.C. § 1–303(c)] to be the signature of a *maker* rather than an indorser, unless there is some indication to the contrary (*e.g.,* a promissory note which begins "I, John Doe, the maker, hereby promise to pay . . . ," followed by Doe's signature and the signature of Sam Surety). [**Philadelphia Bond & Mortgage Co. v. Highland Crest Homes, Inc.,** 288 A.2d 916 (Pa. 1972)]

Chapter Four
Holders in Due Course

Chapter Approach

From common law days, there has been a strong policy in favor of insulating remote holders of an instrument from disputes between the immediate parties to the instrument. This policy has been retained by the U.C.C. The party whom this policy is designed to protect is called the holder in due course ("HDC"). As previously noted, a HDC takes a negotiable instrument free from all but a few of the defenses that could be raised against enforcement of a simple contract that has been assigned.

Whether the transferee of a negotiable instrument qualifies as a HDC will obviously affect the transferee's liability on the instrument and the claims or defenses that may be asserted against him. Thus, in an exam question, once you have established that a negotiable instrument has been properly negotiated, you must determine whether the holder of the instrument qualifies as a HDC. A HDC is:

(i) A *holder* who takes the instrument,

(ii) For *value*,

(iii) In *good faith*, and

(iv) *Without notice* that it is overdue or has been dishonored, or of any defense against or claim to it on the part of any person.

Even if the party holding the instrument in your exam question does not meet these technical requirements, keep in mind that he still may be afforded the rights of a HDC under the "shelter rule," which generally allows any transferee to "step into the shoes" of the HDC who formerly held the instrument.

A. Code Requirements for Due Course Holding

1. In General

According to § 3–302(a)(1) of the U.C.C., a HDC is: (i) a *holder* who takes the instrument, (ii) for *value*, (iii) in *good faith*, and (iv) *without notice* that it is overdue or has been dishonored, or of any defense against or claim to it on the part of any person.

Is the person in possession of the instrument a *holder* (see Negotiation—Becoming a Holder chart, *supra*)?

— NO → The person *cannot be an HDC*.

↓ YES

Did the holder take the instrument for *value* (executed consideration, a security interest, payment for an antecedent debt, a negotiable instrument, an irrevocable obligation to a third person)?

— NO →

↓ YES

Did the holder take the instrument *in good faith* (with honesty in fact *and* compliance with reasonable commercial standards)?

— NO → The holder is *not an HDC* and so generally * will be subject to all defenses that the maker or drawer may have concerning the instrument.

↓ YES

Did the holder take the instrument *without notice* that it is *overdue*, has been *dishonored*, or *of any claims or defenses* at the time(s) the holder gave value *and* took possession?

— NO →

↓ YES

The holder *is an HDC* and can enforce the instrument subject only to *real* defenses.

* Under the shelter rule, discussed at 56, if the holder does not qualify as an HDC but was a transferee of an HDC, the holder will have the rights of an HDC unless the holder was a party to a fraud involving the instrument.

2. Holder

The first requirement of due course holding is that the person in possession thereof *be* a "holder." In other words, the transferee must have possession pursuant to a valid negotiation, free of forgeries of those names necessary to the chain of title (*i.e.*, the payee and any special indorsees). You have to hold to be a "holder."

EXAM TIP   GILBERT

Determining whether a person is a HDC is a two-step process: First, you must determine whether the person is a *"holder"* (*see* p. 26) and second, you must determine whether the person *holds in "due course"* (takes the instrument for value, in good faith, and without notice of overdueness, dishonor, or defenses). However, recall that one cannot be a HDC if the instrument is *nonnegotiable* (*see* p. 8).

---

3. Purchase for Value

A holder takes an instrument for *value* [U.C.C. § 3–303]:

(i)   To the extent that the agreed consideration has been *performed*, or that the holder acquires a security interest in or a *lien* on the instrument otherwise than by legal process; *or*

(ii) When the holder takes the instrument in payment of or as security for an antecedent claim against *any* person, whether or not the claim is due; *or*

(iii) When the holder gives a negotiable instrument for it or makes an irrevocable commitment to a third person (*e.g.*, a letter of credit).

a. Executory Promise Is Not "Value"

U.C.C. § 3–303 makes it clear that an executory promise—*i.e.*, a promise to give value *in the future*—is *not* itself "value" as the Code uses the term in Article 3 (though it would certainly be valid consideration in the meaning of the common law of contracts). Hence, if all the holder has parted with is an unperformed promise, the holder is *not* a HDC. However, if the executory promise includes an *irrevocable commitment* to a third person (such as is made by a bank issuing a letter of credit), value is given as soon as the promise is made.

(1) Rationale

If the holder still owes the consideration for the instrument, the holder can simply not perform the promise upon discovering that there is some defense to the instrument. Because the holder can thereby avoid harm, there is no need to give the holder the extraordinary status of a HDC. Where, however, the holder's promise is binding because of a commitment to a third person, there is no such easy "out," and the promise constitutes current value.

(2) Total vs. Partial Failure of Consideration

Note that one can be a *partial* HDC where only part of the consideration is executory. [U.C.C. § 3–302(d)]

Example: Anne indorses a check to Bill for $20,000, for which Bill pays Anne $8,000, and Bill agrees to cancel Anne's preexisting $12,000 debt *upon the bank's honoring the check.* Bill is a HDC only to the extent of $8,000, because his promise to cancel the debt was executory. [**Halbert v. Horton**, 185 N.W.2d 76 (Mich. 1970)]

Compare: Had Bill accepted the check *as payment* of the antecedent debt, Bill would be a HDC for *the full amount.* [*See* U.C.C. § 3–303]

EXAM TIP   **▉GILBERT**

It is important to understand the difference between a purchase at a discount (*see* p. 50) and partial failure of consideration (which makes the holder a proportional HDC). In the discount case, the holder pays less than the face value of the instrument (*e.g.,* pays $5,000 for a $6,000 note) but pays the *full agreed consideration* ($5,000). The holder is a HDC for the full value ($6,000). However, if the holder pays only part of what he agreed to pay (*e.g.,* pays $2,500 of the agreed $5,000 for a $6,000 note), the holder is a HDC only *in proportion* to the consideration paid ($3,000—half value).

---

(3) "Value" and "Consideration" Distinguished

"Consideration" is essential to a negotiable instrument, as it is to any contract, and the lack or failure of consideration may constitute a valid defense to the instrument's enforcement. An executory promise by itself *is* sufficient "consideration," but it is *not* "value." "Value" is important only to the question of whether the holder can qualify as a HDC.

b. Antecedent Debt as "Value"

The holder takes for "value" when taking the instrument either as security for an antecedent debt or as payment thereof—regardless of whether the debt is then due. The debt may be that of the transferor or any third party.

c. Security Interest in Instrument

The holder also takes for "value" when acquiring a security interest in the instrument *by agreement*, rather than by operation of law.

Example: The payee of a note *pledges* it to a bank as security for a loan, and the pledge agreement gives the bank a security interest therein. The bank is a holder for value to the extent of the value given.

Compare: But an attaching creditor or any other person who acquires a lien by legal process is *not* a holder for "value." [U.C.C. § 3–302(c)]

Example: When the sheriff seized all of a debtor's assets pursuant to a write of execution of a judgment won against the debtor by one of his creditors, the seizure of a promissory note made payable to "bearer" would not be taken by this creditor for value. This is not a voluntary transaction and the creditor acquired the note by operation of law, not by agreement with the debtor.

d. Special Rules Where Holder Is a Bank

When an instrument is negotiated to a bank (other than the drawee) as part of the collecting process, and the bank credits the depositor's account accordingly, is the bank a holder for "value"?

(1) Crediting Depositor's Account

Merely crediting the depositor's account—a bookkeeping transaction—is *not* "value," because the bank certainly would have the right to set aside the credit if the instrument were returned unpaid. [U.C.C. § 4–214]

(2) Permitting Withdrawals from Depositor's Account

However, the bank *becomes* a holder for "value" to the extent that it permits withdrawals of the amount credited to the depositor's account—using the "first-money-in, first-money-out" ("FIFO") rule to determine if the particular item credited has been reached. [U.C.C. §§ 4–211, 4–210(a), (b)]

Example: If the amount of the deposited item was $500 at a time when there was already $1,000 in the account, the bank would become a holder for "value" only to the extent that it permitted withdrawals against the account in excess of $1,000. [**Security Bank v. Whiting Turner Contracting Co.**, 277 A.2d 106 (D.C. 1971)]

(a) Effect

Having permitted withdrawals against the check, the bank is a HDC, with a solid right to insist on payment of the check free and clear of most of the defenses available to the person who issued the check (and who then either stopped payment or failed to cover it).

(3) Security Interest of Collecting Bank as "Value"

Any time the collecting bank has a *security interest* in the item being collected, the bank has given "value." [U.C.C. § 4–211]

(a) Creation of Security Interest

As noted above, a bank has a security interest whenever it has permitted pre-collection withdrawal of the amount of the check (or when the customer has an absolute, contracted-for right to withdraw the money prior to collection). However, the bank can also *contract* for a security interest in the account and thereby give "value" for every check placed in the account.

Example: Bank loans Customer $10,000, and Customer signs an agreement giving Bank a security interest in her checking account, so that Bank may look to the account as collateral for the loan. Because its security interest now attaches automatically to every check placed in Customer's account, Bank has given value on every check, including those which Customer has not drawn against prior to collection. [**Bowling Green, Inc. v. State Street Bank & Trust Co.**, 425 F.2d 81 (1st Cir. 1970)]

VALUE	• *Performance* of the agreed *consideration*
	• Acquisition by the holder of a *lien or security interest* in the instrument
	• Taking the instrument as payment of or security for an *antecedent debt*
	• Giving the instrument in exchange for the incurring of an *irrevocable obligation* to a third person by the person taking the instrument
	• Permitting *withdrawals* from the depositor's account of the amount credited
	• Negotiable instruments acquired by *FDIC* in taking over failed financial institutions
NOT VALUE	• Portion of the agreed *consideration not paid*
	• *Executory promise*
	• Merely *crediting* the depositor's account
	• Purchasing instrument at a *judicial sale*
	• Acquiring instrument in *taking over an estate*
	• Purchasing instrument as part of a *bulk transaction*

e. Special Cases Where Purchaser Is Held Mere Successor to Prior Holder

There are a few exceptional cases in which a holder, even though *having paid* for the instrument, is not accorded the status of an independent purchaser for value. Rather, the holder is held merely to succeed to the rights of his transferor in the instrument in the following situations:

(i) *By purchasing the instrument at judicial sale* (execution sale, bankruptcy sale, etc.) or taking it under legal process;

(ii) *By acquiring it in taking over an estate* (as administrator, etc.); or

(iii) *By purchasing it as part of a bulk transaction* (*e.g.*, corporation buys the entire inventory of predecessor).

[U.C.C. § 3–302(c)]

f. Federal Regulatory Agencies Exception

In spite of the refusal of the U.C.C. in § 3–302(c) to apply HDC status to those taking possession of instruments through legal process or as part of taking over an estate, *federal law* gives HDC status to federal regulatory agencies (*e.g.*, the FDIC) when they take over failed financial institutions. [**Campbell Leasing, Inc. v. FDIC**, 901 F.2d 1244 (5th Cir. 1990)] However, the FDIC cannot be a HDC for *nonnegotiable* instruments. [**Sunbelt Savings, FSB, Dallas, Texas v. Montross**, 923 F.2d 353 (5th Cir. 1991)]

4. Purchase in Good Faith

Basically, the separate requirement of "good faith" means that the holder was acting honestly in the conduct or transaction involved. In both Article 1 and Article 3 the U.C.C. defines "good faith" as *"honesty in fact,"* a purely subjective test and also "the observance of *reasonable commercial standards of fair dealing"* (an objective test). [U.C.C. §§ 1–201(b)(20), 3–103(a)(6)]

5. Without Notice

The holder must purchase the instrument without notice (actual knowledge or reason to know) that it is *overdue*, or has been *dishonored*, or of any *defense* against or claim to it on the part of any person. [U.C.C. § 3–302(a)(2)] Because U.C.C. § 1–202 defines "notice" broadly as including "reason to know," whether a holder has notice is measured by an *objective* (reasonable person) standard as well as what the holder actually knew.

a. Without Notice That It Is Overdue

If the purchaser acquires the instrument with reason to know that it is already overdue, the purchaser cannot qualify as a HDC.

(1) Rationale

Such notice is a *"red flag"* to the purchaser that there may be some defect in, or defense to, the instrument;

(2) Facts Constituting Notice

The purchaser has notice that the instrument is overdue—and hence cannot qualify as a HDC—whenever the purchaser *knows or has reason to know* any of the following [U.C.C. § 3–304]:

(a) Existence of Default

Notice that any part of the *principal* amount is overdue, or that there is an uncured default in payment of another instrument of the *same* series (below) prevents HDC status.

e.g. **Example:** Where an instrument bears a *fixed maturity date*, and the purchaser acquired it after midnight on the date set for its payment, she has notice that it is overdue.

e.g. **Example:** Likewise, if the principal is payable in installments, and the maker has defaulted on *any installment* of principal, a subsequent purchaser has notice of the default and cannot be a HDC.

1) Distinguish—Default in Interest Payments

Knowledge of a default merely in *interest* payments does not prevent due course holding. [U.C.C. § 3–304(c)]

2) Distinguish—Other Obligations

Knowledge of the obligor's default in payment of *other* obligations or instruments does not prevent due course holding, unless the instruments were of the *same series* (*e.g.*, where several notes maturing at different dates were issued at the same time for a single indebtedness).

(b) Acceleration

Notice that an event has occurred that accelerates the maturity date prevents HDC status. [U.C.C. § 3–304(b)(3)]

Example: Ingrid Investor buys a promissory note having a maturity date of February 1, 2025, but payable earlier if George W. Bush should win the Presidency. If Ingrid purchases the note in 2026, she cannot qualify as a HDC—because she has reason to know that the note is overdue.

(c) Demand Instruments

Instruments currently dated, or payable "at sight" or "on demand" become overdue as follows:

1) Checks

Checks become overdue 90 days after their date. Someone first acquiring a check 90 days after its date therefore could not qualify as a holder in due course. [U.C.C. § 3–304(a)(2)]

2) Other Instruments

Other instruments (*e.g.*, promissory notes) that are demand instruments become overdue according to the following factual test: "when the instrument has been outstanding for a period of time after its date which is unreasonably long under the circumstances of the particular case in light of the nature of the instrument and usage of trade." [U.C.C. § 3–304(a)(3)]

b. Without Notice That It Has Been Dishonored

If the purchaser acquires the instrument with reason to know that it has been dishonored, the purchaser cannot qualify as a HDC. Dishonor occurs when the instrument is returned after presentment *without payment or acceptance* within the allotted time (*see* further discussion p. 88).

c. Without Notice of Defenses and Claims

If the purchaser acquires the instrument with reason to know of defenses or claims to the instrument, the purchaser cannot qualify as a HDC.

(1) Time When Notice Received as Affecting HDC Status

To be effective, the "notice" to the purchaser must have been received in such a manner and within such time as to afford the purchaser a *reasonable opportunity* to act upon it; *i.e.*, notice received by a bank president one minute before the bank's teller cashes the check is not effective to prevent the bank from being a HDC. [U.C.C. § 3–302(f)]

(a) Notice to Large Organization

When dealing with any large organization, notice is deemed effective from the time it would have been received if the personnel in the organization had exercised *due diligence*. [U.C.C. § 1–202(f)]

(b) Notice at Time Purchaser Becomes a Holder and Gives Value

The purchaser's "good faith" and "notice" are measured as of the time the purchaser acquires and *gives value* for the instrument *as a holder*. This point is significant where the purchaser of an order instrument neglects to obtain the transferor's indorsement at the time of the purchase. The purchaser cannot be a "holder" until the missing indorsement is obtained. Until that time, the purchaser is a mere transferee in possession of an unindorsed order instrument (*see* p. 30). And if the purchaser is put on notice of some adverse claim or defense to the instrument prior to obtaining the transferor's indorsement, the purchaser can never qualify as a HDC because by the time "holder" status is achieved, he has notice of the existence of a claim or defense.

e.g. **Example:** Mortgage lender sells the promissory note on which it is the named payee to Big Bank for $100,000. Whether Big Bank is a HDC is measured as of the moment at which it gave value for the note (*i.e.*, paid the $100,000). Subsequent notice of problems with the note (such as the defense of the maker of the note that the mortgage lender committed fraud at the time of the loan) will not destroy Big Bank's HDC status once achieved. However, this presumes that at the time of giving value Big Bank was a "holder" on the note. If the mortgage lender failed to indorse the note as payee, we will postpone determining HDC status until that event occurs, because until then the new taker is not a holder. If the payee did not indorse the note when Big Bank paid the $100,000 and Big Bank learns of the maker's defense before getting the payee's indorsement, Big Bank cannot become a HDC because it has notice of a defense before becoming a holder.

EXAM TIP   ◤GILBERT

Remember that in order to attain "holder" status a person must have (i) *possession* of the instrument and (ii) the *right to enforce* the instrument (*see* p. 27). The delivery of an order instrument without the required indorsements may transfer possession but is not a negotiation because the transferee may not enforce the instrument. This can be important on an exam because by the time the transferee gets the indorsements and becomes a holder, she may also have learned of a *claim or defense* to the instrument and thus *cannot be a HDC.*

---

(2) Notice Imputed to Purchaser Where Instrument Incomplete or Irregular ("Red Lights" Doctrine)

As will be seen below, knowledge of facts extraneous to the instrument will not ordinarily be imputed to the purchaser. But the purchaser is charged with knowledge of defenses or claims apparent *from the face of the instrument.* Thus, if the instrument bears "apparent evidence of forgery or alteration or is . . . otherwise so irregular or incomplete as to call into question its authenticity," knowledge of potential defenses or claims is imputed to the purchaser, and thus the purchaser cannot qualify as a HDC. [U.C.C. § 3–302(a)(1)] Such obviously suspicious matters are often referred to as "red lights" which a good faith purchaser would stop to investigate. [**Eldon's Super Fresh Stores, Inc. v. Merrill Lynch, Pierce, Fenner & Smith, Inc.**, 207 N.W.2d 282 (Minn. 1973)]

(a) Effect

In practice, this means that minor erasures or omissions in the instrument (*e.g.*, date of month omitted in a demand note) would not prevent HDC status; however, an omission that raises a question as to the bona fides of the instrument constitutes "notice" of a potential claim or defense to the instrument and thus prevents HDC status.

(3) "Notice"—"Closed Eyes" Doctrine

While mere grounds for suspicion are not enough to constitute "notice," a purchaser cannot ignore the obvious or purposefully avoid finding out the truth. The U.C.C.

specifically provides that a person is **charged with notice** of any fact if from all of the facts and circumstances known to the person at the time in question he has **reason to know** that such fact exists. [U.C.C. § 1–201(25)(c)]

(a) Effect

Thus, where the circumstances are such that the purchaser (subjectively) must have realized that there was some sort of defect in or defense to the instrument, the purchaser cannot close his eyes and escape the truth. The *purposeful* failure to inquire because of a belief or fear of what might be uncovered also shows *lack of honesty* in fact—*i.e.*, *"bad faith."* [**General Investment Corp. v. Angelini**, 278 A.2d 193 (N.J. 1971)]

e.g. **Example:** A cashier's check bears the indorsement "Deposit to A-B Partnership Account," signed by both partners. Bank officer observes Partner A strike the quoted words and then deposit the check in his personal account. Bank's failure to make inquiry from Partner B under such circumstances may be held to be bad faith—motivated by a belief that inquiry would have disclosed that Partner A was acting without authority. [**Christian v. California Bank**, 30 Cal. 2d 421 (1947)]

(4) Limitation—"Close Connection" Doctrine

Moreover, an increasing number of courts take the position that where the holder of an instrument is "closely connected" to the transaction out of which the instrument arose, the holder may be *charged* with knowledge of any defenses or claims involved in the transaction—even though it cannot be shown that the holder had actual knowledge thereof. This doctrine is particularly likely to be applied in *consumer sales financing* transactions, but it has also been used in commercial cases; see **St. James v. Diversified Comm. Fin. Corp.**, 102 Nev. 23, 714 P.2d 179 (1986).

(a) Relevant Factors

The following factors are among those usually relied upon by courts in finding that a holder (creditor) is so "closely connected" to the transaction as to be charged with knowledge of defenses assertable against the seller.

1) Go-participation in the underlying sales transaction, as where the holder has *prepared the instruments* and written assignments thereof before the instruments were even executed. [**Unico v. Owen**, 232 A.2d 405 (N.J. 1967)]

2) The existence of an *agency* relationship whereby the seller acts as an agent of the holder in soliciting the buyers for such transactions. [**Calvert Credit Corp. v. Williams**, 244 A.2d 494 (DC. 1968)]

3) The fact that the seller and holder are actually *owned or controlled* by the same persons or companies. [**Jones v. Approved Bancredit Corp.**, 256 A.2d 739 (Del. 1969)]

4) Continuous dealings between the seller and holder, particularly in the face of the holder having *actual knowledge* that this particular seller has engaged in fraudulent sales practices in the past. [**Security Central National Bank v. Williams**, 368 N.E.2d 1264 (Ohio 1976)]

Example: Paula Proprietor buys a car for her small business on credit from Happy Jack Auto Sales ("HJAS"), signing a promissory note payable to HJAS. The car dealer then discounts (*i.e.*, sells) the note to Happy Jack Finance Company ("HJFC") and declares bankruptcy. The car blows up and injures Proprietor, but HJFC still demands payment on the note as a HDC. It is discovered that HJAS and HJFC have the same officers, stockholders, and place of business, that HJFC bought all HJAS commercial paper, and that HJFC supplied HJAS with forms and ran credit checks on prospective HJAS customers. HJFC would probably be considered too "closely connected" with HJAS to become a HDC of the promissory note, so that Proprietor could assert her defenses when pressed for payment by HJFC.

(b) Bases for Denying HDC Status

When a court denies HDC status to the seller's assignee under the "close connection" theory, it may do so on the ground that: (i) the assignee did not take the paper in *good faith*, (ii) the assignee had *notice*, or (iii) the alleged assignee is the *same entity* as the original seller—so that it was a party to the transaction creating the paper and not an assignee at all. [**Unico v. Owen**, *supra*]

(c) Consumer Protection Statutes

Federal and state consumer protection statutes have adopted the "close connection" doctrine and impute notice to a lender that has an interlocking relationship with the seller. (*See* further discussion p. 56)

WILL THE HOLDER BE CHARGED WITH NOTICE OF DEFENSES OR CLAIMS?	◼GILBERT
"RED LIGHTS" DOCTRINE	Holder is charged with knowledge of defenses or claims apparent *from the face of the instrument.*
"CLOSED EYES" DOCTRINE	Holder is charged with knowledge of any fact if from all of the facts and circumstances she has *reason to know* that such fact exists.
"CLOSE CONNECTION" DOCTRINE	Holder "closely connected" to the transaction is charged with knowledge of defenses or claims *involved in the transaction.*

(5) Notice of Breach of Fiduciary Duty

No one can qualify as a HDC if she takes the instrument from a fiduciary with knowledge that the fiduciary is in breach of his fiduciary duties.

(a) Fiduciary Defined

A fiduciary is defined as an "agent, trustee, partner, corporate officer or director, or other representative owing a fiduciary duty with respect to an instrument." [U.C.C. § 3–307(a)(1)] Thus, if John Jones is the trustee of a trust established for the benefit of Betty Beneficiary, John would be a fiduciary; in this situation Betty would be called the "represented person."

(b) Breach of Fiduciary Duty—Meaning

If the fiduciary is named as such on the instrument ("Pay to the order of John Jones, Trustee for Berry Beneficiary"), those taking the instrument would have notice of breach of the fiduciary's duty if he uses the instrument for his own benefit: *e.g.*, puts it in his individual bank account, uses it as security for his own personal loan, or negotiates it to another to pay a personal debt. [U.C.C. § 3–307(b)] However, a paycheck to John Jones personally made by the trust would not give notice of anything unusual because trustees are entitled to be paid for their services. [U.C.C. § 3–307(b)(3) and Off. Com. 4]

(c) Claim of Represented Person

Where the taker from the fiduciary has notice that the fiduciary is in breach of his duty, not only will the taker not qualify as a holder in due course, but the taker is subject to a *claim* by the represented person, and must surrender the instrument or its proceeds. [U.C.C. § 3–307(b)]

e.g. **Example:** When Aunt died, she left her infant niece Sally a $10,000 certificate of deposit. Sally's parents took the certificate of deposit to Big Bank and used it as collateral for a loan so they could start a business. Big Bank took possession of the certificate of deposit, which the parents, as Sally's guardians, indorsed over to the bank. In this case the bank knows that the parents are misusing the certificate of deposit, so they are breaching their fiduciary duty to Sally. The bank will not be a HDC, and Sally can retrieve the certificate of deposit from the bank without having to repay the loan.

(6) Waiver of Defenses by Contract

Where they are unable to rely on HDC status to avoid defenses to a negotiable instrument, finance companies may seek to accomplish the same result by having the seller provide in the original contract that the buyer (obligor) will complain only to the seller about problems with the underlying transaction and will not assert claims or defenses against the seller's assignee (*i.e.*, the finance company).

(a) Limitations on Waiver of Defense Clauses

These "waiver of defense" clauses are limited by the "good faith" and "without notice" requirements, and also by consumer protection statutes.

1) Limitation—Good Faith

First of all, any such "waiver" of defenses is enforceable only if the assignee purchased the instrument in good faith and *without actual notice* of any defenses or claims that the obligor might have against the assignor-seller. [U.C.C. § 9–403(b)]

a) Form Contracts

Several courts have voided waiver of defense clauses in blank form contracts supplied by a manufacturer to its dealers for use in sales transactions involving its goods (the contracts to be assigned to the manufacturer for financing). Any policy of insulating financers against squabbles as to the quality of the goods sold certainly does not apply where the party financing the sale also manufactures the goods. [**Massey-Ferguson, Inc. v. Utley**, 439 S.W.2d 57 (Ky. 1969)]

b) "Real" Defenses

Even if the assignee meets these tests, the obligor may assert the same "real" defenses that U.C.C. § 3–305 permits against a HDC. [U.C.C. § 9–403(b); and see p. 61]

2) Limitation—Consumer Transactions

U.C.C. § 9–403, regulating waiver clauses, does not apply to transactions in which a *consumer is the obligor.* Hence, consumer contracts containing such clauses have sometimes been declared void as against public policy (*i.e.*, for attempting to create quasi-negotiable instruments without the protections of negotiable instruments law). [**Unico v. Owen**, *supra*, p. 48]

a) State and Federal Regulation

Such clauses may also be forbidden or regulated by state statute [see Uniform Consumer Credit Code § 3.404 (1974 text)], and are now forbidden in most consumer credit sales or closely connected loans by a Federal Trade Commission rule that requires such contracts to contain a prominent notice preserving the consumer's right to assert defenses against later purchasers of the contract. (*See* p. 57)

(7) Other Factors Affecting "Good Faith" and "Notice"

(a) Purchase at a Discount

When the payee sells the instrument to a later holder, the later holder sometimes buys the instrument for less than the face amount, the difference being referred to as the "discount." The existence of a discount does *not* mean that the holder has not given full value for the instrument, nor does a large discount in and of itself constitute lack of good faith or a reason to be suspicious. However, a very large discount together with *other suspicious circumstances* may lead courts to find lack of good faith and/or notice and thus deny HDC status to the holder. [*See* **United States Finance Co. v. Jones**, 229 So. 2d 495 (Ala. 1969)]

(b) Constructive Notice

The filing or recording of a document (such as an Article 9 financing statement) does not constitute notice that will defeat HDC status. [U.C.C. § 3–302(b)]

1) Note

U.C.C. Article 9 provides not only that a creditor's perfected security interest is ineffective against a HDC in possession of the instrument, but also that such a security interest is ineffective against a bona fide purchaser of *nonnegotiable* paper. [U.C.C. §§ 9–308, 9–309; *and see* Secured Transactions Summary]

NOTICE EXISTS IF THE HOLDER KNOWS OR HAS REASON TO KNOW ANY OF THE FOLLOWING FACTS:
• Any part of the *principal* is overdue.
• An *acceleration* has been made.
• More than a reasonable time has *elapsed* after issue of a demand instrument (*e.g.,* 90 days for checks).
• There are *defenses or claims* on the instrument (must have a reasonable opportunity to act upon the notice).
• The fiduciary who transferred the instrument is in *breach of fiduciary duties.*

THE FOLLOWING FACTS DO *NOT* GIVE RISE TO NOTICE:
• The instrument was sold at a reasonable *discount.*
• There is a *public filing or recording* of a document (*e.g.,* security agreement) that concerns the instrument.
• The instrument is *antedated, postdated, or undated* (*see* p. 17).

(c) "Forgotten" Notice

Holders who have received notice of a claim or a defense may nevertheless achieve HDC status if, at the time the holder acquires the instrument, the holder has *forgotten* about the earlier information.

Example: A credit reporting service sends Bank a list of other creditors' dealings with various debtors. Eighteen months later, one of these debtors cashes a check with Bank. Bank is then sued by Creditor, who claims that the earlier report constituted notice to Bank of problems with the check. Given the length of time involved, it may be held that Bank had in *good faith* forgotten the credit information and thereby qualified as a HDC. [**McCook County National Bank v. Compton**, 558 F.2d 871 (8th Cir. 1977)]

1) Application of Doctrine

The U.C.C. definition of "notice" (found in U.C.C. §§ 1–202) does not say how long notice lasts. However, courts are reluctant to apply the forgotten notice doctrine unless a long period of time has elapsed between the receipt of notice and acquisition of the instrument, *and* the holder's good faith is obvious. As one opinion has noted, "a lapse of memory is too easily pleaded and too difficult to controvert to permit the doctrine to be applied automatically. . . ." [**First National Bank v. Fazzari**, 10 N.Y.2d 394 (1961)]

6. Time at Which HDC Status Determined

Whether a holder qualifies as a HDC is determined as of the moment that the instrument is *negotiated* to the holder *and/or* the holder gives *value* therefor, whichever occurs later. Thus, if the transferee of a negotiable instrument acquires notice of a claim or defense to the instrument *prior* to either negotiation or the giving of value, the transferee will not qualify as a HDC.

(e.g.) **Example:** Polly Payee tricks Donald Drawer into giving her a check, which Payee indorses over to her bank. The bank is now a "holder" but not a HDC until it gives value. If Drawer notifies the bank of the fraud prior to the bank's parting with value (*e.g.*, cashing the check), Drawer may reclaim the check from the bank or stop payment.

(cf.) **Compare:** If the bank has given value before Drawer gives notice of the fraud, the bank is a HDC, meaning that Drawer cannot reclaim the check and must pay it if the bank sues him. [**Manufacturers & Traders Trust Co. v. Murphy**, 369 F. Supp. 11 (W.D. Pa. 1974)]

(e.g.) **Example:** Peter Payee of a promissory note signed by Maria Maker sells the note to Finance Company for a discount. Finance Company presents the note to Maker for payment, but Maker raises a defense she had against Payee. Finance Company decides to sue, but discovers that Payee neglected to indorse the note prior to its sale to Finance Company. Even if Payee is now willing to indorse the note, it is too late for Finance Company to become a HDC, because at the time it becomes a "holder" (when Payee indorses the note), Finance Company will have notice of Maker's defense. [U.C.C. § 3–203(c), off. Com. 3; **Cheshire Commercial Corp. v. Messier**, 278 A.2d 413 (Conn. 1971)]

B. Payees as Holders in Due Course

1. Introduction

The original version of U.C.C. § 3–302(2) provided that "a payee may be a holder in due course," thereby settling a controversy under the old N.I.L. The 1990 Revision dropped any statutory discussion of this issue, but Official Comment 4 to § 3–302 indicates that a payee can become a HDC in certain situations, giving examples similar to the ones below.

2. In Practice

As a practical matter, the payee is almost always so involved in the transaction giving rise to the instrument that she will have notice of claims or defenses against the instrument.

3. U.C.C. Provisions

Nevertheless, there are seven situations in which a payee may be sufficiently insulated to qualify as a HDC:

(i) A remitter, purchasing goods from Payee, obtains a bank draft payable to Payee and forwards it to Payee, who takes it for value, in good faith, and without notice as required by U.C.C. § 3–302.

(ii) The remitter buys the bank draft payable to Payee, but it is forwarded by the bank directly to Payee, who takes it in good faith and without notice in payment of the remitter's obligation to Payee.

(iii) Alex and Beth sign a note as co-makers. Alex by fraud induces Beth to sign and, without authority from Beth, delivers the note to Payee, who takes it for value, in good faith, and without notice.

(iv) Alex defrauds the maker into signing an instrument payable to Payee. Payee pays Alex for it in good faith and without notice, and the maker delivers the instrument directly to Payee.

(v) Drawer draws a check payable to Payee and gives it to his agent to be delivered to Payee in payment of Drawer's debt. The agent delivers it to Payee, who takes it in good faith and without notice in payment of the agent's debt to Payee. But as to this case, *see* § 3–307(b), which may apply. (*See* p. 49)

(vi) Drawer draws a check payable to Payee but blank as to the amount, and gives it to his agent to be delivered to Payee. The agent fills in the check with an excessive amount, and Payee takes it for value, in good faith, and without notice.

(vii) Drawer draws a check blank as to the name of the payee, and gives it to his agent to be filled in with the name of Alex and delivered to Alex. The agent fills in the name of Payee, and Payee takes the check in good faith, for value, and without notice.

[U.C.C. § 3–302, Off. Com. 4]

C. Successors to Holders in Due Course

1. Introduction

In certain circumstances, a transferee can acquire the *rights* of a HDC without actually qualifying as a HDC.

2. Shelter Rule

It is a basic rule of commercial law that a transferee acquires *whatever rights the transferor had.* The transferee is said to take "shelter" in the status of the transferor and this principle is known as the "shelter" rule.

a. U.C.C. Provision

The shelter rule appears at several points in the U.C.C. The relevant provision in Article 3 reads as follows: "Transfer of an instrument, whether or not the transfer is a negotiation, vests in the transferee any right of the transferor to enforce the instrument, including any right as a holder in due course, but the transferee cannot acquire rights of a holder in due course by a transfer, directly or indirectly, from a holder in due course if the transferee engaged in fraud or illegality affecting the instrument." [U.C.C. § 3–203(b)]

(1) Effect

Subject to the "washing through exception" (below), this allows any transferee to "step into the shoes" of the HDC who formerly held the instrument and to obtain the rights of a HDC, even though the transferee otherwise clearly fails to meet the requirements of due course holding (*e.g.*, because he did not give value or because he was aware of claims or defenses).

e.g. **Example:** A promissory note is held by Holder, who qualifies as a HDC. Holder makes a gift of the note to Son. Because Son paid no consideration for the note, he obviously would not otherwise qualify as a HDC; however, because his father had that status, Son succeeds to the rights of a HDC too. The result would be the same even if Son *knew* of some defense to the instrument.

(2) Rationale

The underlying reason for the shelter rule is to protect the free negotiability of commercial paper. Once the instrument comes into the hands of a HDC, defenses that could not be asserted against the HDC cannot be allowed against any transferee. Otherwise, the obligor could, by putting all potential transferees on notice of claimed defenses, vastly restrict the HDC's market for the instrument and thereby interfere with the free passage of commercial paper. [**Kost v. Bender**, 25 Mich. 515 (1872)]

b. Parties to Fraud or Illegality—the "Washing Through" Exception

The shelter rule never grants HDC rights to persons who were parties to fraud or illegality affecting the instrument, whether or not such persons are prior holders of the instrument. A party so implicated cannot sell the instrument to a HDC and reobtain it (*i.e.*, "wash" the instrument through the hands of the HDC) in order to be free from a defense of fraud or illegality. [*See* U.C.C. § 3–203, Off. Com. 4]

3. HDC Rights and Remote Transferees

Once a person has qualified as a HDC, *all subsequent transferees* will acquire the same HDC rights no matter how far down the chain of transferees they may be—*unless* they are transferees after a transferor who failed to obtain HDC rights because the transferor was a party to fraud or illegality affecting the instrument.

Example: Maker signs a promissory note payable to Adam, who negotiates it to Ben, a HDC. Ben makes a gift of the note to Carla, who makes a gift of it to Delilah, who in turn donates the note to Erik. Carla, Delilah, and Erik do not qualify as HDCs in their own right because none has paid value. Nevertheless, Carla obtained Ben's HDC rights under the shelter rule; and when Carla gave the note to Delilah, Delilah likewise received all of Carla's rights (which include Ben's HDC rights). Erik then took shelter in Delilah's status, which included acquisition of Ben's HDC rights.

Compare: If, in the prior example, Adam (the original payee) had defrauded Maker, sold the note to Ben (a HDC), and reacquired it from Ben's donee, Carla, Adam (as a party to fraud) does not obtain Ben's HDC rights through Carla. Nor will Adam's subsequent negotiation to an innocent purchaser convey Ben's HDC rights because Adam's purchaser will receive only Adam's rights.

a. But Note

The purchaser from a defrauding payee might qualify as a new HDC if he meets the usual requirements for HDC status. (*See* p. 38)

EXAM TIP   **GILBERT**

If you find that a particular person does *not qualify for HDC status*, don't stop there. Be sure to see if some holder *farther up the chain* of transfers was a HDC because if so, those rights as a HDC continue down to later transferees unless cut off by a holder who was a party to a fraud involving the instrument.

D. Burden of Proof as to Holding in Due Course

1. In General

In any action to enforce an instrument, the burden is ultimately on the holder to establish HDC status (*i.e.,* that the holder or someone through whom the holder claims title acquired the instrument as a HDC). However, it becomes necessary for the holder to prove HDC status only when (and if) the defendant has established some defense to the instrument that a HDC would cut off. This is because anyone who qualifies as a *holder* of the instrument (whether or not a HDC) is entitled to recover on the instrument until the defendant-obligor proves some defense. The Code not only allows a mere holder to enforce the instrument, but it also gives parties other than a holder the right to sue. These include a nonholder who (because of the shelter rule) has the rights of a holder, the former holder of an instrument that has been lost or destroyed, and a person from whom a mistaken payment was recovered. These are all "persons entitled to enforce the instrument." [U.C.C. § 3–301]

2. Burden of Establishing Defenses

The U.C.C. provides: "If the validity of signatures is admitted or proved and there is compliance with subsection [§ 3–308(a)—regarding proof of signatures], a plaintiff producing the instrument is entitled to payment if the plaintiff proves entitlement to enforce the instrument under § 3–301, unless the defendant proves a defense or claim in recoupment," [U.C.C. § 3–308(b)]

a. Effect

This results in a *presumption* that every *holder* is entitled to recover. If the plaintiff can establish that she *is* a holder (*i.e.,* the transferee in possession of a bearer instrument, or the indorsee in possession of an order instrument), and can *produce the instrument* and establish the validity of the signatures thereon, the burden is on the defendant to prove a defense.

(1) Rationale

The purpose of requiring production of the instrument is to prove that the plaintiff is the holder at the time of the suit and has not assigned the instrument. [**Blair v. Halliburton Co.,** 456 S.W.2d 414 (Tex. 1970)]

b. Where Plaintiff Cannot Produce Instrument

The owner of an instrument can win without producing the instrument, but failure to produce it will prevent the attachment of the presumption under § 3–308. The burden is then on the plaintiff to prove due execution, negotiation, and each fact essential to the validity of the instrument and the claim of ownership.

(1) Missing Instruments

If the original instrument has been lost, stolen, or destroyed, the owner may recover by proving up its terms together with the facts why the original cannot be produced. (*Note:* In such cases, the court may also require the owner to *indemnify* the defendant against loss by reason of any future claims if the instrument should show up.) [U.C.C. § 3–309]

3. Burden of Establishing Due Course Holding

The U.C.C. likewise provides that "[i]f a defense or claim in recoupment is proved, the right to payment of the plaintiff is subject to the defense or claim, except to the extent the plaintiff proves that the plaintiff has rights of a holder in due course which are not subject to the defense or claim." [U.C.C. § 3–308(b)] Thus, HDC status is not presumed, but must be proved by the person so claiming.

E. Statutory Erosion of HDC Doctrine

1. Background

The original purpose of the HDC doctrine was to insulate lenders from squabbles between the immediate parties to the instrument. However, there has been considerable dissatisfaction with the doctrine in consumer credit transactions: Unscrupulous sellers could victimize consumers by selling shoddy goods on credit, then discount the consumers' payment contracts to "innocent" lenders or finance companies who would qualify as HDCs under the U.C.C. requirements. If the goods proved defective and the consumers were unable to obtain repairs or replacement from the seller (who might be out of business by that time), the consumers were left "on the hook"—*i.e.,* forced to pay the finance company notwithstanding that they had valid defenses against the seller.

2. State Consumer Protection Statutes

To eliminate this unfairness, statutes have been enacted in many states that eliminate or restrict the HDC doctrine in consumer financing transactions. These statutes vary widely as to their coverage and effect.

a. Some statutes simply *prohibit waiver of defense* clauses in sales or leases of consumer goods.

b. Some statutes allow such clauses but give the consumer the power to preserve defenses against any assignee by *notifying* the assignee of claims against the seller within a specified period of time (*e.g.,* within 10 days after learning that the contract has been assigned). [*See* Ariz. Rev. Stat. § 44–145]

c. Other statutes actually *eliminate* the HDC doctrine by providing that *any* assignee of a retail installment contract *takes subject to* whatever defenses the retail buyer had against the seller. [*See* Cal. Civ. Code § 10804.2]

d. Still others reach the same result by *prohibiting the use of negotiable instruments* in consumer financing, or by permitting only a single document to be used to evidence the contract and debt, so that the seller's contract obligations are apparent on the face of the instrument assigned—which thereby destroys negotiability. (*See* p. 18)

e. Finally, some courts will *impute notice* even to "interlocking" direct lenders—those who have some degree of participation in the consumer transaction. (*See* discussion of "close connection" doctrine, p. 47)

3. Federal Regulation

The lack of uniformity in state regulation has also prompted federal regulation in this area. The Federal Trade Commission ("FTC"), pursuant to its power to prohibit "unfair or deceptive acts or practices in or affecting interstate commerce" [15 U.S.C. § 45], has promulgated a Trade Regulation Rule "Preserving Consumers' Claims and Defenses."

a. Notice Requirement

The Rule basically requires that any *consumer credit* contract contain a *notice* that any holder or assignee is "*subject to all claims and defenses* which the debtor could assert against the seller of the goods or services" covered by the contract. [16 C.F.R. § 433.2]

(1) Effect

Although the Rule does not expressly prohibit the use of waiver of defense provisions, that is clearly its intended purpose and effect.

(2) Scope of Notice Requirement

The notice requirement is not limited to contracts that the retailer plans to assign. It applies equally to retail installment notes or contracts that the seller keeps and collects.

(3) U.C.C. Provision

If the notice is added to the note, it would become nonnegotiable because the maker has not made an "unconditional" promise. (*See* p. 11) However, the U.C.C. contains an express statement that in spite of the inclusion of such a notice preserving the consumer's defenses, Article 3 still applies to the instrument even though there can be no HDC of an instrument bearing this notice. [U.C.C. § 3–106(d)]

b. Scope of Rule

(1) Interstate Commerce Requirement

FTC authority is limited to interstate commerce. However, practically any transaction that is completed through use of the mails or telephone may be deemed to "affect" interstate commerce. (*See* Constitutional Law Summary.) Hence, only purely local transactions would be unaffected, and these may still be subject to state consumer protection statutes (above).

(2) "Consumer Credit Contract"

The term "consumer credit contract" covers either *purchase or lease* of consumer goods and services.

(3) Purchase Money Loans

The Rule also applies to *direct lender loans* made to a consumer by a lending institution (bank, finance company) *affiliated* with the seller (by common control, etc.) or that has had consumers *referred* to it by the seller on a regular basis. Any consumer contract covered by such "purchase money" loans must contain the FTC notice provision stated above.

(4) Credit Card Transactions Excluded

The Rule specifically *excludes* consumer sales financing transacted through credit cards.

(a) Rationale

A credit card holder already could assert most defenses against the card issuer under the Federal Truth in Lending Act. [15 U.S.C. § 1643; Regulation Z, 12 C.F.R. § 226.12(c)]

c. Remedies Under FTC Rule

Where an instrument contains the FTC notice, the consumer may raise any defense to payment of the instrument that he or she has. In addition, the consumer may sue for damages and recover from the assignee as well as the seller, up to the amount the consumer has *paid* on the contract.

(1) Instrument Without Notice

Where the instrument does *not* contain the required notice and has come into the hands of a HDC, the consumer must *pay* the instrument unless the consumer has a defense that can be raised against a HDC. *Rationale:* Only the FTC can prosecute a violation of its rules. [**Holloway v. Bristol-Myers Corp.**, 485 F.2d 986 (D.C. Cir. 1973)]

(2) State Statutes

Some state consumer deceptive sales acts make violation of FTC rules a violation of state statute. In such jurisdictions, an instrument arising in a transaction subject to the statute would have to bear the FTC warning or be deemed a deceptive practice under the state statute.

Chapter Five

Claims and Defenses on Negotiable Instruments

Chapter Approach

While a HDC takes a negotiable instrument free from most defenses, some defenses are available even against a HDC. Defenses available against a HDC are called *real defenses* and include:

(i)   *Infancy*;

(ii)   *Incapacity* to contract;

(iii) *Illegality*;

(iv)   *Duress*;

(v)   *Fraud in the factum*;

(vi)   *Discharge in insolvency proceedings*;

(vii) *Discharges known* to the HDC;

(viii) *Suretyship* (if the HDC knows of the suretyship);

(ix)   *Alteration* of the instrument; and

(x)   *Forgery.*

All other defenses are *personal defenses* and are not available against a HDC. Thus, in an exam question, if a party to an instrument has a defense to its payment, you must determine whether the defense is real or personal in order to decide whether it is available against a HDC.

Even if the suing party is not a HDC, not all personal defenses are available to the defendant. As explored below, the defenses of third parties ("jus tertii") are not generally available to a defendant. Thus, if your exam question does not involve a HDC, then you will have to decide whether the personal defense can be asserted by the defendant in a lawsuit on the instrument without joining other parties.

A. Introduction

1. HDC vs. Non-HDC

There are substantial differences in the legal effects that flow from the transfer of a negotiable instrument to one who is a HDC, as compared to a transfer to any other type of transferee. As discussed in this chapter, claims and defenses against the instrument may be cut off where a HDC is involved—whereas a non-HDC transferee is forced to litigate the claims and defenses of other parties to the instrument.

2. Basic Definitions

a. "Claim"

A claim to a negotiable instrument is an *affirmative cause of action* for recovery on the instrument, based upon superior ownership rights of the claimant. A HDC takes the instrument free of *all* such claims. [U.C.C. § 3–306]

b. "Defense"

A defense is a ground for *refusing to pay* all or part of a negotiable instrument. The few defenses that can be asserted against a HDC (as well as non-HDC transferees) are called "real" defenses, and most are set forth in U.C.C. § 3–305(a)(1) (below). Defenses that *cannot* be asserted against a HDC (but that are good against non-HDCs) are called "personal" defenses.

c. Claim in Recoupment

A claim in recoupment is a right of someone who owes a debt to *subtract* from the amount due damages arising from the *same* transaction that gave rise to the instrument. For example, if Buyer buys a stereo from Seller and gives Seller a $500 promissory note as payment, and the stereo proves defective so that a warranty is breached, and Buyer spends $50 to remedy the breach, Buyer has a $50 claim in recoupment. A claim in recoupment may be asserted against any non-HDC, but may be asserted against a HDC only if the claim is against the HDC. [U.C.C. § 3–305(a)(3), (b) and Off. Com. 3]

B. Real Defenses

1. In General

A HDC takes free of most defenses to the instrument. The few defenses that may be asserted against a HDC are commonly called *real defenses.* [U.C.C. § 3–305(a)(1)] Defenses that may not be asserted against a HDC are commonly called personal defenses. [U.C.C. § 3–305(a)(2), (a)(3)] The following defenses are real defenses, and may therefore be asserted against *both* HDC and non-HDC transferees of the instrument in question.

2. Infancy

Infancy is a real defense (and therefore assertable against a HDC) if it would be a defense *under state law* in a simple contract action. If state law does *not* make the contracts of an infant void or voidable, infancy would be only a personal defense (not assertable against a HDC). [U.C.C. § 3–305(a)(1)(i), Off. Com. 1]

e.g. **Example:** State law makes the contracts of infants (*i.e.,* those under 18 years of age) voidable at the option of the infant unless the infant has lied about age. Tom Thumb, age 17, buys a car for business purposes and signs a promissory note, which the seller negotiates to a HDC. If Tom is sued on the note, he may refuse to pay the HDC on grounds of infancy, unless he lied about his age when buying the car.

3. Incapacity to Contract

Under state law, persons other than infants may also lack the capacity to contract. For example, persons declared incompetent by judicial proceedings (because, for example he/she is mentally ill) or corporations that have failed to take the necessary legal steps to transact business within the state may lack such capacity.

a. Contract Must Be Void

Before such incapacity will constitute a real defense, however, state law must render the contract *void* from its inception, rather than merely voidable. [U.C.C. § 3–305(a)(1)(ii),

Off. Com. 1; **Universal Acceptance Corp. v. Burks**, 7 U.C.C. Rep. 39 (D.C. 1969)] If the obligations of the incompetent are merely voidable at the option of the incompetent, such incompetency is a personal defense and cannot be raised against a HDC.

b. Distinguish—Infancy

The distinction between void and voidable obligations applies only to incapacity, illegality, and duress; this distinction is *not* relevant to the infancy defense. Thus, the contract of an infant may be merely voidable under state law, but infancy is nevertheless a real defense. [U.C.C. § 3–305(a)(1)(i)]

4. Illegality

If some illegality in the underlying transaction renders the obligation *void* (as opposed to merely voidable), this is a real defense assertable against a HDC even if the HDC had nothing to do with the illegality. If the obligation is merely voidable under state law, the illegality is a *personal* defense. [U.C.C. § 3–305(a)(1)(ii)]

Example: Minnesota Chubby loses a game of pool to Paul Hustler and pays off his gambling wager with a check. State law makes gambling debts void from their inception. Minnesota Chubby stops payment on the check after it has been negotiated to Hustler's bank. Even if the bank qualifies as a HDC, Chubby can assert the illegality to avoid payment.

Compare: A state consumer protection law provides that notice of the fabric content of all garments must be firmly affixed to the garments. Summer buys four swimsuits from Beach Mart, a retail store, and pays by check. The swimsuits do not have the required fabric content labels. The illegality here merely renders the contract voidable (Summer can keep the swimsuits if she wants to), and so the illegality is only a personal defense.

5. Duress

Duress occurs in a contract situation where one party acts *involuntarily.* It is sometimes a real and sometimes a personal defense.

a. U.C.C. Provision

Article 3 provides that duress "is a matter of degree. An instrument signed at the point of a gun is void, even in the hands of a HDC. [However,] one signed under threat to prosecute the son of maker for theft may be merely voidable, so that the defense is cut off [against a HDC]." [U.C.C. § 3–305, Off. Com. 1]

6. Fraud in the Factum (Real Fraud)

Under the U.C.C., there are two kinds of fraud: real and personal. "Real" fraud (fraud in the factum) is assertable against a HDC and is defined as "fraud that induced the obligor to sign the instrument with neither knowledge nor reasonable opportunity to learn of its *character or its essential terms.*" [U.C.C. § 3–305(a)(1)(iii)]

a. Other Types of Fraud

Any other type of fraud—which would encompass *most* types—is a *personal* defense not assertable against a HDC.

Example—fraud in the factum: Hans Immigrant, who cannot read English, signs a promissory note after his attorney tells Hans that it is a credit application. Even in the hands of a HDC unaware of this lie, the note is not enforceable against Hans if he asserts fraud in the inducement. [**Schaeffer v. United Bank & Trust Co.**, 360 A.2d 461 (Md. 1976)]

cf. **Compare—personal fraud:** Honest John tells Cathy Consumer that the car he is selling has been driven only by a little old lady to Sunday church services. After paying for the car by check, Cathy discovers that the auto was formerly a police car and stops payment on the check. If the check is now held by a HDC, Cathy's defense cannot be raised; she knew she was signing a negotiable instrument, so her fraud defense is personal only.

b. Requirement of Excusable Ignorance

Even where the defendant was unaware that the document was a negotiable instrument, fraud in the factum cannot be asserted if the defendant failed to take reasonable steps to ascertain the nature of the transaction. Official Comment 1 to U.C.C. § 3–305 states in relevant part:

The test of the defense is that of excusable ignorance of the contents of the writing signed. The party must not only have been in ignorance, but must also have had no reasonable opportunity to obtain knowledge. In determining what is a reasonable opportunity all relevant factors are to be taken into account, including the intelligence, education, business experience, and ability to read or understand English of the signer. Also relevant is the nature of the representations that were made, whether the signer had good reason to rely on the representations or to have confidence in the person making them, the presence or absence of any third person who might read or explain the instrument to the signer, or any other possibility of obtaining independent information, and the apparent necessity, or lack of it, for acting without delay. Unless the misrepresentation meets this test, the defense is cut off by a holder in due course.

e.g. **Example:** Salesman Fast Buck tells Husband and Wife that new aluminum siding for their home will cost nothing because his company wishes to use the finished job in advertising its siding. Buck hands them a promissory note which he refers to as a "television authorization," and which Husband and Wife sign without reading. A subsequent HDC of the note could probably enforce it against Husband and Wife, unless they show a valid reason for not reading the paper before signing. [**Burchett v. Allied Concord Financial Corp.**, 396 P.2d 186 (N.M. 1964)]

EXAM TIP　　　　　　　　　　　　　　　　　　　　　　　　　　**GILBERT**

It is important to remember that *most* types of fraud are personal defenses. Fraud is a real defense only when it causes the obligor to sign an instrument *without knowledge or reasonable opportunity to learn of its character or essential terms*.

---

7. Discharge in Insolvency Proceedings

"Insolvency proceedings" include an assignment for the benefit of creditors (a state liquidation proceeding) and "any other proceeding intending to liquidate or rehabilitate the estate of the person involved." [U.C.C. § 1–201(22)] By far the most common example of such proceedings is discharge in a federal *bankruptcy proceeding*, which excuses the debtor from most of the debts listed in the bankruptcy petition. Under U.C.C. § 3–305(a)(1)(iv), such a discharge is a real defense assertable against a HDC.

Example: Douglas Debtor borrows $10,000 from Nightflyer Finance Company, signing a promissory note for that amount. The following day Douglas files a petition in bankruptcy, listing the promissory note as an unpaid debt; shortly thereafter, the court discharges the debt in bankruptcy. One year later, National Bank presents the note to Douglas for payment. Even if the bank is a HDC, Douglas has a real defense based on his discharge in bankruptcy.

a. Effect—Shifting of Loss

If the defense is asserted, the creditor can probably pass its loss on to its transferor in a contract action (p. 74) or a warranty suit (p. 100).

8. Discharge Known to HDC

The U.C.C. provides: "Notice of discharge of a party, other than discharge in an insolvency proceeding, is not notice of a defense ... but discharge is effective against a person who became a holder in due course with notice of the discharge. Public filing or recording of a document does not of itself constitute notice of a defense, claim in recoupment, or claim to the instrument." [U.C.C. § 3–302(b)] The word "discharge" here refers to the events by which a party to the instrument is excused from his obligation, as illustrated below. [*See also* U.C.C. § 3–601]

a. Cancellation of Liability

A holder may cancel the liability of a prior party by striking out the signature of that party. [U.C.C. § 3–604(a)] Such an action would not itself give a later purchaser notice of a problem with the instrument (so as to keep her from becoming a HDC), but it *would* give the HDC notice that the person whose name is stricken is no longer liable on the instrument. Hence, the discharge of that person is a real defense assertable by that person against the HDC.

Example: Fenton Hardy purchases a promissory note and notices many names indorsed on the back of the instrument. Included are the names of his sons, Frank and Joe, who were prior holders of the note. Fenton draws a line through their names, thus discharging their liability. The note later comes into the possession of Dixon, a HDC. If Dixon attempts to collect the note from Frank or Joe, they have a real defense of "discharge of which the holder has notice."

(1) Consideration Not Necessary for Valid Cancellation

A holder who strikes out the liability of a prior party discharges that party even if the holder receives no consideration in return. [U.C.C. § 3–604(a); *and see* U.C.C. § 1–107]

b. Agreement Not to Sue

An agreement that would discharge liability on a simple contract also discharges liability on a negotiable instrument. [U.C.C. § 3–601(a)] Such an agreement would be a real defense under U.C.C. § 3–302(b) against any later HDC who knew of the agreement before acquiring the instrument. [*See also* U.C.C. § 3–601(b)]

Example: Fenton becomes the holder of a note on which his sons Frank and Joe are prior indorsers. When he sells the note to Dixon, Fenton obtains Dixon's agreement not to sue either Frank or Joe on the instrument. This agreement is a discharging event under U.C.C. § 3–601(a) and, because Dixon knew of it when he acquired the note, the discharge is a real defense against him.

c. Discharge Usually a Personal Defense

Unless the discharge of a prior party is apparent from the face of the instrument (as in the case of a line drawn through an indorsement to cancel it out) or the HDC knows of the discharge, discharge is a personal defense and therefore not assertable against a HDC. [U.C.C. § 3–601(b)] For example, *payment* by a party discharges that party [U.C.C. § 3–602(a)], but unless the payment was apparent on the instrument, a later HDC could compel payment again.

Example: After 20 years, Peter Pumpkin finally pays off the mortgage on his house. He asks the mortgagee, National Bank, for his promissory note and is very upset to learn that the bank sold it long ago but failed to tell Peter. If the note is later presented to Peter by a HDC for payment, Peter must pay again—because his discharge by payment is only a personal defense.

(1) But Note—Recovery Against Payee

However, the original discharged party should be able to pass his additional liability on to the original payee in a quasi-contract action for money had and received. U.C.C. § 1–103 preserves such common law actions. (*See* Contracts Summary.)

(2) 2002 Amendments Change Payment Rules

In jurisdictions adopting the 2002 proposed amendments to Articles 3 and 4, the obligor on an instrument may continue to pay the original payee until notified that the instrument has been transferred to another, and is discharged up to the amount of these payments. Even a HDC takes subject to the defense of payment in this situation. [U.C.C. § 3–602(b)–(d)]

Example: When Joe Lawstudent was ready to make his final payment on his student loan he sent it, as usual, to the original lender (and payee on the promissory note he had signed), and then threw a party to celebrate. He was very upset when New Lender, Inc. sent him a notice that it was the current holder of the promissory note, having bought it two years ago from the original lender, and it was demanding the missed final payment (which, apparently the original lender had failed to forward to New Lender). Does Joe have to pay again? Yes in jurisdictions (the majority of the country) where the 2002 amendments to Article 3 have not been adopted. Payment is a personal defense. No in jurisdictions adopting the 2002 revision of this section, which allows Joe to keep paying the original lender until notified of the note's assignment to a new payee.

d. Caution—Notice of Certain Discharging Events Prevents HDC Status

Some of the discharging events in the U.C.C. arise in situations that also give notice of problems with the instrument. This in turn may prevent "due course" holding for the purchaser. (*See* p. 44) One such event is delay in presenting an instrument for payment, which may result in the discharge of prior parties. (*See* p. 90) Here, notice of the delay given to a later potential purchaser not only alerts that person to the possibility of discharge of prior parties but also gives notice that the instrument is overdue and that there are defenses to it. That notice, if apparent before the holder acquires the instrument, prevents the taking from being "in due course."

9. Suretyship as a Real Defense

If a HDC *knew* prior to acquiring a negotiable instrument that some of the prior parties were sureties ("accommodation parties"; *see* p. 80), the HDC takes subject to the right of these parties to raise their suretyship defenses (*see* p. 79).

a. Note

On the other hand, if the HDC did not know that a prior party had signed as a surety, the suretyship defenses—being *personal*—cannot be raised. [U.C.C. § 3–605(h)]

10. Alteration of Instrument

An "alteration" is a change in the terms of the instrument. For example, a thief may alter the amount of a check from "$10.00" to "$1000" by eliminating the decimal point. In certain circumstances (discussed p. 137), a HDC may be able to collect only the original amount, so that the alteration is a partial "real" defense. In other situations, the HDC may be able to collect on the instrument as altered.

EXAM TIP   🔲 GILBERT

Remember that there is a difference between *alteration* (changing the terms that the maker or drawer inserted in the instrument) and *unauthorized completion* (filling in blanks left by the maker or drawer). Generally, the maker will *not* be liable for the *altered amount* but *will* be liable for the full amount of the *unauthorized completion* (see p. 140).

---

11. Forgery

a. Forgery of Name Necessary to Negotiation

If the name of the *payee* or any *special indorsee* is unauthorized (*i.e.,* forged or signed by a nonagent), no subsequent taker can be a HDC because there is no "negotiation," which is necessary to qualify as a "holder." However, if the person whose name was forged *ratifies* the unauthorized signature or is *estopped* from denying it (*see* p. 137), subsequent takers can qualify as HDCs (provided they meet the other requirements of U.C.C. § 3–302 for due course holding).

b. Forgery of Names Not Necessary to Negotiation

The names necessary to a proper negotiation of an instrument are those of the payee and any special indorsee. (*See* p. 28, p. 32) The forgery of any other name (*e.g.,* maker, drawer, acceptor, or indorsers on a bearer instrument) does *not affect negotiation or holder status*; subsequent takers may qualify as HDCs if they meet the usual tests. Even so, a party whose name was either forged or placed on the instrument by a nonagent has a real defense of *unauthorized signature* unless that person has ratified the signature or is estopped from denying it. (*See* p. 137)

(1) Statutory Basis for Real Defense

The U.C.C. provides that no person is liable on an instrument unless that person has *signed* the instrument. [U.C.C. § 3–401] § 3–403—the basic "forgery" rule—adds that an unauthorized signature is not effective as that of the person whose name is signed (absent ratification or estoppel), but does operate as that of the forger or nonagent. Finally, U.C.C. § 3–305(a)(2) frees HDCs only from the defenses of "a party to pay the instrument" in § 3–302. Because a person whose name is forged is not a "party to the instrument" under §§ 3–401 and 3–403, that person may raise the defense of unauthorized signature against the HDC.

> **Example:** Fingers Fagin steals a blank check from Ronald Rich and forges Rich's name as drawer. The check ends up in the possession of Collecting Bank, a HDC. If Rich is sued for payment by Bank, he may defend on the basis that he is not a "party to the instrument." [U.C.C. § 3–305] Collecting Bank will have to sue Fagin, who is liable under § 3–403 just as if he had signed his own name instead of "Ronald Rich."

C. Claims Against Negotiable Instruments

1. Non-HDC Subject to Valid Claims

Unless the transferee of a negotiable instrument is a HDC or has the right of a HDC under the "shelter" rule (*see* p. 53), the transferee takes the instrument subject to all valid claims to it. [U.C.C. § 3–306]

2. What Constitutes a Valid Claim

As noted previously, a claim is an affirmative right to a negotiable instrument because of *superior ownership.* For example, if a check is stolen from the payee and the payee's name is forged thereon, the payee is still the true owner of the check and may bring a replevin action ("give it back to me") to claim it from the person who now possesses it. In this case, the possessor cannot be a HDC, because he/she cannot qualify as a "holder." (*See* p. 28)

D. Personal Defenses

1. Definition

Personal defenses cannot be asserted against anyone having the rights of a HDC. They may be viewed as "all defenses other than real defenses," including every defense available in ordinary contract actions. [U.C.C. § 3–305(a)(2)] Any transferee of a negotiable instrument without HDC rights thus takes the instrument subject to all such personal defenses.

2. Common Examples of Personal Defenses

The U.C.C. does not specifically list personal defenses, but instead refers to any "defense . . . that would be available if the person entitled to enforce the instrument were enforcing a right to payment under a simple contract." [U.C.C. § 3–305(a)(2)]

a. Consideration and Negotiable Instruments

A negotiable instrument must be supported by sufficient consideration. However, the existence of consideration is not technically a prerequisite to negotiability. Rather, its absence (lack or failure of consideration) is a valid defense to an instrument in the hands of anyone *other than a holder in due course.* [U.C.C. § 3–303(b)]

(1) Complete vs. Partial Defense

Where there is only a *partial* failure of consideration, such failure is a pro tanto (*i.e.,* by that much) defense, whether or not the failure is in an ascertained or liquidated amount. [U.C.C. § 3–303(b)]

EXAM TIP GILBERT

Whenever a question deals with *partial consideration,* pay particular attention to the parties involved with the instrument. Remember, if a holder pays only part of the agreed consideration, he will be a proportional HDC (*see* p. 40). However, if a non-HDC is involved, he may assert partial failure of consideration as a defense.

---

(2) "Consideration" Defined

"Consideration" is generally defined in the same terms as it is under ordinary contract law—basically, a bargained-for exchange that results in a legal detriment to the promisor, or a legal benefit to the promisee. [U.C.C. § 3–303(b); *and see* Contracts Summary]

(a) Antecedent Debt

Prior to the U.C.C., there was a split on whether an antecedent debt constitutes sufficient consideration. The U.C.C., however, expressly provides that it does. [U.C.C § 3–303(a)(3)]

(3) Burden of Proof as to Consideration

Because lack or failure of consideration is an affirmative defense to enforcement of the instrument, it follows that the burden of proof thereof is on the *defendant-obligor.* This is made clear by U.C.C. § 3–308, which provides that once the signatures on the instrument are established, the holder is entitled to recover unless the defendant-obligor establishes a valid defense (such as lack of consideration). (*See* p. 55)

(a) Effect

Every negotiable instrument is deemed *prima facie* to have been issued for valuable consideration, and every obligor (maker or indorser) is presumed to have become a party thereto for value.

EXAM TIP GILBERT

Probably the most common personal defense on exams is that the contract out of which the commercial paper arose was not properly or fully performed. Remember that this defense cannot be used *against a HDC,* but it *can* be used against a non-HDC.

---

b. Claims or Defenses of Another ("Jus Tertii")

In defending a lawsuit, one must rely on his *own* defenses and cannot use the claims or defenses of third parties ("jus tertii") as a defense. "[T]he obligor may not assert against the person entitled to enforce the instrument a defense, claim in recoupment, or claim to the instrument (§ 3–306) of another person, but the other person's claim to the instrument may be asserted by the obligor if the other person is joined in the action and personally asserts the claim against the person entitled to enforce the instrument." [U.C.C. § 3–305(c)]

Example: Martha Maker signs a promissory note as maker. Years later, the current holder, Panther Finance, presents the matured note to Martha and demands payment. Martha receives a phone call from Harry Holdit, a prior indorser of the instrument, who asks Martha not to pay on the note because Panther Finance defrauded Harry when he negotiated the note to Panther. Unless Harry is willing to defend Panther's lawsuit against Martha himself, she may not raise the "jus tertii" rights of Harry if she is sued.

(1) "Payment" Rule

The liability of any party on an instrument is discharged by a *good faith* payment to a *holder*, even though some other person asserts a claim to the instrument. [U.C.C. § 3–602] If that other party wants to stop payment, that person must obtain a court order or supply indemnity (*e.g.*, a bond or collateral) to protect the payor in the event that payment is eventually ordered. [U.C.C. § 3–602(b)]

(a) Rationale

A person seeking to make payment and be discharged from liability should not have to become, in effect, an arbiter of competing claims to the instrument.

(2) Exceptions Where "Jus Tertii" Can Be Raised

There are some situations in which the claims and defenses of a third person are available as a defense in actions by a non-HDC, and which must be investigated before payment would be deemed to be in "good faith" and result in a discharge.

(a) Theft

A defense that the non-HDC acquired the instrument by theft from another, *or* that the title of the non-HDC is derived from a theft, must be raised by one making payment (if known), at the risk of continued liability. Payment without raising this issue would be in bad faith and would not discharge the payor from liability. [U.C.C. § 3–305(c)]

Example: In the previous hypothetical, if Harry tells Martha that Panther Finance *stole* the bearer note from him, she should raise this issue before paying Panther. One possibility would be to pay the money into court in an *interpleader* action.

(b) Violation of Restrictive Indorsement as Permissible "Jus Tertii"

The same duty of the payor to investigate upon penalty of continued liability exists where a third person claims that there was no compliance with a restrictive indorsement. (*See* p. 108)

Example: When she got her paycheck, Wilhelmina Worker indorsed it on the back and added the words "For Deposit Only" (a restrictive indorsement—*see* p. 108). Before she could deposit the check, it was stolen from her by Harry Thief, who placed his indorsement below Wilhelmina's and then presented the check to the bank on which it was drawn, which dishonored it because Wilhelmina's employer had insufficient funds in its account. When Harry tries to sue the employer on its drawer's obligation (*see* p. 87), the employer may raise Wilhelmina's defense that paying Harry would violate the restrictive indorsement.

1) Policy

The policy both here and where theft is involved is to prevent innocent parties from being exposed to the possibility of having to pay twice.

(c) Surety's Use of Principal's Defenses

The Code allows a surety to raise the same defenses as the principal has with the following three exceptions (all situations where the surety was meant to bear the risks): an accommodation party cannot raise as a defense *the principal's* discharge in insolvency proceedings, infancy, or lack of legal capacity, because these are matters that frequently led to the demand for a surety in the first place. [U.C.C. § 3–305(d)]

COMMERCIAL PAPER DEFENSES	GILBERT
REAL DEFENSES	**PERSONAL DEFENSES**
May be raised against HDC	May *not* be raised against HDC
• *Alteration* of instrument	• Simple contract defenses (*e.g.*, lack of consideration, failure of consideration, breach of warranty, fraud in the inducement, etc.)
• *Discharge in insolvency* proceedings	
• *Discharges known to HDC*	• Must be one's *own* defenses except the payor must raise the defense of theft if known
• *Duress* (depending on degree)	
• *Forgery* of names necessary to negotiation	
• *Fraud in the factum*	
• *Illegality*	
• *Incapacity* to contract	
• *Infancy*	
• *Suretyship* defenses	

Chapter Six
Liability of the Parties

CONTENTS	PAGE

Chapter Approach

Even if a HDC is not involved, an issue may arise on your exam as to the type of lawsuit that can be brought in connection with a negotiable instrument. You must become sensitive to the various theories of liability available. Liability can be based (i) on the **underlying obligation,** rather than on the instrument itself, but beware of the **merger rule,** which at least temporarily suspends the cause of action on the obligation; (ii) on the **instrument;** (iii) on a **warranty;** or (iv) on **conversion** of the instrument. When the suit is "on the instrument," liability depends on the party involved; *i.e.,* the maker, indorser, drawer, surety, etc., each incurs a different obligation. Remember especially that the maker is primarily liable, while the drawer or indorser is secondarily liable and thus entitled to the procedural rights of presentment and notice of dishonor before being sued. Similarly, warranty liability differs depending on whether the warranty arises from transfer or presentment. A suit "off the instrument" means a cause of action that arises outside of Article 3 of the Uniform Commercial Code as a matter of common law or other statutes.

All of these concepts are explored below. Keep in mind that the different theories of liability may all exist simultaneously, so that parties to the instrument may have a number of ways of passing on any harm they have suffered.

A. Introduction

1. Theories of Liability

When a dispute arises over commercial paper, it must first be determined whether the instrument is technically "negotiable" so as to come within the scope of U.C.C. Article 3. If so, the U.C.C. authorizes the following types of lawsuits on the instrument:

(i)   Suits on the instrument's contractual **obligations;**

(ii) Suits in property, based on **implied warranties** arising upon transfer or presentment of the instrument; and

(iii) Suits in tort for **conversion.**

In addition, suits outside Article 3 may be available, such as actions based on the **underlying transaction** (below). In analyzing the liability of parties on any of these theories, one must always be alert to whether a party is a HDC and whether this affects relevant **claims or defenses** in the lawsuit (discussed in the previous section).

EXAM TIP   GILBERT

When faced with a question dealing with liability of the parties on an instrument, you should first *identify the status of each party* (*e.g.,* maker, indorser, etc.), and then discuss each party's liability. If the fact situation is complex, make a chart of the transfer chain.

B. Suits on the Underlying Obligation—the Merger Rule

1. The Merger Rule

A negotiable instrument is issued for a reason, typically to pay an obligation. When the instrument is issued, the obligation becomes **merged** into the instrument and, **unless the parties have agreed otherwise,** it is not available as a cause of action (at least temporarily; *see* below). [U.C.C. § 3–310(b)]

2. Suspension of Underlying Obligation

Where a negotiable instrument is accepted as conditional payment for the underlying obligation, that obligation cannot be the basis of a cause of action **until the instrument is presented for payment and dishonored.** [U.C.C. § 3–310(b)]

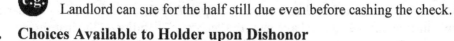 **Example:** Tenant delivers a rent check to Landlord. Tenant's rent obligation is suspended until the check is presented for payment to Tenant's bank. If the bank pays the check, the rent obligation is discharged. If the bank refuses payment (*e.g.,* because Tenant has stopped payment on the check), Landlord can sue on the check, on the underlying lease agreement, or on both.

Note: This suspension of the underlying obligation has major implications for mortgage foreclosure issues. See p. 76.

a. Partial Payment

If the parties understand that the instrument is merely partial payment of the underlying obligation, then the obligation is suspended only "pro tanto" (*i.e.,* by that much). [U.C.C. § 3–310(b)]

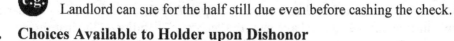 **Example:** If Tenant gives Landlord a check for one-half of the rent owed, Landlord can sue for the half still due even before cashing the check.

b. Choices Available to Holder upon Dishonor

If a negotiable instrument is dishonored, the holder may sue **on** the instrument (*see* p. 74), on the underlying obligation, or on both. Of course, the holder is entitled to only one recovery, whichever course is selected.

c. Discharge of Instrument—Merger Rule

If liability on the instrument is discharged in any way (by payment, cancellation, alteration, bankruptcy, etc.), liability is also discharged on the underlying obligation. **Rationale:** Because the instrument and the obligation have become merged, discharge of the instrument also discharges the underlying obligation. [U.C.C. § 3–310(b)] For that reason this is sometimes called the "merger rule."

3. Cancellation of Underlying Obligation

Where the party primarily liable on a negotiable instrument is a **bank** (as in the case of a cashier's check, certified check, or certificate of deposit; *see* p. 5), the underlying obligation is **completely discharged** as long as the person who owed the obligation is not liable **on** the instrument (*see* below). [U.C.C. § 3–310(a)]

a. Rationale

Banks are more solvent and trustworthy than most individuals, so their paper is deemed to have the same effect as money (unless the parties agree otherwise). Moreover, many courts have held that payment cannot be stopped on bank obligations of this kind.

Example: Ralph gives $1,000 in cash to his bank and asks it to draw up a check payable to his ex-wife Louella to meet his $1,000 monthly alimony payment. The bank does so, signing its name as drawer and the wife's name as payee. When Louella takes this check, Ralph's alimony obligation is discharged. If the check bounces, Louella must look to the bank rather than Ralph for relief. *Note:* Ralph may be listed on the bank check as "remitter"—*i.e.,* the person actually making payment. However, this does not affect his liability on the instrument or the fact of his discharge.

Compare: If the bank had listed Ralph as *payee* on the check and he had indorsed it over to Louella, the underlying (alimony) obligation would *not* be canceled—because Ralph's indorsement created recourse against him *on* the instrument (*see* below).

EXAM TIP   ◢GILBERT

Keep the merger rule in mind whenever the question deals with an instrument that has not yet been presented for payment. Remember, a party can sue on the underlying obligation only *after* the instrument has been *dishonored.*

C. Contract Suits—Suits "on the Instrument"

1. Commercial Paper "Contracts"—in General

In the original 1962 version of Article 3, the term "contract"—when used to describe the liability of the parties—referred to contracts *implied in law. Any* person who signed a negotiable instrument was said to have incurred "contract" liability *on* the instrument, whether or not such liability was intended. The 1990 Revision does not use the word "contract" but substitutes instead the word "obligation." The idea, however, is the same. Anyone signing a negotiable instrument (except in an innocuous fashion, *e.g.,* "John Doe, Witness") undertakes to pay the instrument under certain circumstances, the person's actual intent being irrelevant.

a. Scope of Suits "on the Instrument"

Aside from express obligations written into the terms of the instrument, implied U.C.C. obligations are the only types of lawsuits that are said to be "on the instrument."

b. Procedural Rights

There are a number of parties who may be liable on an instrument simply because their names appear on the instrument. However, some of those parties are entitled to the technical procedural rights of "presentment" or "notice of dishonor" prior to being sued. (*See* p. 87) A party having the benefit of the procedural rights is said to be *"secondarily" liable* on the instrument because these procedures must be either complied with or excused before U.C.C. contract liability arises. *Drawers and indorsers* are typical examples of such secondary parties. Parties not accorded these rights are said to be *"primarily" liable* because of their vulnerability to immediate suit.

2. "Obligation" of a Maker

The maker of a promissory note has none of the technical procedural rights referred to above. The maker's obligation is a simple one: The maker promises to pay the note according to its terms as of the moment of signature to a person entitled to enforce the instrument. [U.C.C. § 3–412] As discussed infra at p. 77, this is the major suit brought in foreclosure of a mortgage, where the failure to present the note to the maker may prevent the foreclosure entirely.

a. Defenses Available to Maker

If sued on the note, the maker can assert whatever claims or defenses are available against the party suing. [U.C.C. § 3–305]

e.g. **Example:** When Dan's promissory note comes due, he pays the full amount to the payee, Nightflyer Loan Company, but fails to demand return of the note (*see* p. 87). The following month the note is again presented for payment by Stonewall Loan Company, the new holder. Dan's obligation to pay the note according to its original terms (implied under U.C.C. § 3–412) does not prevent him from raising his defense of discharge by payment—which will prevail unless Stonewall qualifies as a HDC.

EXAM TIP   📕GILBERT

Recall that only **real defenses** are available against a HDC (*see* p. 61). They are (i) **alteration,** (ii) **discharge in insolvency,** (iii) **discharge known to the HDC,** (iv) **duress,** (v) **forgery,** (vi) **fraud in the factum,** (vii) **illegality,** (viii) **incapacity** to contract, (ix) **infancy,** and (x) **suretyship.** On the other hand, non-HDCs are subject to both **real and personal defenses** as well as **valid claims** (*i.e.,* claims of superior ownership).

---

b. Incomplete Instruments

If the maker signs an incomplete note (one having blanks or spaces), the maker is bound by the terms *as subsequently filled in.* [U.C.C. §§ 3–412, 3–115, 3–406, 3–407; *and see* p. 145]

c. Co-Makers

If two or more persons sign as co-makers in the same transaction, they are *jointly and severally liable* (*i.e.,* each can be sued individually for the entire amount). This is true even if the body of the note fails to use plural pronouns, as in a note beginning "I promise to pay," that is signed by more than one maker. [U.C.C. § 3–116(a); **Ghitter v. Edge,** 165 S.E.2d 598 (Ga. 1968)]

(1) Right of Contribution

If one co-maker is forced to pay the full amount to the holder, the co-maker may seek pro rata reimbursement from the other co-makers. [U.C.C. § 3–116(b); Simpson, Suretyship 243–244]

(2) Suretyship

If the co-maker forced to pay the full amount is a surety for one of the other co-makers, he/she may seek *complete* reimbursement from the principal. [U.C.C. § 3–419(e); *see* p. 81]

Example: Huey, Dewey, and Louie all sign a promissory note as makers in return for a $3,000 loan. At maturity, the holder collects the entire $3,000 plus interest from Huey. Huey has a right of contribution for $1,000 *each* (plus one-third of the interest) from Dewey and Louie; if Huey was only a surety when he signed as co-maker (*i.e.,* Dewey and Louie got all the loan money), he is entitled to recover the *full amount* ($3,000 plus interest) from either of them.

3. Mortgage Foreclosure and the Obligation of the Maker on the Promissory Note

a. The Basic Concepts

When a new owner buys a home, that person will sign two primary documents at the closing ceremony: (1) a *promissory note* in which the buyer ("maker" of the note) promises to pay the lender (the payee on the note) the amount borrowed to finance the purchase of the property, and (2) a *mortgage contract* (plus the mortgage deed that goes with it) by which the buyer contractually grants the lender a real estate mortgage lien on the purchased property. The mortgage deed is filed in the county real property records so that subsequent parties can see that the lender has an interest in the real property that must be satisfied before the property can be transferred to another. The mortgage contract is the "underlying obligation" as defined above; the promissory note is the *primary document* because it embodies the promise to pay the loaned amount. These two documents (the mortgage contract and the promissory note) should be kept together if and when the original lender sells ("assign") them to another entity, which is commonly done. Unfortunately those in the business community do not always appreciate this, and they often assign the mortgage contract and neglect to pass the promissory note along with it. What happens to the promissory note? It is often lost, misplaced, or (in one egregious legal mess) destroyed in a "paper reduction" effort. See Whaley, Mortgage Foreclosures, Promissory Notes, and the Uniform Commercial Code, 39 W. St. U. L. Rev. 313 (2012), explained in the text below.

b. "Security Follows the Debt"

It had always been a maxim of the common law that "security follows the debt," meaning that collateral (the mortgage) goes wherever the debt obligation (the promissory note) goes. Those in the mortgage industry did not always understand this, and in fact did the opposite: they sold the mortgage and ignored the note. The common law would say that whoever has the note automatically has the mortgage, not the other way around, because "security follows the debt." **Deutsche Bank Nat. Trust Co. v. Byrams**, 275 P.3d 129 (Okla. 2012).

c. Merger Rules Stops Foreclosure on Mortgage Contract Until Note Dishonored

If the homeowner who signed the mortgage promissory note as a maker fails to make the payments as agreed, the note goes into default and the current holder of the note may then initiate foreclosure proceedings (which are governed by independent state laws, with half the states allows foreclosure without going through a court proceeding, and the other half requiring a judicially guided foreclosure process). But can the foreclosing entity prevail if it only is the assignee of the mortgage contract but doesn't have the promissory note in its possession? *No, it can't* (at least if the courts pay attention to the rules of the Uniform Commercial Code). Why not? Because the mortgage contract that has been assigned is the "underlying obligation" as defined above, and per the "merger rule" described above is *suspended* as a cause of action until there's a default on the *original promissory note*.

"Security follows the debt" and so the security can't be foreclosed upon until the debt is due and not paid. Thus only a "person entitled to enforce" [PETE] the promissory note is entitled to payment on the note, and that means a person who has possession of the promissory note and is either a holder, someone who takes holder rights via the shelter rule, or someone who has lost the note an can recreate it by use of the Code's lost instruments section. **In re Miller**, 666 F.3d 1255 (10th Cir. 2012). Until the promissory note in the hands of a PETE is dishonored, the underlying mortgage contract is suspended; Official Comment 3 to § 3–310.

d. **Standing to Foreclose**

Only a holder in possession of the original promissory note is the *real party in interest* and therefore eligible to foreclose. The Uniform Commercial Code will not allow someone to declare a debt in default (and hence trigger the right to foreclose) unless that person is in possession of the original promissory note. **U.S. Bank Nat. Ass'n v. Kimball**, 27 A.3d 1087 (Vt. 2011) ("It is neither irrational nor wasteful to expect a foreclosing party to actually be in possession of its claimed interest in the note, and to have the proper supporting documentation in hand when filing suit"). A **copy** of the original note is not enough (there might be hundreds of copies, but only the person with the original can foreclose); **In re Veal**, 450 B.R. 897 (9th Cir. BAP 2011) (dueling creditors attempting to foreclose each held only a copy of the note, but not the original); **In re Adams**, 204 N.C. App. 318, 693 S.E.2d 705 (2010) (copy of note sufficient as long as possession of the original note is alleged, but if possession challenged it must be proven, along with a valid chain of indorsements to demonstrate proper negotiation).\

e. **Policy to Protect from Double Payment**

The reason for the rule is that if the maker of the note pays the wrong party (someone not in possession of the original promissory note) the maker is still liable to the right party, someone in possession who is a "person entitled to enforce the note" per § 3–301. The Code is clear that payment to the wrong party does not discharge the liability to make payment to the proper party; §§ 3–601 and 3–602, **Leyva v. National Default Servicing Corp.**, 255 P.3d 1275 (Nev. 2011); **HSBC Bank USA v. Thompson**, 2010 WL 3451130 (Ohio App. 2010) . If the foreclosure fails, the homeowner/maker still owes the debt, and the mortgage lien continues to cloud the real estate title and prevent sale of the home until the debt is paid and the lien released.

f. **Lost Instruments**

If the promissory note has been lost or destroyed, § 3–309 allows the court to recreate the lost instrument on proving that it otherwise is a "person entitled to enforce" the instrument and also the circumstances of the note's destruction (along with giving "security" to the obligors on the instrument to protect them from double liability); **In re Carter**, 681 S.E.2d 864 (N.C. App. 2009). Once the instrument is thus judicially recreated the foreclosure can then proceed.

g. **Remedy if Foreclosure Is Forbidden**

If the entity attempting to foreclose cannot produce the promissory note nor prove the circumstances of its destruction or loss, foreclosure is not permitted, but the entity can recover from whoever sold it the unenforceable mortgage contract by using the warranties made during the assignment of that contract, one of which is that the assigned contract is enforceable; Restatement of Contracts (Second) § 333(b).

4. "Obligation" of an Indorser

Indorsing one's name to the back of a negotiable instrument makes the indorser a type of surety for all prior parties (including the maker or drawer). By indorsing the instrument, the indorser promises to pay it to a "person entitled to enforce" the instrument (PETE), but this promise is *conditioned* on the indorser *first* being accorded the technical procedural rights of *presentment and notice of dishonor.* [U.C.C. § 3–415]

EXAM TIP   ❦GILBERT

Remember that there are five types of indorsements: (i) *special* (names a particular person as indorsee); (ii) *blank* (does not name a particular person as indorsee); (iii) *qualified* (limits liability by the words "without recourse"); (iv) *restrictive* (limits payment); and (v) *anomalous* (made by a person who is not a holder for suretyship purposes).

---

a. Indorsement "Without Recourse"—the Qualified Indorsement

An indorser who does not wish to incur the above liability may add the words "without recourse" to the indorsement and thereby avoid any promise of payment. Indorsing in this manner is called a "qualified" indorsement, and has the effect of negotiating the instrument without incurring liability.

Example: "Hot Check" Harry gives Rhonda a check for a debt he owes her. Rhonda is afraid the check may bounce, so she signs her name on the back and cashes it at Local Grocery Store. If the check bounces, the store may collect from Rhonda on her indorser's obligation without suing Harry first or even joining him in the suit. However, if Rhonda had made a qualified indorsement on the check (*i.e.,* signed her name and wrote "without recourse"), the store would have no action against her.

b. Indorsement of Bearer Instruments

Indorsements are not needed to negotiate bearer instruments. Nevertheless, prospective transferees of such instruments may insist on unqualified indorsements from their transferors in order to acquire their indorsers' liability.

c. Multiple Indorsers

The common law presumed that if one person indorsed an instrument after someone else had done so, they were "subsureties," meaning that the later one could get full reimbursement from the prior indorser. Only where the indorsers agreed (expressly or impliedly) to share liability would they become "co-sureties" and have proportionate liability. Section 3–116 now reverses this presumption in certain situations:

(1) Joint Payees

If the instrument is made payable to joint payees ("Pay to the order of John and Mary Doe") and they both indorse the instrument, they are presumed to be co-sureties and liable *to each other only for their respective shares.* However, the law presumes that they are both *"jointly and severally liable" to the rest of the world,* meaning that they can be sued together *or* each individually for the full amount of the instrument. [U.C.C. § 3–116(a)]

(2) Anomalous Indorsers

Similarly, if there are multiple anomalous indorsers (*see* p. 34), they are deemed to be co-sureties and have only proportionate liability to one another. For example, both Brother and Sister become sureties on Dad's promissory note, both signing on the back; if Brother is forced to pay the note, he could only get reimbursement from Sister for her share, and not the entire amount. [U.C.C. § 3–116(a)]

(3) Co-Makers

Unless they have agreed otherwise, or one is clearly the surety for the other, co-makers are jointly and severally liable for the entire debt to the holder of the note, and between themselves can seek only proportionate liability. [U.C.C. § 3–116(a)]

(4) Reacquisition and Cancellation

Reacquisition occurs if an instrument reenters the hands of a *prior indorser.* Upon reacquisition, the reacquirer may cancel indorsements that were made between the time he formerly held the instrument and the present. This cancellation has the effect of discharging the indorsers whose signatures were canceled, and the discharge is effective against *any subsequent holder,* including a HDC. [U.C.C. § 3–207] Of course, reacquisition has the *automatic* effect of canceling *intervening indorsers'* liability to the reacquirer because the intervening indorsers would have an action back against the reacquirer based on her prior indorsement.

> **Example:** Pat Payee negotiates a note to Sara Supplier by special indorsement as payment for some goods. Pat immediately discovers that the goods are defective and returns them to Sara. Sara has already indorsed the note, but offers to return it to Pat if he promises to strike Sara's indorsement. Pat agrees and does in fact strike Sara's indorsement. He then negotiates the note to Stan Storeowner, another goods supplier. Sara has no liability on the note because her indorsement was canceled. If Pat had not canceled Sara's indorsement, she would owe indorser liability to Stan, but not to Pat.

d. Available Defenses

The obligation of an indorser is not absolute, and (like the maker) an indorser may raise all available claims and defenses. [U.C.C. § 3–305]

5. "Obligation" of a Surety

A surety is a "favorite of the law," whose obligations are construed strictly in favor of the surety. In addition to the U.C.C. rules on suretyship, most states give the surety additional statutory rights, such as the right to compel the creditor (at maturity of the obligation) to use "due diligence" in pursuing the principal or lose the liability of the surety. Sureties also have a host of common law rights.

a. Common Law Rights

(1) Exoneration

At maturity of the obligation, the surety may bring an equitable action to compel the principal to pay the debt and thereby exonerate the surety from liability.

(2) Subrogation

If the surety is forced to pay the principal's debt to the creditor, the surety is subrogated *to (i.e.,* acquires) any rights the creditor had—such as rights to other collateral or the right to a preferred position in the principal's insolvency proceeding.

(3) Reimbursement

Upon paying the principal's debt to the creditor, the surety may sue the principal for reimbursement. This right is also codified in U.C.C. § 3–419(e).

(4) Contribution

If there is more than one surety on the instrument, sureties signing as part of the same transaction are entitled to recover pro rata from each other. In other words, the parties are presumed to be *co-sureties*. [U.C.C. § 3–116]

b. U.C.C. Rights

(1) In General

(a) U.C.C. Terminology

The U.C.C. refers to the surety as an *"accommodation* party," while the principal is called the *"accommodated* party." If the surety adds words of guaranty to the signature (*e.g.,* "Jane Doe, guarantor"; "I, Jane Doe, guarantee this obligation"), the surety becomes a *"guarantor."*

1) Guarantor

A guarantor is a special party under the U.C.C, and the nature of the guarantor's contract is discussed below (*see* p. 85). Bear in mind, however, that the guarantor is *also a surety,* with the usual common law and U.C.C. rights accorded sureties. [U.C.C. §§ 1–201(40); 3–419, Off. Com.]

ARTICLE 3 TERMINOLOGY REGARDING SURETIES	GILBERT
ACCOMMODATION PARTY	Surety
ACCOMMODATED PARTY	Principal
GUARANTOR OF COLLECTION	Surety who adds words of guaranty and thus gets the right to have payment sought first from the maker or acceptor

(b) Obligation of the Accommodation Party

A surety who signs in the place where a maker usually signs incurs the same obligation as a maker does. [U.C.C. § 3–412] Similarly, a surety who signs in the place where an indorser usually signs (*i.e.,* the back of the instrument) makes the obligation of an indorser. [U.C.C. § 3–415] Accommodation makers and accommodation indorsers therefore have the U.C.C. rights of nonsurety makers and indorsers plus the special common law and U.C.C. rights given to sureties. [U.C.C. § 3–419]

(c) Proof of Surety Status

Oral proof of the accommodation nature of a surety's signature may be introduced, except against a HDC with no notice of surety status. (*See* p. 66) If the instrument itself indicates that one of the signatures was meant to accommodate another party (*i.e.,* "John Doe, surety"), even a HDC takes subject to suretyship defenses. [U.C.C. § 3–605(h)]

1) Anomalous Indorsements

If an indorsement seems out of place in the usual chain of title (*e.g.,* maker or drawer to payee to special indorsee, etc.), every subsequent taker of the instrument is conclusively presumed to know that the indorsement was meant as a surety's signature. The Code calls such a signature an *anomalous indorsement.* [U.C.C. § 3–205(d)]

Example: A promissory note is signed by the maker and made payable to the order of Clark Kent. On the back of the note at the top is the signature of Bruce Wayne, *followed by* Clark Kent's signature. The Kent signature would normally be at the top, since Kent is the payee. Hence, the "Bruce Wayne" signature means that Wayne signed as an accommodation indorser. [*See* U.C.C. § 3–419(c)]

(2) Surety Not Liable to Principal

The surety is not liable to the accommodated person, regardless of the place in which the surety has signed the instrument. [U.C.C. § 3–419(e)] This section likewise codifies the right of reimbursement (*see* p. 80) *on the instrument*—again, regardless of the order in which the parties have signed.

Example: "Hot Check" Harry wants to buy an auto, but Honest John Used Cars will not accept his check. Harry then persuades his friend "Good Natured" Gloria to write the check for him, payable to Honest John. Harry signs as an indorser, and obtains the car. When Honest John tries to cash Gloria's check, it bounces. If Honest John collects the amount of the check from Gloria, she may seek reimbursement from Harry even though check drawers may not usually sue the indorsers on their U.C.C. § 3–415 obligations (*i.e.,* because indorsers sign subsequent to drawers). Similarly, if Honest John collected the money from Harry, Harry would have no right to sue Gloria on her drawer's obligation (although indorsers usually have this right). Both of these results occur because Gloria was in fact a surety for Harry, even though Harry signed as the indorser of her check. [*See* **Gibbs Oil Co. v. Collentro & Collentro, Inc.,** 252 N.E.2d 217 (Mass. 1969)]

EXAM TIP   **GILBERT**

Remember that although an accommodation party (the surety) is never liable to the party accommodated (the principal), but *is liable to other parties* in the capacity in which the accommodation party signed (*e.g.,* maker, indorser, etc.).

---

(3) Tender of Payment

The tender of payment rule [U.C.C. § 3–603] acts to protect sureties and anyone else (*e.g.,* indorsers) who would have a right of recourse against some prior party if forced to pay on the instrument. (Indorsers have a right of recourse against the maker/drawer and/or prior indorsers.) The rule has two parts:

(a) Tender by the Surety or Indorser

If, at maturity, the surety (or an indorser) tenders payment to the holder of the instrument and the holder refuses to accept the money, the surety (or indorser) is still liable for the full amount, but is not liable for any subsequent *interest*. [U.C.C. § 3–603(c)]

(b) Tender by the Principal

If the tender is made by the principal (or by the party against whom the indorser has a right of recourse), the surety or indorser is *completely discharged*. [U.C.C. § 3–603(b)]

Example: Luke Skywalker's promissory note is payable to Darth Vader, and indorsed first by R2D2 and then by C3PO. When the note matures, R2D2 tenders payment but Vader refuses to accept, stating, "I want the money from Skywalker himself." This refusal invokes § 3–603 and discharges C3PO because he had a right of recourse against R2D2, but it leaves R2D2 liable for the tendered amount.

Example: If Luke had tendered payment and Vader had refused (*e.g.,* "I'll collect it next month"), Luke would still be liable for the tendered amount (but not for any subsequent interest, costs, or attorneys' fees). However, *both* accommodation indorsers would be discharged because both had a right of recourse against Luke on his maker's contract. [*See* U.C.C. §§ 3–415, 3–419(e)]

(4) Impairment of Collateral

As discussed above, it is a common law maxim that "security follows a debt," meaning that the transferee of an obligation is entitled to whatever *collateral* supports the obligation. Because this is one of the rights to which a surety is subrogated on payment (*see* p. 79), the holder of a negotiable instrument has a duty to **protect** any collateral securing the debt. If the holder "impairs" the collateral by failing to take reasonable care of it (so that it is lost, destroyed, or loses value), this impairment discharges—up to the amount of the collateral—all nonconsenting parties who would have had a right to the collateral if forced to pay on the instrument. [U.C.C. § 3–605(e); U.C.C. (2002) § 3–605(d); *and see* U.C.C. § 9–207]

Example: Gertrude borrows money from Careless Finance Company, signing a promissory note and giving Careless her diamond ring as security. Gertrude's friend Alice also signs the note as an accommodation maker. If Careless subsequently loses the diamond ring, the loss will discharge Gertrude's obligation up to the value of the ring. Moreover, because Alice (if forced to pay) would have had a right of recourse against Gertrude (and would thus have been entitled to the ring on payment), Alice is also discharged up to the value of the ring.

(a) Failure to Perfect Security Interest

If a creditor fails to take the steps required by law (usually Article 9 of the U.C.C.) to perfect a security interest in the collateral, and if this failure results in the collateral's being unavailable as security (*e.g.,* seized by a bankruptcy trustee), an impairment of the collateral has likewise occurred. [U.C.C. § 3–605(g)]

Remember the defense of impairment of collateral whenever the surety is forced to pay the creditor for a debt secured by collateral that has **changed** (*e.g.,* has lost value) or is **no longer available** (*e.g.,* was lost, destroyed, or an unperfected security interest).

(5) Agreements Between Creditor and Principal

Both at common law and under the U.C.C, the failure of the creditor to press the principal for payment at maturity of an obligation does *not* discharge the surety (at least in the absence of a complaint by the surety).

(a) Agreements to Extend Time of Payment

An agreement to extend the time of payment discharges nonconsenting sureties *only if they can prove harm* caused to them by the extension. [U.C.C. § 3–605(c)]

Example: Alice signed a promissory note, payable to Bank on April 1, and her father, John, indorsed the note on the back as a guarantor. Alice talked the bank into extending the time of payment to December 1. The bank is not required to give John *notice* of this change (although it would be smart to do so). John remains liable on the note as a surety except to the extent he can prove that the extension agreement caused him damages (which he could do if Alice's financial situation deteriorated significantly between April and December). The Official Comment to § 3–605 has other examples of all of these surety discharge rules, including the ones that follow.

1) Distinguish—2002 Revision

Under the 2002 revision of Article 3, the rules are similar but more complicated. The surety is bound by the extension when pursuing rights against the principal (so that, *e.g.,* the surety could not bring an exoneration action requiring the principal to pay on the original date), but also gets the benefit of the extension *vis-a-vis* the creditor (unless the extension agreement says otherwise). In any event, the surety is discharged by the extension agreement to the extent of any *loss* the surety can prove it caused. The surety is free to ignore the extension agreement and pay the creditor as of the original date (thus stopping the running of interest). [U.C.C. (2002) § 3–605(b), (h); *and see* Official Comment 5 for examples]

(b) Agreements Not to Sue

An agreement by the holder of the note not to sue the principal does *not discharge* nonconsenting sureties at all. Official Comment 3 explains that typically the principal settles with the creditor by paying a percentage of the debt due in return for a release of all liability, and the creditor then looks to the sureties for the rest. Because the settlement with the principal does not excuse the principal from his liability to the sureties, the sureties are not harmed by the creditor's discharge of the principal's liability. [U.C.C. § 3–605(b)]

Example: Alice signed a $5,000 promissory note, payable to Bank on April 1, and her father, John, indorsed the note on the back as a guarantor. Early in January, Alice told the bank that she was considering filing for bankruptcy, but would forego doing so if the bank would accept $3,000 and forgive the rest of the debt. The bank agreed and took the $3,000. John still owes the bank $2,000. He can then try to get reimbursement from Alice. [U.C.C. § 3–419(f)]

1) Distinguish—2002 Revision

Under the 2002 revision of Article 3, the rules are different. The release also discharges the surety's liability to the creditor unless the release agreement clearly says otherwise (*"rights are reserved against the surety"* is the common language). The surety cannot pursue the released principal unless the release agreement allows this, but the surety is discharged by the release agreement to the extent that the surety can prove loss caused by it. [U.C.C. (2002) § 3–605(a), (h); *and see* Official Comment 4 for examples]

(c) Agreements to Modify the Terms of the Instrument

If the principal and the creditor agree to a modification of the loan agreement other than a release of the principal or an extension of time (*e.g.,* by changing the amount the principal owes, or altering the repayment schedule), nonconsenting sureties *are discharged* up to the amount of *harm* suffered by the modification, which is presumed to be the amount the surety owes unless the creditor can prove a lesser amount of harm. [U.C.C. § 3–605(d)]

Example: Alice borrowed money from the bank, and her father, John, indorsed her promissory note as a guarantor. The note required equal monthly payments until the note was paid, but one year after the note was signed, Alice and the bank agreed to change the payment schedule so that she only had to make one payment a year. John is completely discharged of liability to the bank unless he agreed to this change or the bank can prove he is not harmed so completely by the change.

1) Distinguish—2002 Revision

Under the 2002 revision of Article 3, the surety gets the benefit of any modification, and is bound by it *vis-a-vis* the principal. However, the surety is discharged to the extent the surety can prove loss by reason of the modification. If the surety decides to pay the debt, the surety may ignore the modification and pay according to the original terms. [U.C.C. (2002) § 3–605(c), (h); *and see* Official Comment 6 for examples]

(d) Consent by Surety

If the surety—or a party with a right of recourse, such as an indorser—*consents* to an extension/suspension agreement, that person is *not discharged*. [U.C.C. § 3–605(i)]

1) Implied Consent

Such consent may be *implied* from the circumstances. In the typical case, the president of a corporate maker who is individually liable on the company's note negotiates the extension agreement for the company and is thereby held to have consented to an extension of his personal liability as an accommodation party. [**London Leasing Corp. v. Interfina, Inc.,** 53 Misc. 2d 657 (1967)] This idea is codified in U.C.C. (2002) § 3–605(f).

2) Express Consent in Instrument

The terms of a note may likewise bind all sureties in advance to an extension without notice.

(e) New Notes and the Merger Rule

If the maker gives the holder either a new note or a postdated check as a means of paying the original note, the merger rule (*see* p. 73) *suspends* the maker's liability on the original note. In effect, this is the same thing as an extension of time in which to pay the original note, and has the legal consequences mentioned in p. 83, *supra:* Nonconsenting sureties and indorsers would be discharged only to the extent they could prove loss by reason of the extension.

e.g. **Example:** Uncle signed Nephew's promissory note as an accommodation maker. When the note came due, the payee bank presented it to Nephew, who paid it by giving the bank a new promissory note (which Uncle did not sign) payable six months in the future. The second note suspends the first one, thus working an extension of time for payment. To the extent that Uncle can prove damages by this delay to which he did not consent, he is discharged in that amount.

(6) Obligation of Guarantor of Collection

If a surety adds words to the signature indicating that he/she is guaranteeing collection (*see* p. 80), there is a special contract. Before a guarantor of *collection* can be required to pay the instrument, the holder must first pursue the maker or acceptor to an unsatisfied judgment or show that such action would be useless (as where the maker is insolvent). [U.C.C. § 3–419(d)]

COMMON LAW RIGHTS	*Exoneration*—may compel principal to pay debt
	Subrogation—acquires rights of creditor upon forced payment to creditor
	Reimbursement—may sue principal for the amount of the debt
	Contribution—may recover pro rata from co-sureties
U.C.C. RIGHTS	*Tender of payment*—not liable for *interest* if surety's payment is refused, and *completely discharged* if payment is tendered by *principal*
	Impairment of collateral—discharged to extent of impairment or loss
	Material alteration of agreement *without consent* (express or implied) of surety
	• Extension of time—*complete* discharge *if can prove harm*
	• Release of principal—*no discharge*
	• Modification of terms of instrument—discharge up to *amount of harm*

(a) Collection Guarantee Must Be Clear

If the surety is labeled a "guarantor," that alone in no way changes the usual obligation of a surety. Sureties who call themselves "guarantors" are only garden-variety accommodation parties whose liability depends on the capacity in which they sign (*i.e.,* as accommodation makers or accommodation indorsers), unless they make it clear they are guaranteeing *collection,* in which case their liability is limited to that stated in U.C.C. § 3–419(d) (*i.e.,* guarantor is not liable until collection attempts prove futile against principal).

c. Notice to Cosigner

Under the Credit Practices Rule adopted by both the Federal Trade Commission and the Federal Reserve Board, in credit extension to consumers, the surety (here called a "cosigner") must be warned of liability on a separate document given prior to becoming obligated. The warning must read as follows:

Notice to Cosigner:

You are being asked to guarantee this debt. Think carefully before you do. If the borrower doesn't pay the debt, you will have to. Be sure you can afford to pay if you have to, and that you want to accept this responsibility.

You may have to pay up to the full amount of the debt if the borrower does not pay. You may also have to pay late fees or collection costs, which increase this amount.

The creditor can collect this debt from you without first trying to collect from the borrower. The creditor can use the same collection methods against you that can be used against the borrower, such as suing you, garnishing your wages, etc. If this debt is ever in default, that fact may become a part of your credit record.

This notice is not the contract that makes you liable for the debt.

[16 C.F.R. § 444; 12 C.F.R. § 227]

6. "Obligation" of a Drawer

The obligation incurred by the drawer of a draft is similar to that of an indorser (p. 78), in that the drawer promises to pay the draft only if first accorded certain technical procedural rights (described below). [U.C.C. § 3–414]

a. Effect of Adding "Without Recourse"

The drawer can *eliminate* contractual liability on the instrument by adding "without recourse" to his/her signature. [U.C.C. § 3–414(e)]

b. Defenses Available to Drawer

When sued, the drawer may raise all appropriate claims and defenses to avoid liability. [*See* U.C.C. § 3–305]

7. Presentment and Notice of Dishonor—Technical Procedural Rights

U.C.C. § 3–501 *et seq.* describe the technical procedural rights that may *condition* the contractual obligations of parties to a negotiable instrument. While indorsers retain significant technical rights, drawers, for the most part, do not.

a. Presentment

Presentment is a demand for payment or acceptance made by (or on behalf of) the *holder* of the instrument. Presentment is made at the place of business or residence of the maker or drawee, or at the location specified in the instrument; it can be made through the mails or through a clearinghouse. [U.C.C. § 3–501(a)]

(1) To Whom Made

In the case of promissory notes, presentment is made to the *maker.* Where a draft is involved, presentment is made to the *drawee.* [U.C.C. § 3–501(a)]

(2) Rights of Presentee (Maker or Drawee)

(a) Authorized Demands

When presentment is made, the maker or drawee may demand the following [U.C.C. § 3–501(b)(2), (3)]:

1) *Exhibition* of the instrument;

2) *Reasonable identification* from the person making presentment;

3) *Evidence of the presenter's authority,* if presentment of the instrument is made on behalf of another;

4) *Production* of the instrument *at a reasonable place and hour,*

5) *A signed receipt* on the instrument for any partial or full payment (*but note:* the presentee is entitled only to a signed receipt, *not* the unqualified indorsement of the presenter); and

6) *Surrender* of the instrument if the presentee pays it in full.

(b) Effect of Failure to Comply with Demands

If the presenter cannot or will not comply with one or more of the above demands (*e.g.*, cannot produce identification when seeking payment on a check from the drawee's bank), a "presentment" has not occurred, and the presentee's refusal to pay on the instrument is therefore not a "dishonor" (*infra*). [U.C.C. § 3–501(b)]

(3) Time for Presentment of Domestic Checks

A reasonable time for presenting (or initiating collection on) uncertified checks drawn and payable in the United States and not drawn up by a bank is presumed to be 30 days after their date for both drawers and indorsers. [U.C.C. §§ 3–414(f), 3–415(e)]

b. Dishonor

Dishonor occurs when the maker of a note or the drawee of a draft returns it after presentment without paying or accepting within the allowed time.

(1) Time Allowed for Decision Regarding Checks and Drafts

(a) Presentment Across the Counter

If a check or draft is presented to the drawee across the counter for immediate payment, it must be paid or returned by the close of business on that day. If paid, a check is canceled and returned to the drawer. If the check is returned, a dishonor has taken place. If neither occurs, the drawee has converted the instrument and is liable for the amount of the instrument as if the drawee had agreed to pay it. [U.C.C. §§ 3–502(b)(2), 3–420(a)]

(b) Presentment Through Bank Collection Channels ("Midnight Deadline" Rules)

Using local clearinghouse agreements or Federal Reserve System mechanisms, banks typically collect checks from each other by making a provisional settlement on their own books *before* presenting a check to the drawee bank (the "payor bank" in U.C.C. Article 4 terminology). This provisional settlement allows the drawee bank an extra day within which to decide whether to pay the item—in which case it simply lets the time for dishonor expire, whereby the provisional settlement becomes final (and payment is made by remittance draft)—or to dishonor and return it. In the latter case, the provisional bookkeeping entries on the books of the collecting bank are reversed ("charged back"). This system of giving drawee banks until their *midnight deadline* (defined in U.C.C. § 4–104(h) as midnight of the banking day *following* the banking day of receipt) within which to dishonor an item is called "deferred posting." [U.C.C. § 4–301, Off. Com. 1]

Example: A check drawn by Drawer on Antitrust National Bank ("ANB") is deposited by Payee in her bank, Payee's State Bank ("PSB"). PSB (pursuant to prior agreement with ANB) marks its books as if ANB has already paid the check, and then presents it to ANB for payment on Monday, June 1. If ANB does nothing, its deadline will expire at midnight on June 2, at which time ANB will become accountable (*i.e.,* liable) for the item. This is true even if ANB *meant* to dishonor (where, *e.g.,* the drawer's account at ANB did not contain enough money to pay the check). [**Rock Island Auction Sales, Inc. v. Empire Packing Co.**, 204 N.E.2d 721 (Ill. 1965)]

1) Rationale

The policy here is to force the drawee to act quickly or assume liability for the amount of the check. Quick action helps to cut down on "float" (the period of time in which a check is in transit).

2) What Constitutes a "Banking Day"

A "banking day" is defined as that part of a day in which the bank is open to the public for carrying on substantially *all* banking functions. For purposes of clearing up paperwork, however, U.C.C. § 4–108 permits a bank to establish a cutoff hour (2:00 p.m. or later) and to treat items received after that hour as if they were received on the *next* banking day. This can have the effect of moving the midnight deadline back one day. (For more on the midnight deadline rule, *see* p. 126)

e.g. **Example:** If a drawee bank has a 2:00 p.m. cutoff, a check presented by another bank at 3:30 p.m. on June 1 would have a midnight deadline of June 3.

c. Notice of Dishonor

Notice of dishonor can be given to any person who may be liable on a negotiable instrument. Once given, it operates for the benefit of *all* parties who have rights on the instrument against the party notified. [U.C.C. § 3–503(b)]

(1) Form of Notice

The notice of dishonor may be oral and may be given in any reasonable manner. It must identify the instrument and state that it has been dishonored. [U.C.C. § 3–503(b)]

(2) Time for Giving Notice

Banks must give notice before the expiration of the *midnight deadline.* (*See* p. 88) Parties other than banks have 30 days in which to give notice of dishonor. [U.C.C. § 3–503(c)]

(3) Federal Notice of Large Check Return

Under Federal Reserve Board Regulation CC, the dishonoring bank must send a *direct notice* to the depositary bank (the first bank to which an item is transferred for collection) any time it decides not to pay a check in the amount of $2,500 or more. This is called the "federal notice of large check return." The notice must be received at the depositary bank by 2:00 p.m. (depositary bank time) on the second business day following the banking day on which the check was presented to the payor bank. The notice must include the name of the paying bank, the name of the payee, the amount, the reason for return, the date of the indorsement of the depositary bank, the account number of the depositor, the branch where the item was first deposited, and the trace number on the item of the depositary bank, unless these matters cannot be reasonably determined from an examination of the item itself. [12 C.F.R. § 229.33]

d. Protest

"Protest" is the name given to a *certificate* stating that a dishonor has occurred. [U.C.C. § 3–505(b)]

(1) When Required

Protest is *never* required. Nonetheless, because protest simplifies the evidentiary burden of proving presentment and notice of dishonor, it continues to be used, particularly where dishonor of large items occurs or when presentment is made in a foreign country, and/or anytime a lawsuit is likely. [U.C.C. § 3–505(a)]

(2) Form

A protest must identify the instrument, state that presentment was made (or explain why it was excused; *see infra*) and state that the instrument was dishonored. It may (but need not) add that notice of dishonor was given to some or all of the parties to the instrument. The protest must be signed by a U.S. consul or vice consul, a notary public, or some other person so authorized by the law of the place where dishonor occurs. [U.C.C. § 3–505(b)]

e. Necessity for Presentment and Notice of Dishonor

(1) Indorsees Liability

Because the indorser's obligation under U.C.C. § 3–415 is conditioned upon notice of dishonor, presentment and notice of dishonor—unless excused—are necessary to bind indorsers. Indorsers are released from liability if these are not properly accomplished. [U.C.C. §§ 3–415(c), 3–503(a)]

(2) Drawer's Liability

The Code does not require that the drawer be given notice of dishonor in most circumstances [*see* U.C.C. § 3–503(a)], but does require that checks be presented to the drawee for payment within 30 days of their date. If presentment is delayed beyond that period and the drawee becomes insolvent during the period of delay, the drawer's liability is excused upon assigning to the holder the drawer's rights against the drawee. [U.C.C. § 3–414(f)]

e.g. **Example:** Joe writes a check to Master Credit in order to pay his charge card bill. An employee of Master Credit accidentally drops the check behind a filing cabinet, where it remains hidden for three years before being found and presented to the drawee for payment. As long as Joe's bank is solvent, Joe remains liable on this drawer's contract.

(a) Stale Checks

If a *noncertified* check is presented more than six months after its date, it is said to be "stale." A bank that dishonors a stale check may not be sued for wrongful dishonor by the drawer. (*See* p. 112) Where the bank acts in *good faith* it may pay a stale check; although most courts and commentators agree that if the bank should have noticed that the check was stale, it would be bad faith to pay the check without first checking with the drawer. [U.C.C. § 4–404; **New York Flameproofing Co. v. Chemical Bank**, 15 U.C.C. Rep. 1104 (N.Y. 1974)]

TO DETERMINE WHETHER A SECONDARILY LIABLE PARTY MAY BE FORCED TO PAY ON AN INSTRUMENT, THE FOLLOWING MUST BE SATISFIED:

☑ *Presentment* (demand for payment made by a person entitled to enforce the instrument)

☑ *Dishonor* (failure to pay within the allowed time)

☑ *Notice of dishonor* (may be given in any reasonable manner)

Exceptions: There are a few circumstances in which technical procedures are excused (*see* p. 91)

f. Situations in Which Technical Procedures Are Excused

Compliance with the technical procedures of presentment and notice of dishonor is excused in the circumstances discussed below.

(1) Delay in Compliance Excused

(a) Bank Collection Delays

1) Circumstances Beyond Bank's Control

Payor and collecting banks are excused from compliance with Article 3 and Article 4 time limits if the delay is caused by circumstances beyond the bank's control (*e.g.*, interruption in communication facilities, insolvency of another bank, war, etc.) and *if the* bank uses reasonable diligence under the circumstances to avoid the problem. [U.C.C. § 4–109(b); **Port City State Bank v. American National Bank**, 486 F.2d 196 (10th Cir. 1973)—computer breakdown excused payor bank from having to dishonor checks by its midnight deadline]

2) Showing Required

A bank claiming excuse under U.C.C. § 4–109(b) has the burden of showing: (i) the cause of the delay, (ii) that the cause was beyond the bank's control, and (iii) that the bank exercised the diligence required under the circumstances. [**Sun River Cattle Co. v. Miners Bank**, 521 P.2d 679 (Mont. 1974)—breakdown of armored truck prevented payor bank from dishonoring checks prior to midnight deadline]

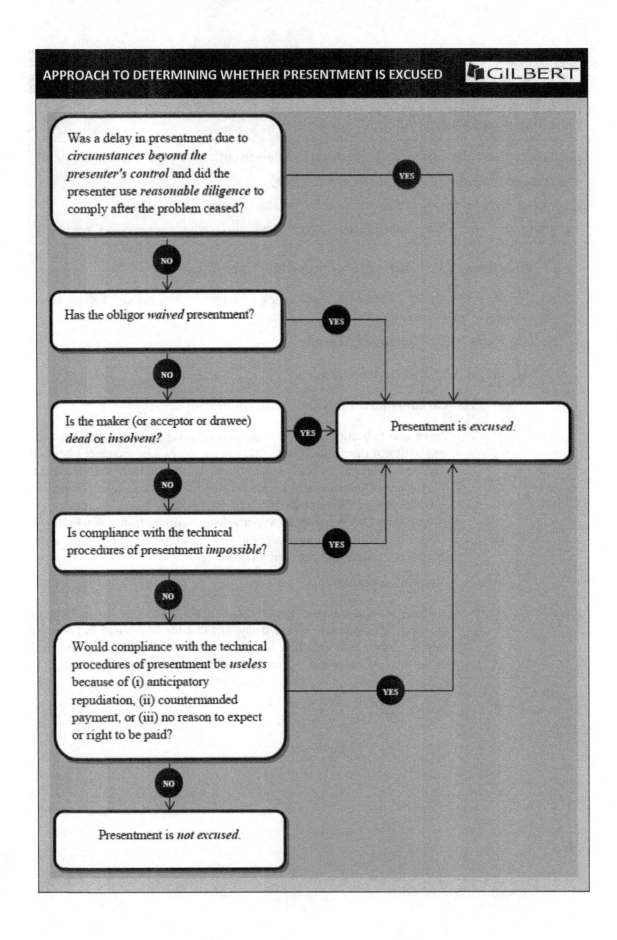

Was a delay in presentment due to *circumstances beyond the presenter's control* and did the presenter use *reasonable diligence* to comply after the problem ceased?

YES →

NO ↓

Has the obligor *waived* presentment?

YES →

NO ↓

Is the maker (or acceptor or drawee) *dead* or *insolvent*?

YES →

NO ↓

Is compliance with the technical procedures of presentment *impossible*?

YES →

NO ↓

Would compliance with the technical procedures of presentment be *useless* because of (i) anticipatory repudiation, (ii) countermanded payment, or (iii) no reason to expect or right to be paid?

YES →

NO ↓

Presentment is *excused*.

Presentment is *not excused*.

(b) Article 3 Rule on Delay

U.C.C. § 3–504(c) excuses delay in complying with the technical procedures whenever the delay is caused by circumstances beyond the control of the relevant party and *reasonable diligence* is exercised to comply after the problem ceases to exist. [*See* **Polk v. Spinks**, 45 Tenn. (5 Cold.) 431 (1868)— a leading pre-Code case in which the Civil War made it "difficult" for a Yankee holder to present a note to a Rebel maker; the court held that literal impossibility was not required, merely obstacles that would deter a reasonable person]

(2) Compliance Excused Completely

Compliance with the technical procedures is ***completely excused*** in the following situations:

(a) Waiver

The right to presentment and notice of dishonor can be waived in the instrument or by conduct of the parties. A waiver written into the body of the instrument binds all parties, while a waiver written above the signature of an indorser binds only that indorser. [U.C.C. § 3–504(a), (b)]

1) Waiver by Conduct

Waiver can also be *implied* from the circumstances. For example, a president of a corporation who dishonors the company's promissory note is typically not entitled to a separate notice of dishonor in order to fix indorser liability. [**Makel Textiles, Inc. v. Dolly Originals, Inc.**, 4 U.C.C. Rep. 95 (N.Y. 1967)]

(b) Unavailability of Primary Party

If the maker, acceptor, or drawee is dead or the subject of insolvency proceedings, presentment is excused except as to documentary drafts. [U.C.C. § 3–504(a)(ii)]

(c) Impossibility

Compliance with the technical rights is also completely excused where such compliance would be *impossible* despite reasonable diligence. [U.C.C. § 3–504(a)(i)]

(d) Where Compliance Would Be a "Useless Thing"

It is a legal maxim that "the law does not require the doing of a useless thing." The U.C.C. applies this principle to technical procedural rights and excuses compliance wherever their performance would be a futile act.

1) Anticipatory Repudiation

If a party announces in advance that he/she will not pay the instrument at maturity, no presentment is necessary. [U.C.C. § 3–504(a)(ii)]

2) Countermanded Payment

A party who has *stopped payment* or has requested another to do so has no right to presentment or notice of dishonor, and is not discharged from liability upon failure to get them. [U.C.C. § 3–504(a)(v); **Klein v. Tabatchnick**, 418 F. Supp. 1368 (S.D.N.Y. 1976)]

3) No Right to Expect Payment

Finally, a party who has "no reason to expect or right to require that the instrument be accepted or paid" cannot complain about failure to receive the technical procedural rights. [U.C.C. § 3–504(a)(iv); *and see* **American National Bank v. Foodbasket**, 497 P.2d 546 (Wyo. 1972)— indorser who knew drawer had written check on insufficient funds had no right to receive notice of dishonor prior to expiration of payor bank's midnight deadline]

8. "Obligation" of a Drawee or Acceptor

A drawee incurs no U.C.C. contractual liability merely by being named as such by the drawer. This result stems from two basic principles: the signature rule [U.C.C. § 3–401] and the "no assignment" rule [U.C.C. § 3–408].

a. Signature Rule

The U.C.C. provides that: No person is liable on an instrument unless that person has signed it. [U.C.C. § 3–401] This rule excuses the drawee from liability to the holder of a draft because the drawee's name thereon is not a "signature"; *i.e.,* it was not written *by the drawee. (See* p. 9)

b. "No Assignment" Rule

Under the U.C.C, the creation and issuance of a check or draft does *not* work an immediate assignment of the drawer's funds in the possession of the drawee, so as to give the holder of the draft a cause of action against the drawee. [U.C.C. § 3–408]

e.g. **Example:** Dan Drawer gives Paula Payee a check drawn on Drawer's account with Antitrust National Bank (" ANB"). Payee presents the check to ANB, but the bank wrongfully refuses to pay it. Payee has no cause of action against ANB, but can sue Drawer on two theories: his drawer's obligation (p. 87), and/or the underlying obligation (the reason Drawer gave Payee the check; *see* p. 73). *Drawer* has a cause of action against ANB for wrongful dishonor. (*See* p. 112)

RULES OF DRAWEE LIABILITY	◢GILBERT
SIGNATURE RULE	Drawee is not liable to holder because it *did not sign* its name (even if drawee's name is listed on the negotiable instrument, *e.g.,* "National Bank")
"NO ASSIGNMENT" RULE	Drawee is not liable to holder because issuance of negotiable instrument does *not* work an *immediate assignment* of the drawer's funds (*e.g.,* drawee not liable to holder for wrongful dishonor)

c. Liability Outside U.C.C.

The drawee may take some action that creates liability *in tort or contract* to the payee. However, such suits are regulated by the law merchant and the common law rather than by the U.C.C. [*See* U.C.C. § 1–103]

(1) Special Agreements with Drawer

If the drawee agrees with the drawer to deliver a check or its proceeds to the payee, the payee becomes a *third-party beneficiary* of this promise and may sue to enforce it. [**Livingston Industries, Inc. v. Walker Bank & Trust Co.**, 565 P.2d 1117 (Utah 1977)]

(2) Liability in Tort

Similarly, oral statements by officials of a drawee bank assuring the payee that a check will clear can create liability for *negligence* [**Faulkner v. Hillside Bank & Trust Co.**, 526 S.W.2d 274 (Tex. 1975)] or fraud [**Union Bank v. Safanie**, 427 P.2d 146 (Ariz. 1967)].

d. Obligation of the Acceptor

(1) "Acceptor" Defined

An acceptor is a drawee who becomes liable *on* the instrument by signing it (typically across the face of the draft, but sometimes on the reverse side). [U.C.C. § 3–409(a)]

(2) "Acceptance" Defined

Acceptance is the drawee's signed agreement to honor the draft as presented. It may consist of the drawee's signature alone, written on the draft. If the draft is a check, the drawee bank's acceptance is called "certification." [U.C.C. § 3–409(c)]

(3) Purpose of Acceptance

Acceptance by the drawee creates an acceptor's *obligation* (below) to honor the draft when presented for payment. Following acceptance, the acceptor *returns* the draft to the holder who has presented it, and it may then be further negotiated. Once it contains the obligation of the acceptor, the draft has greater commercial worth and is more easily sold. For this reason, parties frequently make a *presentment for acceptance* on both checks and nonbank drafts, with a subsequent presentment for payment.

e.g. **Example:** Elton wants to buy a piano from neighbor John, but John will not sell unless Elton's personal check is certified. Elton draws a check payable to John and presents it to his own bank for certification (acceptance). After the bank certifies the check, the bank returns the check to Elton, who gives it to John in return for the piano.

e.g. **Example:** Buyer orders 1,000 widgets from Seller, asking 90 days after delivery in which to pay. Seller draws up a draft with Buyer listed as the drawee and stating, "Pay to bearer 90 days after sight." When the widgets are delivered to Buyer, Seller presents Buyer with the draft and asks her to sign it (thus becoming an acceptor). Buyer does so, and this presentment for acceptance starts the running of the 90-day period. During the next 90 days, the accepted draft can be negotiated to new holders and presented to Buyer for payment at the end of the period.

Recall that a drawee cannot have any liability unless and until she signs the instrument. Thus, a holder generally cannot force a drawee to pay out on a draft. However, once the drawee *signs* the instrument, she becomes an acceptor and incurs acceptor *(primary)* liability.

---

(4) Characteristics of Acceptor's Obligation

The acceptor's signature on a draft creates *primary liability* identical with that of the maker of a promissory note (p. 75). In other words, the acceptor promises to pay the instrument according to its terms at the time accepted (or, if then incomplete, as subsequently completed). [U.C.C. § 3–413]

(a) Defenses Available to Acceptor

When sued on the obligation, an acceptor may raise all available defenses. [U.C.C. § 3–305]

1) Exception for Certified Checks

Many courts hold that a certified check should be treated like money, so that an acceptor bank *must pay* the check when presented for payment—even if the bank has a defense or the drawer has tried to stop payment. [*See* U.C.C. § 4–303; **Dziurak v. Chase Manhattan Bank**, 58 App. Div. 2d 103 (1977)] The Revision strongly urges banks issuing cashier's, teller's, and certified checks to pay them on presentment by making the bank liable for consequential damages and other expenses (in addition to the amount of the check) for wrongful dishonor. The bank may avoid this liability by showing that the dishonor was reasonable under the circumstances. [U.C.C. § 3–411]

(5) Acceptance Varying Draft

If the drawee refuses to accept a draft unless some alteration is made in its terms, the presenter (holder) may treat this as a dishonor and, after giving notice of dishonor, may proceed against prior parties. If the presenter agrees to the drawee's conditional acceptance, all prior nonconsenting parties are *discharged.* [U.C.C. § 3–410]

e.g. **Example:** Collecting Bank presents to Buyer a sales draft drawn on Buyer as drawee by Seller (along with a bill of lading representing the goods being sold). Buyer refuses to accept the draft unless its terms are changed from "pay to bearer 60 days after sight" to "pay to bearer 90 days after sight." If Collecting Bank agrees to this change, the drawer (Seller) and all prior indorsers will be discharged from their contracts unless they affirmatively assent. If Collecting Bank will not agree to the change, a dishonor has occurred and Collecting Bank should so notify Seller (and obtain instructions on what should be done with the goods). [U.C.C. §§ 3–410, 4–501, 4–503]

(a) Exception for Domiciling the Draft

If the drawee merely wants to name a *place* where the draft should be presented for payment (*i.e.,* a domicile for the draft), this addition does not vary the terms of the draft as to constitute a dishonor or discharge nonconsenting parties. *Rationale:* It may be very useful for a nonbank drawee to domicile the draft because this provides a place at which the acceptor can tender payment and stop the running of interest. [U.C.C. §§ 3–410(b), 3–604(c); *and* see p. 82, p. 90]

(6) Check Certification

When a drawee bank agrees to certify a check, it typically freezes a like amount in the drawer's account so that funds will be available when the check is presented for payment. Once the bank has certified the check and either returned it to the presenter *or* notified the presenter of the certification, the bank becomes *primarily liable* thereon by incurring the obligation of an acceptor, and it is too late for the drawer to stop payment. [U.C.C. §§ 3–409, 3–413, 4–303(a)(1)]

(7) Discharge by Certification

No matter who procures certification, the *drawer and indorsers* are immediately *discharged* from all liability by the act of certification. [U.C.C. §§ 3–414(c), 3–415(d)]

LIABILITY OF THE PARTIES		**GILBERT**
PARTY	**LIABILITY TO HOLDER**	**NOTICE OF DISHONOR REQUIRED?**
MAKER	Primary	No
INDORSER	Secondary	Yes
SURETY	Depends on capacity in which party signed	Depends on capacity in which party signed
DRAWER	Secondary	No
DRAWEE	None*	No
ACCEPTOR	Primary	Yes, if acceptor is a bank
* If the drawee signs the instrument, the drawee becomes an acceptor and is primarily liable on the instrument. The drawer's liability is discharged.		

9. Liability of an Agent

The signature rule (p. 94) provides that no one is liable on an instrument unless that person has *signed* the instrument. However, a signature can be made by an agent on behalf of the principal. [U.C.C. § 3–402(a)]

a. Authority of Agent

An agent's authority to act may be established through the usual common law rules of agency. Thus, authority may be express, implied, or apparent. [U.C.C. § 3–402(a); *and see* **Senate Motors, Inc. v. Industrial Bank**, 9 U.C.C. Rep. 387 (D.C. 1971)] No specific formalities are required to establish the agent's authority [*e.g.,* the grant of authority need not be in writing).

e.g. **Example:** George asks his wife, Martha, to cash his paycheck and deposit part of it in his checking account. Martha phones George from the bank to tell him that he has forgotten to indorse the check, whereupon George tells Martha to sign his name to the check. This makes Martha George's agent, and he is bound by her signing of his name. It makes no difference whether Martha signs her own name or indicates that George did not personally write the signature purporting to be his.

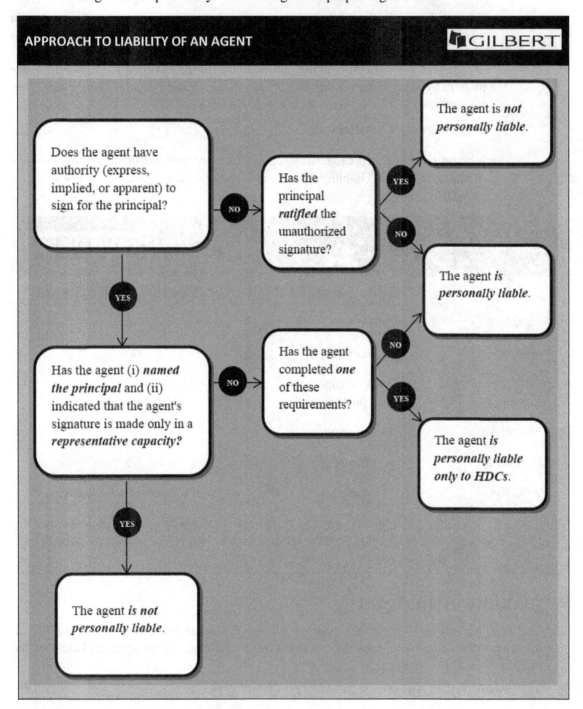

APPROACH TO LIABILITY OF AN AGENT   **GILBERT**

b. Unauthorized Signatures

An unauthorized signature usually does *not bind the person whose name is purportedly signed,* but it does act as the signature of the person who signs. [U.C.C. § 3–403(a)]

(1) Ratification

However, an unauthorized signature can be *ratified,* thereby making the principal liable on the same basis as if the principal had authorized the signature. [U.C.C. § 3–403(a)] Ratification occurs when a principal knowingly adopts a signature as his/her own or when, with full knowledge of the circumstances, the principal appropriates the benefit of the unauthorized signing or fails to deny the validity of the signature, knowing that silence may mislead others. (*See* Agency, Partnership & Limited Liability Companies Summary.)

(2) Criminal and Civil Liability of Forger

Ratification does *not* relieve the forger of criminal liability, nor insulate the forger from civil liability to the person whose name was forged. [U.C.C. § 3–403(c)]

c. Personal Liability of Agent

(1) Ambiguous Signature

A signature on a negotiable instrument that does not clearly indicate some other capacity or intention is *conclusively presumed* to be an *indorsement,* and no one may introduce evidence to the contrary. [U.C.C. § 3–204(a), Off. Com. 1]

(2) Signature as Agent

It follows that an agent must be very careful to sign in such a way as to bind the principal but not the agent. Otherwise, the agent may be personally liable on the instrument and unable to introduce evidence of agency status.

(a) Requirements

To escape liability against all persons (even a HDC), an agent must:

(i) *Name the principal, and*

(ii) Indicate that the agent's signature is made *only in a representative capacity.*

[U.C.C. § 3–402]

1) Official Title

The name of the agent followed by the agent's official title and coupled with the name of the principal is sufficient to relieve the agent of liability (unless the parties agree that the agent shall still be liable). [*See* **Trenton Trust Co. v. Klausman**, 296 A.2d 275 (Pa. 1972); U.C.C. § 3–402(b)(1)]

Example: A promissory note is signed: "X Corporation, Mary Money, Pres." Because this names the principal and indicates that the other signature is that of an agent, Mary Money is not liable on the note.

2) Use of the Word "by"

The word "by" in front of a signature is usually sufficient to indicate that the signer is an agent of the named principal. [*See* U.C.C. § 3–402(b)]

(b) Effect of Failure to Complete One of Two Requirements

Under § 3–402(b), if the agent indicates representative capacity but fails to name the principal, or names the principal but fails to indicate representative capacity, the agent is personally liable *only to a HDC,* but in a lawsuit with a non-HDC is permitted to prove that the original parties did not intend for the agent to be personally liable.

(c) Unidentified Principal

If someone signs a negotiable instrument on behalf of someone else, the principal is bound (as long as the principal authorized the agent to do this), and this is true even if the principal is not named in the instrument.

e.g. **Example:** John Jones is the purchasing agent for Business Corporation. For the corporation he contracts to buy a shipment and pays for it by signing a promissory note. He signs only his own name, and the note nowhere even mentions Business Corporation. Nonetheless, Business Corporation is liable on the note.

(d) Agent's Signature on Checks

Agents signing checks frequently fail to add representative capacity to their signature on the drawer's line. The check itself typically names the principal by printing the principal's name as the account holder. Nonetheless, at common law some courts held that the failure to indicate representative capacity as part of the drawer's signature made the agent personally liable on the check. [*See, e.g.,* **Griffin v. Ellinger**, 538 S.W.2d 97 (Tex. 1976)] The Code keeps the agent from personal liability on checks as long as the principal's name is printed on the check as the account holder. [U.C.C. § 3–402(c), *and see* Off. Com. 3]

D. Warranty Suits

1. Introduction

Warranty suits involving a negotiable instrument arise *off the instrument.* The plaintiff in an action for breach of warranty need not possess the instrument because liability arises from implied warranties created automatically when the instrument is physically shifted from one party to another. Furthermore, an implied warranty on a negotiable instrument is a *property right* and does not depend upon the intentions of the parties. Moreover, the plaintiff need not qualify as a "holder" of the instrument—a prerequisite to suit on any of the commercial paper "obligations" discussed above.

2. Stages in Life of a Negotiable Instrument

A negotiable instrument typically goes through three stages in its commercial "life": *issuance* (p. 26), *transfer* (p. 26), and *presentment* (p. 87). The warranties arising at each of these stages are mutually exclusive, so that, *e.g.,* the implied warranties made on transfer are *not* also made at the moment of presentment.

3. No Warranties on Issuance

No implied warranties are created by the issuance of a negotiable instrument (*i.e.,* the first delivery to the payee).

4. Warranties on Transfer

Any movement of an instrument *other than* an issuance or presentment is a transfer. The U.C.C. provides substantially identical implied transfer warranties in Article 3 and Article 4. [U.C.C. §§ 3–416, 4–207]

a. Person Entitled to Enforce Instrument

The first transfer warranty is a warranty that the transferor is a "person entitled to enforce the instrument" [PETE]. [U.C.C. § 3–416(a)(1)] That phrase has been defined elsewhere (*see* p. 27), but in the transfer warranty context its primary meaning is that the transferor has taken the instrument pursuant to a *valid negotiation* and is therefore a "holder" (*see* p. 26), a warranty that would be breached if there were a forgery of the payee's name or that of any special indorsee.

Example: Dino Drawer writes a check payable to the order of Patty Payee and gives ("issues") it to Payee. Before Payee can sign it, the check is stolen from her, and her name is forged on the back by Fred Forger. Forger then transfers the check to Gullible Grocery, which deposits it at Grocer's State Bank ("GSB"). GSB in turn sends the check to the drawee ("payor") bank, Antitrust National Bank ("ANB"). At the moment they transferred the check, both Forger and Gullible Grocery breached the transfer warranties in § 3–416(a)(1), (2), and (4) (as to right to enforce, *supra,* validity of signatures, *infra,* and defenses, *infra*). GSB did not breach a transfer warranty when it sent the check to the drawee, because that act is a *presentment.*

b. Valid Signatures

The second transfer warranty is that *all* signatures are authentic and authorized. This warranty would be breached by forged signatures on a bearer instrument, even though the forgeries would not create negotiation problems. [U.C.C. §§ 3–416(a)(2), 4–207(a)(2); *compare* § 1–201(18)]

c. No Alterations

The third transfer warranty is a warranty against alterations. An alteration is any change in the terms of the instrument—as, *e.g.,* "raising" the amount from $10.00 to $1,000 by erasing the decimal point (*see* p. 144). [U.C.C. §§ 3–416(a)(3), 4–207(a)(3); *compare* § 3–407]

d. No Defenses Good Against the Transferor

The fourth transfer warranty is that there are no legal defenses or claims in recoupment that are good against the transferor. [U.C.C. § 3–416(a)(4)] This is a warranty that there are no legal problems being transferred along with the instrument.

Example: Pamela Payee defrauds Myron Maker into giving Payee a promissory note, which Payee promptly negotiates to Loan Company. Because Maker could successfully defend a suit on the note by Payee, transfer of the note to Loan Company breached the warranty that there was no defense good against Payee.

(1) Transfer to HDC

In the previous example, the transfer warranty would have been breached even if Loan Company qualified as a HDC—because there would still be a defense good against the transferor (Payee). It is no answer that Loan Company, as a HDC, might have enforced the instrument; the warranty "gives the transferee the option of proceeding against the transferor rather than litigating with the obligor on the instrument the issue of the holder-in-due-course status of the transferee." [U.C.C. § 3–416, Off. Com. 3]

e. No Knowledge of Insolvency Proceedings

Finally, there is a transfer warranty that at the moment of transfer the transferor has *no knowledge* of any insolvency proceeding (*e.g.,* bankruptcy) instituted by or against the party from whom payment is expected (the maker, acceptor, or drawer of an unaccepted draft).

(1) But Note

A warranty of "no *knowledge* of insolvency proceedings" is not a warranty that no such proceedings exist. [U.C.C. §§ 3–416(a)(5), 4–207(a)(5)]

f. Warranties Depend on Receipt of Consideration

Transfer warranties are made *only* by transferors *who receive consideration;* a transferor who receives no consideration (*e.g.,* a person who gives a check as a gift) makes *no* transfer warranties. [U.C.C. §§ 3–416(a), 4–207(a)]

---

g. Parties to Whom Warranties Extend

If the transferor has received consideration, the various transfer warranties described above are made by the transferor to the immediate transferee. However, the U.C.G. provides different rules in Articles 3 and 4 as to whether *later* transferees may also sue for breach of warranty.

(1) Article 3—Indorsement Required

Only if the transferor *indorses* the instrument are later good faith transferees beneficiaries of the warranties under Article 3. [U.C.C. § 3–416(a)]

(2) Article 4—All Collecting Banks Protected

Article 4 transfer warranties are first made by the customer who initiates bank collection on a negotiable instrument. The provisional settlements routinely made thereafter as a part of bank collection (*see* p. 88) furnish the consideration necessary for transfer warranties, and the warranties therefore run in favor of all subsequent collecting banks which take the item in good faith. No indorsement is required. [U.C.C. § 4–207, Off. Com.]

(3) Article 4 Controls

When both Article 3 and Article 4 apply to a given transaction, Article 4 controls in the event of a conflict. Thus, once someone begins bank collection, the Article 4 transfer rules apply. [U.C.C. § 4–102(a)]

EXAM TIP   GILBERT

If you encounter a question involving a person (i) *transferring an instrument* (*i.e.,* any movement of possession of the instrument other than issuance or presentment) (ii) *for consideration,* remember that the transferor makes the following *five transfer warranties:* (i) the transferor is *entitled to enforce* the instrument; (ii) *all* of the signatures are *authentic and authorized;* (iii) the instrument has *not been altered;* (iv) *no defenses* are good against the transferor; and (v) the transferor has *no knowledge of insolvency proceedings.*

---

5. Warranties on Presentment

The warranties made on presentment for payment or acceptance are considerably *narrower* than transfer warranties. This is largely attributable to the common law doctrine developed in Price v. Neal (*infra*).

a. Doctrine of Price v. Neal—Drawee's Responsibility

In the landmark English case of Price v. Neal, Lord Mansfield held that as between an innocent holder and a drawee who had both been duped by an unauthorized drawer's signature, the *drawee* must bear the loss and could not recover what the drawee had paid the holder on presentment. The opinion stated that the drawee was responsible for knowing the drawer's signature, so that if the drawee were mistaken the drawee could not seek restitution from the innocent presenter. [**Price v. Neal**, 97 Eng. Rep. 871 (1762)]

(1) Expansion of Rule

The traditional rule that a drawee must know the drawer's signature has been expanded by subsequent court decisions and statutes so that a drawee who pays on an instrument takes the risk of *any mistakes* other than problems covered by the various presentment warranties (discussed below). Such mistakes would include the fact that there were insufficient funds in the drawer's account, that there was no such account, or that the drawer had stopped payment. [*See* U.C.C. § 3–418, Off. Com. 1]

(2) Effect of Final Payment

Once *final payment* has occurred (*see* p. 122), the foregoing doctrine indicates that the drawee (or the maker in the case of promissory notes) cannot undo the transaction and recover the money paid unless a presentment warranty has been breached or the person who received payment was not acting in good faith. [U.C.C. §§ 3–418, 4–215]

(a) Unjust Enrichment Exception

The above final payment rule applies only if the person paid acted in *good faith.* If good faith is lacking, any final payment under Article 4 is canceled and the now-dishonored instrument is returned to the person from whom payment was recovered. Section 3–418 broadly adopts the common law of restitution, so as to allow recovery against those who would otherwise be unjustly enriched. [U.C.C. §§ 3–418, Off. Com.; 4–302(b)]

b. Same Presentment Warranties in Articles 3 and 4

The U.C.C. provides for nearly identical presentment warranties in both Articles 3 and 4.

(1) Person Entitled to Enforce Instrument

The first presentment warranty is that the warrantor is a "person entitled to enforce" the instrument. [U.C.C. §§ 3–417(a)(1), 4–208(a)(1)] That phrase has been defined elsewhere (*see* p. 27), but in the presentment warranty context its primary meaning is that the transferor has taken the instrument pursuant to a *valid negotiation* and is therefore a "holder" (*see* p. 26), a warranty that would be breached if there were a forgery of the payee's name or that of any special indorsee.

e.g. **Example:** David Drawer gave Pandora Payee a $1,000 check drawn on Octopus National Bank. The check was stolen from Payee by Thadeus Thief, who forged Payee's name as payee on the back of the check and cashed it at Wonder Drug Store. The drug store deposited the check in its bank, Merchants Bank, which presented it to Octopus National and was paid. When all of this was discovered, Octopus National recredited Drawer's account (the check was not "properly payable"—*see* p. 114). Octopus National now may sue Thief, Wonder Drug Store, and/or Merchants Bank, all of whom will have breached the warranty that they were persons entitled to enforce the instrument. The only person entitled to enforce this instrument was Payee. Following the forgery of her name as payee, no one else could qualify as a "holder," and therefore no one met the definition in § 3–303 of a "person entitled to enforce the instrument." Whoever gets stuck with the liability here can use *transfer* warranties to pass the loss back to the wrongdoer. (*See* p. 101)

(2) No Alterations

The second presentment warranty is that there has been no alteration of the instrument. (*See* p. 144) However, this warranty is not given to makers of notes or acceptors of drafts. [U.C.C. §§ 3–417(a)(2), 4–208(a)(2)]

(3) No Knowledge That Signature of Drawer or Maker Is Unauthorized

The third presentment warranty is that at the time of transfer or presentment the presenter has *no knowledge* that the signature of the drawer or maker is unauthorized. (Note that this is not a warranty that the drawer's (or maker's) name *is* genuine.) [U.C.C. §§ 3–417(a)(3), 4–208(a)(3)] Note that this warranty is not made to makers of notes nor to acceptors of drafts.

Example: Thadeus Thief stole a blank check from David Drawer's checkbook and forged Drawer's name to the drawer's line. He made the check out to himself as payee and then deposited the check in his own account at Merchants Bank, which presented the check to the drawee, Octopus National Bank, which paid it. When the canceled check was returned to Drawer, he protested immediately and the bank put the money back in his account (as it must do because the check was not "properly payable"—*see* p. 114). The bank cannot sue anyone but Thief for breach of presentment warranties, because the presentment warranty dealing with the signature of the drawer is a warranty that those handling the check had **no knowledge** at the time they handled it that the drawer's name was forged, and only Thief breached this warranty. The policy here is that of **Price v. Neal** (p. 103), that the drawee is supposed to know the drawer's signature, and on making a mistake as to this the drawee cannot pass the loss back to innocent parties.

(a) Other Presentment Warranties Not Breached Either

In the above example, none of the other two presentment warranties was breached. A forgery is not an alteration, so U.C.C. § 4–208(a)(2) is irrelevant. The first presentment warranty is that the warrantors are each a "person entitled to enforce the instrument," but it is not breached here for the following technical reason. *Thief* is the true drawer of this instrument because § 3–403(a) states that an unauthorized signature acts as the signature of the unauthorized signer only (*see* p. 137), meaning that the forgery of Drawer's name is the same as if Thief had foolishly signed his own name. Later parties are persons entitled to enforce *Thief's* check, so the first presentment warranty is not breached.

(b) Forgery of Maker's Name

The same result occurs when a *maker's* name is forged to a promissory note and the maker mistakenly pays it when it is presented. In this situation U.C.C. § 3–417(d) states that the only warranty made by those handling the instrument is that they were "persons entitled to enforce" the instrument, which they will be if only the maker's name is forged since they are entitled to enforce the *forger's* obligation. The maker is supposed to know his/her own signature, and making a mistake as to this, will have to go against the forger for restitution. [U.C.C. § 3–418]

EXAM TIP

Note the difference in result between a forged drawer's signature and a forged indorser's signature. If a bank pays out on a forged **drawer's** signature, payment is final and the bank cannot recover the money back from the party paid because no presentment warranty is broken (the forgery is treated as a valid signature **of the forger** and thus the presenter had the right to enforce the forger's instrument as against the forger). But if the bank pays out on a forged **indorser's** signature, a presentment warranty is broken (the presenter did not have the right to enforce against the drawer because of the forgery).

---

(4) Persons Deemed to Make Presentment Warranties

Everyone who *transfers* a negotiable instrument automatically makes presentment warranties, as does the party who physically receives payment or acceptance. This permits the payor to sue anyone in the chain for breach of presentment warranties. [U.C.C. §§ 3–417(a), 4–208(a)]

Example: Delilah Drawer writes a check to the order of Pancho Payee, who loses the check. Payee's name is forged thereto by Felicity Forger, who transfers the check to Gullible Grocery ("GG"). GG cashes the check at Grocer's State Bank ("GSB"), which sends it to the Federal Reserve Bank ("FRB"). FRB in turn presents the check to the payor bank, Antitrust National Bank ("ANB"), and receives payment. At the moment when FRB made presentment, *all* prior transferors made the presentment warranties. Thus, when ANB learns that Payee's name was forged, it must repay the money to Payee and may then sue FRB, GSB, GG, or Forger for breach of the presentment warranty that they were persons entitled to enforce the instrument. If it sues and recovers from GSB, GSB may in turn recover from GG for breach of the *transfer* warranties. The loss proceeds up the chain until it rests with Forger (or, if she is unavailable or insolvent, with the first person who trusted her).

EXAM TIP

The general rule is that *payment of a negotiable instrument is final—i.e.,* the payor cannot recover payment back from the party paid. However, there are two exceptions to the general rule. The payor can recover from the party paid if: (i) that party *neither took for value nor in good faith*, nor detrimentally relied on the payment; or (ii) the party paid *breached a transfer warranty* (*see* p. 101) *or a presentment warranty*. Remember that there are two sets of presentment warranties: those made to a drawee on an *unaccepted draft* (the presenter is entitled to enforce the instrument, the instrument has not been altered, and the presenter has no knowledge that the drawer's signature is unauthorized) and those made to a payor of *any other instrument* (the presenter is entitled to enforce the instrument).

---

6. Notice Requirement

For both transfer and presentment warranties, the Code requires that notice of claim of breach be given to the warrantor *within 30 days* after the claimant has reason to know of the breach. Failure to give notice within that period discharges the liability of the warrantor to the extent of any loss caused by the delay in giving notice. [U.C.C. §§ 3–416(c), 3–417(e), 4–207(d), 4–208(e)]

7. Statute of Limitations

The statute of limitations for warranty claims is three years after the cause of action accrues, and a cause of action for warranty claims accrues when the claimant has reason to know of the breach. [U.C.C. §§ 3–118(g), 3–416(d), 3–417(f), 4–111, 4–207(e), 4–208(f)]

8. Damages for Breach of Warranty

The Code, in all four of its warranty sections, permits recovery of the loss suffered as a result of the breach, but no more than the amount of the instrument, plus expenses and loss of interest. The Official Comments to these sections leave to "other state law" the issue of whether "expenses" includes the recovery of attorney's fees. [U.C.C. §§ 3–416(b), 3–417(b), 4–207(c), 4–208(b)]

9. 2002's Remotely Created Consumer Items

The 2002 revision of Article 3 adds both transfer and presentment warranties dealing with what are called *remotely created consumer items*. These are defined in new § 3–103(a)(16) as checks drawn on a consumer account, not created by the payor bank, and which do not bear the handwritten signature of the drawer. They are sometimes called by other names: preauthorized drafts or telechecks.

Example: Consumer Betty Buyer succumbed to a telemarketing pitch to buy a new watch from Nightflyer Watch Company. To pay for the watch, Buyer supplied the telemarketer with all the information that was magnetically encoded across the bottom of the checks that she was given by her bank, Octopus National. Nightflyer Watch Company then created a check payable to itself, drawn on Octopus National Bank, and in lieu of Buyer's signature as drawer it simply marked "Maker's Signature on File" in the usual place for the drawer's signature. Nightflyer then deposited this check with its bank, which collected the check from Octopus National. This check, created by the payee on a consumer's account and not bearing the actual signature, qualifies as a remotely created consumer item.

COMMERCIAL PAPER WARRANTIES		GILBERT
	THE PRESENTMENT WARRANTIES	
THE TRANSFER WARRANTIES	*UNACCEPTED* DRAFTS	OTHER INSTRUMENTS
1. Entitled to enforce	1. Entitled to enforce	1. Entitled to enforce
2. Signatures are authentic and authorized	2. No alteration	
3. No alterations	3. No knowledge that drawer's signature is unauthorized	
4. No defenses are good against the transferor		
5. No knowledge of insolvency proceedings (against maker, acceptor, or drawer of unaccepted draft)		

a. The New Warranties

To deal with these pesky checks (and there are a lot of them out there), the drafters of the 2002 revision to Articles 3 and 4 created new transfer and presentment warranties that the purported drawers of the check really did authorize the issuance of the check. If the drawer did not do so, these warranties allow the banks to pass the liability back to the telemarketer or its own bank. [U.C.C. (2002) §§ 3–416(a)(6), 3–417(a)(4), 4–207(a)(6), 4–208(a)(4)] The Federal Reserve adopted similar warranties for remotely-created checks in § 229.34 of Regulation CC.

E. Conversion

1. Definition

At common law, "conversion" is the unauthorized assumption and exercise of the rights of ownership over personal property belonging to another. It is no defense to a conversion action that the converter acted in the good faith belief that he/she was entitled to exercise dominion over the property and was nonnegligent in so believing.

2. Common Law Preserved

Instead of listing the many different ways a negotiable instrument can be converted, U.C.C. § 3–420(a) simply preserves the common law of conversion and allows it to govern most problems. Thus, the theft of a negotiable instrument (whether payable to order or bearer) would be conversion, and so would any other wrongful taking of the instrument. (*See* Torts Summary.)

3. Restrictive Indorsements

A restrictive indorsement is—obviously—an indorsement accompanied by a restriction. Violation of the restriction results in conversion, but Article 3 cuts down the possible lawsuits severely.

a. Restrictions on Transfer

An indorsement accompanied by a restriction on further transfer has no effect to prohibit further transfers. Thus, a restriction saying "Pay A and only A" would not prohibit A from negotiating the instrument to later parties. [U.C.C. § 3–206(a)]

b. Conditional Indorsements

Conditions accompanying indorsements are effective only between the original parties thereto and do not bind later parties. Thus, a payee who indorses "Pay A only if A goes to his mother's funeral" has no binding effect on parties taking the instrument after A, and later parties may ignore the condition (and need not investigate A's attendance at the funeral). [U.C.C. § 3–206(b)]

c. "For Deposit Only" Indorsements

If the payee (or later parties) adds "For Deposit Only" (or similar language) to an indorsement, this restriction means that the very next indorsement should be that of the depositary bank. If not, the instrument has been converted. The common law permitted the payee to sue everyone who handled the instrument after the "For Deposit Only" indorsement was violated, but banks rightly protested that this was too big a burden to place upon them. The Code's rule is that only the *first bank* that sees the check after the "For Deposit Only" indorsement is placed thereon is liable in conversion (because at the first bank, typically the depositary bank, a human being—the teller—should examine the check manually and make sure this restriction is followed). Later banks (such as the drawee bank, assuming it is not the first bank to handle the check) are excused from conversion liability. *Note: **Nonbank entities,*** no matter how innocent or far down the transfer chain, have no such exemption and are liable in conversion on taking a check bearing such a restriction that did not make it into the appropriate bank account. [U.C.C. § 3–206(c)]

d. Trust Indorsements

If the restriction is for the benefit of another person ("Pay A in trust for B"), later takers who are unaware of any breach of fiduciary duty (*see* p. 48) may assume that the restriction was complied with and escape conversion liability if it was not. [U.C.C. § 3–206(d)]

4. Forged or Missing Indorsements

The most important kind of conversion of a negotiable instrument occurs where there is a forgery of an indorsement. Section 3–420(a) provides that where an instrument is taken by transfer *other than a negotiation* or a bank makes payment to someone not entitled thereto, a conversion occurs. This language means that a conversion occurs anytime there is a forgery of a necessary indorsement (the payee or any special indorsee's name—*see* p. 28, p. 32) or such a necessary indorsement is *missing*. All transfers and payments thereafter would be conversions.

e.g. **Example:** Donna Drawer drew a check payable to the order of John and Mary Doe. John took the check and signed his own name to the back thereof and forged Mary's name below his. He cashed the check at Big Drug Store, which deposited the check in its bank, which forwarded the check to the drawee bank for payment. Because Mary's valid signature had to be on the check for there to be a true *negotiation*, she may sue in conversion the following entities: John (who is guilty of common law theft), Big Drug Store, Big Drug Store's bank, and the drawee bank. Whoever is sued will use warranty theories to pass the loss back to John (*see* p. 101). The same result would follow if John did not sign Mary's name at all because her valid signature is still required before a negotiation occurs.

a. Plaintiffs in Such Suits

The appropriate plaintiff in conversion suits based on forged or missing indorsements is the person whose property rights are being violated by the transfers. In the above example, that was Mary. The drawer (Donna) is not an appropriate plaintiff because she has no property rights in the check—it belongs to John and Mary; Donna's suit would be against her own bank for violation of the "properly payable" rule (*see* p. 114). Section 3–420(a) expressly states that conversion actions may not be brought by the issuer or acceptor of an instrument. Here Donna was the issuer (*see* p. 26).

b. Necessity of Delivery

Settling a controversy arising under the original version of Article 3, § 3–420(a) also provides that a payee may not sue in conversion unless the payee received *delivery* of the instrument either directly, through an agent, or through a co-payee. In the above example, Mary could sue in conversion because her co-payee (John) received delivery of the instrument. If neither Mary nor John had received the check (*e.g.,* it was stolen from the mails) and their names were forged thereon, they could not sue in conversion. However, because they never received the check, the merger rule (*see* p. 73) would not be in effect, and they could still sue Donna (the drawer) on the underlying obligation from which the check arose.

5. Damages in Conversion Suits

Under the original version of Article 3, if the conversion suit was brought against the *drawee*, there was a *conclusive presumption* that the damages were equal to the face amount of the instrument. Where other parties were sued, they were allowed to show that the damages were a lesser amount. Under the Revision, the presumption is not conclusive, and damages are limited to the plaintiff's interest in the instrument (so that co-payees are entitled to half each, for example). [U.C.C. § 3–420(b)]

GILBERT

ON THE UNDERLYING OBLIGATION	Underlying obligation generally *merges* into the instrument upon issuance. Cannot sue on underlying obligation until *after* instrument has been *dishonored*.
ON THE INSTRUMENT	Liability depends on the *party* involved. Secondarily liable parties are entitled to *presentment, dishonor, and notice of dishonor*.
ON A WARRANTY	Liability depends on whether the warranty arises from *transfer* (entitled to enforce, authentic/authorized signatures, no alterations, no defenses, no knowledge of insolvency) or *presentment* (entitled to enforce, no alteration, no knowledge that drawer's signature unauthorized).
ON CONVERSION	Common law tort action. Payee must have received *delivery* in order to maintain this action.

Chapter Seven
Bank Deposits and Collections

CONTENTS	PAGE

Chapter Approach

When someone opens a checking account and begins using it, both U.C.C. Article 4 and the Federal Expedited Funds Availability Act regulate the legal issues that arise from the passage of checks through the bank collection machinery. In addition, the Federal Reserve Board has promulgated various regulations that apply to checking accounts, and the common law has a few rules of its own on point. Federal rules will prevail over inconsistent Article 4 provisions pertaining to the bank collection process.

For exam purposes, the two most important rules to remember when dealing with an instrument drawn on or deposited in a bank are:

(i) A bank may charge a customer's account only if an item is *"properly payable"*; and

(ii) Once *"final payment"* has been made, a bank loses the right to return items.

The details of what constitutes a properly payable item and when final payment occurs are outlined below, together with various other rules regarding a bank's liability for wrongful dishonor, its right to pay items after the death of a customer, its right to set off, the customer's duty to examine statements, and the timing of availability of a customer's deposits.

A. Introduction

1. Article 4 Governs the Bank Collection Process

U.C.C. Article 4 ("Bank Deposits and Collections") amplifies or alters the Article 3 provisions governing negotiable instruments where items (particularly checks) become part of the bank collection process. In the event of a conflict between Article 3 and Article 4, *Article 4 prevails.* [U.C.C. § 4–102(a)] The two basic parts of Article 4 are the rules governing the relationship between a bank and its customers, and the rules governing the check collection process among banks.

B. Relationship Between Banks and Depositors

1. Introduction

U.C.C. § 4–400 *et seq.* deal with the contractual relationship between a drawee bank (a "payor bank" [*see* U.C.C. § 4–105(3)]) and the drawer (the "customer"), and define the rights and duties stemming from that relationship.

2. Wrongful Dishonor

If a check or other item is properly payable from the drawer's account but the bank wrongfully refuses to honor it, the drawer has a cause of action against the bank for "wrongful dishonor." [U.C.C. § 4–402]

a. Only Drawer May Sue

Because the drawer—through the contract creating the account—is the only one in privity with the payor bank, only the drawer may sue for wrongful dishonor. Other parties cannot sue the payor bank unless it has accepted the instrument. (*See* p. 94)

EXAM TIP　　　　　　　　　　　　　　　　　　　　　　　　**█GILBERT**

Recall that under the *"no assignment" rule* (*see* p. 94), the creation and issuance of a check does not give the holder any immediate rights in the drawer's checking account funds. Also, the drawee bank has no liability to the holder until the bank pays or accepts the check. Of course, the drawee bank is bound by the terms of its agreement with its customer (the drawer) and may be liable to the drawer for wrongful dishonor.

---

b. Damages for Wrongful Dishonor

A court may award the drawer actual and consequential damages for wrongful dishonor. Noncompensatory damages, such as punitive damages, are awarded only for outrageous conduct by the bank.

(1) Proximate Cause Limitation

Only those damages that are *proximately caused* by the wrongful dishonor may be recovered by the drawer. However, such damages may include consequential damages for arrest and prosecution of the customer. Whether a particular item of damages is proximately caused is a question of fact in each case.

(2) Damages at Common Law—the "Trader Rule"

Common law courts did not require that a merchant drawer (a "trader") prove damages for dishonor. Automatic ("punitive") damages were *presumed* because the dishonor was deemed to cause widespread damage to the drawer's credit rating and this type of damage was very hard to establish. This presumption of damages was known as the "trader rule."

(3) Damages Under the Code

The drafters of the U.C.C. wanted to kill the trader rule, so § 4–402(b) requires injured drawers to *prove actual damages.* Official Comment 1 says that punitive damages, if recoverable, must be sought under other theories than mere wrongful dishonor. Nonetheless, courts have awarded punitive damages where the dishonor is indefensible and outrageous. [*See* **Twin City Bank v. Isaacs**, 672 S.W.2d 651 (Ark. 1984)—$45,000 punitive damages where bank froze the account for four years because it wrongly believed that its depositor was involved in check forgery; **Beshara v. Southern National Bank**, 928 P.2d 280 (Okla. 1996)—punitive damages where bank placed a three-year hold on customer's account on discovering irregularities caused by an embezzlement done by its own bank employee]

3. Death or Incompetence of Customer

At common law, an agent's authority to act *terminates* with the death of the principal, so that thereafter the agent's actions are unauthorized even if done in ignorance of the principal's demise. The same rule applies where the principal is adjudged incompetent. (*See* Agency, Partnership & Limited Liability Companies Summary.) Because a bank can be both a collecting agent and a paying agent for its customers, their death or incompetence could cause problems for bankers. U.C.C. section 4–405 attempts to solve this difficulty.

a. Pre-Knowledge Actions

A bank's collection or payment actions taken prior to knowledge of the death or incompetency of a customer are *valid.* [U.C.C. § 4–405(a)]

(1) What Constitutes "Knowledge"

"Knowledge" means *actual knowledge* of the bank employee whose job it is to close down such accounts, plus a *reasonable time* within which to act. [U.C.C. §§ 1–201(25)–(27), 4–405(a)]

b. Post-Knowledge Actions

Even where it has knowledge of a customer's death, a bank may elect to pay or certify checks *for 10 days following the death.* [U.C.C. § 4–405(b)]

(1) Rationale

Payment of outstanding checks avoids the inconvenience of submitting small matters to probate proceedings. [*See* U.C.C. § 4–405, Off. Com. 2]

(2) Stopping Payment

However, *any person* who claims an interest in the customer's account, whether or not the claim is valid, may order the bank not to pay or certify checks during the 10-day period, and such an order *terminates the bank's authority* to do so. [U.C.C. § 4–405, Off. Com. 3]

(3) Impact of State Tax Laws

And regardless of their rights under U.C.C. section 4–405, most banks will freeze an account upon learning of the customer's death because of state tax law requirements.

EXAM TIP   ◆GILBERT

On an exam, if you see a question where a bank's customer dies or is adjudged incompetent, remember that the ordinary agency rules do not apply to revoke the bank's authority. Instead, the customer's death does *not revoke* the bank's authority to pay a check *until* the bank (i) *knows* of the death and (ii) has a *reasonable time to act* on the knowledge. Even with such knowledge, the bank may continue paying checks for *10 days* after the date of death unless someone claiming an interest in the account orders that payment be stopped.

---

4. Requirement That Item Be "Properly Payable"

A bank may charge a customer's account for an item (check, note, etc.) only if the item is "properly payable." If the item is not "properly payable," the bank usually must replace the money in the account if the customer complains within relevant time limits (*see infra*). Whether an item is *"properly payable"* depends on: (i) the terms of the deposit contract between the customer and the bank, (ii) who presents the item, (iii) the terms of the item, and (iv) the usages of trade (*i.e.,* common understanding, *see* U.C.C. section 1–205(2)). [U.C.C. § 4–401(a)]

a. Overdrafts

If payment of the item in question would overdraw the customer's account, the bank need not pay but *may* do so—even where the bank and its customer have no agreement concerning overdrafts. [U.C.C. §§ 4–401(a), 4–402(a)]

EXAM TIP   ◤GILBERT

In the case of *insufficient funds* in the drawer's account, remember that the bank does not have to honor the check. If the bank chooses to do so, the customer is liable to the bank for the overdraft and may also be charged a fee.

---

b. Altered and Completed Items

If an item has been altered (*e.g.,* the amount changed), the bank may charge the account only according to the *original terms* of the item unless the customer's negligence led to the alteration, in which case the bank may pay the item as altered. [U.C.C. § 4–402(d)(1)] If a customer leaves blanks in the item that are later filled in, the bank may assume that the item as completed is proper (unless it knows otherwise), and the account may be charged accordingly. [U.C.C. § 4–401(d)(2)]

c. Contract of Deposit

When an account is opened, the customer may sign a contract with the bank regulating when and how an item will be "properly payable." The U.C.C. does not have detailed regulation of such contracts of deposit, but it does provide that the contract *cannot disclaim* bank liability for *bad faith or failure to exercise ordinary care.* [U.C.C. § 4–103]

(1) Parties May Set Standards

The parties may agree that the actions of the bank or the customer must meet certain standards, as long as the standards are not manifestly unreasonable. An action taken pursuant to Federal Reserve Board regulations is insulated from attack. Action pursuant to agreements between banks (such as bank clearinghouse rules) is at least considered *prima facie reasonable*, as is compliance with any general banking usage not forbidden by Article 4. [U.C.C. § 4–103(b), (c)]

(2) Contract May Not Disclaim Article 4 Provisions

Whatever terms are provided, a contract of deposit may not change the explicit rules of Article 4. Thus, for example, an agreement that the bank has no liability for failing to honor stop payment orders from the customer would be invalid. [U.C.C. §§ 4–103(a); 4–403, Off. Com. 7]

d. Proper Presenter

The payor bank may charge its customer's account with the amount of an item only if it pays a person who qualifies as a "person entitled to enforce the instrument" (usually a "holder")—*i.e.,* someone in possession of the instrument to whom the instrument has been validly negotiated (*see* p. 27). [U.C.C. §§ 3–301, 4–401]

(1) Rationale

If the bank makes payment to a nonholder, it does so without authority—because it has not followed the customer's order, which was to "pay to the order of [payee]."

Example: Donna Drawer writes a check on her account in Antitrust National Bank ("ANB") payable to the order of John Doe. The check is stolen from Doe, and his name is forged thereon. The forger cashes the check at his bank, Forgers State Bank ("FSB"), which in turn presents it to ANB for payment. Meanwhile, John Doe reports the loss of the check to Donna Drawer and she so notifies her bank. ANB must return the money to Donna's account because the item was not "properly payable." Donna had ordered the bank to pay to the order of John Doe, and Doe had not ordered further payment to anyone (so negotiation stops with him). After recrediting Donna's account, however, ANB may proceed against FSB (or the forger) for breach of the presentment warranty that it was a person entitled to enforce the instrument. (*See* p. 104)

e. Postdated Checks

Under the original 1962 version of section 4–401(1), a postdated check was *not properly payable before its date.* Because the date of the check is not magnetically encoded on the check so that modern check-processing equipment can read it, this rule meant that many banks had no chance to catch postdated checks prior to their payment. Thus, the Code now provides that postdated checks *are properly payable unless* the customer gives the bank *notice* of the postdating before the bank pays or certifies the check. [U.C.C. § 4–401(c)] Most people don't know this and wrongly assume that a postdated check cannot be paid prior to its date.

f. Stop Payment Orders

An item on which a customer has stopped payment is no longer "properly payable."

(1) No Stop Payment on Bank Obligations

In the case of cashier's checks (checks drawn by the bank on itself as drawee), teller's checks (drafts drawn by a bank on another bank), and certified or accepted items, customer may *not* stop payment nor may the issuing bank do so; such items remain "properly payable" in spite of a stop payment order by the customer ("remitter"). [U.C.C. §§ 4–303(a)(1), 3–411]

(a) Rationale

A certified check or similar item is commonly believed to be "as good as cash," so the law gives the same legal effect to its transfer. Further, the bank itself is primarily liable on these types of checks, so the customer has no ability to interfere with that liability.

(b) Lost Cashier's Checks, Teller's Checks, or Certified Checks

If a person (typically the remitter who buys a cashier's check) loses it, § 3–312 creates a procedure that gives that person some rights to access the missing funds. The person who loses the check is required to fill out a "declaration of loss" explaining the circumstances causing the check to be missing, and the bank that is primarily liable on the check (the "obligated bank") then waits for 90 days after the date of the check. If the check is not presented during that period, the obligated bank refunds the money to the person losing the check, and has no further obligation on the missing check, even if it turns up in the hand of a holder-in-due-course. In the latter case, the HDC would have to seek relief by going after the person filing the declaration of loss.

(2) Requirement of Reasonable Notice

For other items—*e.g.,* ordinary checks, domiciled promissory notes, sales drafts, and the like—a customer may stop payment by giving notice that *reasonably identifies* the item and is received sufficiently before payment that the bank has a *reasonable opportunity* to act on it. [U.C.C. § 4–403(a)]

(a) Oral Notice

The customer's stop payment notice may be *oral,* but an oral notice is good for *only 14 days* unless renewed in writing within that period. [U.C.C. § 4–403(b)]

(b) Written Notice

A written stop payment notice is good for *six months,* but it may be renewed in writing for further six-month periods. [U.C.C. § 4–403(b)]

(3) Customer Has Burden of Proving Loss

If the bank pays an item in spite of a stop payment order, the *customer* has the burden of proving that a loss has occurred and the amount of the loss. If there is an HDC in the chain of transferees of the item, the customer cannot recover—because even if payment *had* been stopped, the customer would have had to pay the HDC. [U.C.C. § 4–403(c), Off. Com. 7]

e.g. **Example:** Dion Drawer gives a check to his nephew as a gift, but decides to stop payment. The nephew cashes the check at his bank, Nephew's State Bank ("NSB"), which presents it to the payor bank. The payor bank, carelessly failing to obey Drawer's stop order, makes the payment. Drawer has no loss because NSB was an HDC (having given value for the check by cashing it); and if the payor bank *had* dishonored the check, Drawer would still have been liable to NSB. [*See* **Universal C.I.T. Credit Corp. v. Guaranty Bank & Trust Co.**, 161 F. Supp. 790 (D. Mass. 1958)]

g. Right of Subrogation

If an item is not "properly payable" for any of the reasons previously discussed but the bank nevertheless pays it, the bank is subrogated to ("steps into the shoes of") any person connected with the instrument (drawer, payee, holder, or HDC) to the extent necessary to prevent *unjust enrichment.* [U.C.C. § 4–407]

e.g. **Example:** The payor bank in the previous example (p. 117) may avoid recrediting Drawer's account by asserting NSB's HDC rights against Drawer.

e.g. **Example:** If a bank pays an item in the face of a stop payment order and there is no HDC in the chain, the bank may resist the drawer's request to recredit by asserting whatever rights the *payee* could have asserted against the drawer. Or, if the bank does recredit the account, it may sue the payee in the position of the drawer (to whose rights it is also subrogated).

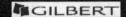
A BANK *CANNOT* CHARGE A CUSTOMER'S ACCOUNT:

☑ For more money than the original order (*alteration* of amount by third party).

☑ If there is no order by the depositor (*forged* signature of drawer).

☑ I the bank pays the wrong person (*forgery* of payee or indorsee's signature).

☑ If the item is postdated, the customer gives the bank *notice of postdating*, and the bank pays the item *before* the stated date.

☑ If the customer has *stopped payment* on the item.

5. Right of Setoff for Bank

Traditionally, banks (as "debtors," with the customer being the bank's "creditor") have exercised a common law right available to all debtors to subtract ("set off") from the amount owed the customer any debt the customer owes the bank. This is the right of "setoff" generally referred to by bankers as an "offset." [**Walter v. National City Bank**, 330 N.E.2d 425 (Ohio 1975)]

e.g. **Example:** Little Orphan Annie misses a payment on the school loan she has borrowed from her bank, so the bank pays itself out of her checking account. Annie has no recourse, even if the withdrawal causes her outstanding check for her dog Sandy's food to bounce.

a. No Setoff for Credit Card Debts

Note, however, that the Federal Fair Credit Billing Act of 1975 [part of the Truth in Lending Act, 15 U.S.C. § 1601 *et seq.*] *prohibits* banks from setting off the unpaid credit card debts of their customer-cardholders. Banks usually don't understand that this is the law, and the rule is constantly violated, even though the Truth in Lending Act provides for significant penalties for such a violation.

b. Notice Not Required

Banks need not notify the customer prior to a setoff.

c. Applies Only to General Accounts

A bank's right of setoff may be exercised only against a *general* checking or savings account. If the account is earmarked for a special purpose (*e.g.*, tax accounts), there can be no setoff of unrelated debts from it. [*See* **Commercial Discount Corp. v. Milwaukee Western Bank**, 214 N.W.2d 33 (Wis. 1974)]

d. Effect of Final Payment

If the bank has certified an item or has made "final payment" thereon (*see* p. 124), it is too late to set off a claim against the amount necessary to pay that item. [U.C.C. § 4–303(a)(1)]

Remember that when a bank is owed money by its customer, it can "set off" the amount owed (*i.e.,* help itself to the funds in the customer's general accounts), but the bank *cannot* make setoffs (i) for unpaid *credit card debt,* (ii) against *special accounts,* or (iii) for items that have been *certified or for which payment is final.*

6. Customer's Duty to Examine Bank Statements

After a bank pays items, it cancels them and returns the items to the customer with a statement of account. Failure by the customer to use reasonable care in promptly examining the statement and reporting any unauthorized signatures or alterations on an item may validate the improper payment. [U.C.C. § 4–406, and see discussion of forgery p. 137]

C. Bank Collection Procedures

1. Deposit Availability Under Federal Law

If a bank customer puts money or checks in an account, a federal statute, the Expedited Funds Availability Act ("EFAA"), regulates how quickly the customer must be allowed to draw against that account. The federal government decided to act in this matter because it believed that banks were unfairly using the "float period" (the period of time that the check travels from one bank to another). The EFAA commands the Federal Reserve Board to issue a regulation implementing the statute, and as a consequence the Board has issued Regulation CC (for "check collection"). All subsequent citations are to Regulation CC. [12 C.F.R. Part 229] Regulation CC sets the following time limits for deposit availability.

a. Government Checks and Bank Checks

Funds from government checks that are deposited in a bank account must be made available on the *next business day.* This includes checks issued by any branch of government: federal, state, or local. The same one-day availability period is mandated for the deposit of checks drawn on the same bank in which deposited, cashier's checks, certified checks, teller's checks, or similar bank-generated checks, and for wire transfers. [Reg. CC § 229.10]

b. The $200 Availability Rule

The customer must be permitted to withdraw $200 of a day's deposit (not counting checks already requiring next business day availability) on the business day after deposit. [Reg. CC § 229.10(c)(1)(vii)]

c. Withdrawals

For checks the funds must be available for *withdrawal by check* payable to third parties no later than two business days after deposit. For *cash withdrawals,* the customer must be permitted to take out $200 on the business day after the date of deposit (*see* above), must be permitted to withdraw up to $300 more by 5 p.m. on the second business day after deposit, and must be allowed to withdraw all the rest as cash on the next business day. [Reg. CC § 229.12(d)]

Example: Assume $900 worth of checks are deposited on a Monday. Two hundred dollars in cash of the aggregate amount of such checks would be available at the opening of business on Tuesday, the next business day. By no later than 5 p.m. on Wednesday, an additional $300 of cash would be available. The remaining balance of funds for purposes of cash withdrawal represented by the checks ($00) would then be available at the opening of business on Thursday.

d. ATM Deposits

For deposits made at an Automated Teller Machine ("ATM") owned or controlled by the depositary bank, the above rules apply except items requiring next-day availability are given an extra day. For deposits made at what the statute calls a "nonproprietary ATM" (*i.e.,* one not owned, controlled, or in close physical proximity to the depositary bank), checks, cash, and government checks so deposited must be available for withdrawal no later than two business days after deposit. [Reg. CC § 229.12(f)]

e. Safeguard Exceptions

Congress recognized that the early availability schedules described above could be misused by some bank customers, so it gave the banks a few escape valves:

(1) New Accounts

During the first 30 days of the existence of a new account, there must be next day availability for cash or wire deposits, for government checks, and for bank-generated checks (cashier's checks, etc.). However, if a government check or a bank-generated check exceeds $5,000, the depositary bank may put a hold on the amount that exceeds the $5,000 for up to nine business days. There are no rules that describe the time period for the availability of local or nonlocal checks; thus, the U.C.C. rules described below would apply. [Reg. CC § 229.13(a)]

(2) Large Checks

To the extent a day's deposit exceeds $5,000, the bank may hold the excess for a further reasonable time (presumed to be five business days for checks over the usual time period. [Reg. CC § 229.13(b), (h)]

(3) Redeposited Checks

Unless the check was returned for a missing indorsement or because it was postdated, and these problems have since been cleared up, the bank may hold a redeposited check for a further reasonable time (presumed to be five business days) over the usual time period. [Reg. CC § 229.13(c), (h)]

(4) Repeated Overdrafts

If a customer repeatedly overdraws an account in any given six-month period, then for the next six months thereafter the bank may hold deposited checks for a further reasonable time (presumed to be five business days) over the usual time period. An account is considered repeatedly overdrawn if the balance in it was negative (or would have been if the bank had paid all items drawn against it) for six or more banking days in the six-month period *or* if the account was negative on two or more banking days in that period in the amount of $5,000 or more. [Reg. CC § 229.13(d), (h)]

(5) "Reasonable Cause" Exception

If a bank has "reasonable cause" to believe that a check is uncollectible, it may ignore the usual rules if it gives the notice to the customer described below, telling the customer when the funds will be made available. A bank has "reasonable cause" whenever there exist "facts which would cause a well-grounded belief in the mind of a reasonable person." Such reasons must be included in the notice. The Official Commentary to Regulation CC gives as examples of "reasonable cause" the following: suspicion of check kiting, receipt of the payor bank's notice of dishonor (*see* p. 89), and the fact that the check is "stale" (meaning that is over six months old). [Reg. CC § 229.13(e)]

(6) Emergency Conditions

If the bank suffers emergency conditions beyond its control (*e.g.,* war, computer failure, failure of other banks, etc.), the bank may hold the deposited funds until the emergency has ended. [Reg. CC § 229.13(f), (h)]

(7) Notice

Except in the "new accounts" situation (*see* p. 120), where a bank plans to take advantage of any of these exceptions, the depositor must be notified as soon as possible of the date the funds will be made available. [Reg. CC § 229.13(g)]

SAFEGUARD EXCEPTIONS 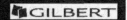 GILBERT

A BANK DOES *NOT* HAVE TO FOLLOW THE EFAA IN THE FOLLOWING CIRCUMSTANCES

☑ *New accounts*—during first 30 days, bank must follow EFAA for cash, government checks, and bank-generated checks up to $5,000, but may hold excess for nine business days

☑ *Large deposits*—bank may hold excess of $5,000 for a reasonable time*

☑ *Redeposited checks*—bank may hold for a reasonable time* unless check returned for missing indorsement or it was postdated

☑ *Repeated overdrafts*—bank may hold for a reasonable time* during six months following six months of repeated overdrafts

☑ *Reasonable cause* to doubt collectibility

☑ *Emergency conditions*—bank may hold during emergencies beyond its control

* A *reasonable time* is presumed to be five business days for local checks and six business days.

---

f. Civil Liability

A bank that does not follow the statute or the regulations promulgated there under by the Federal Reserve Board can be sued by an injured customer for any actual damages, punitive damages (not greater than $1,000 or less than $100, although in a class action the upper figure is the lesser of $500,000 or 1% of the net worth of the bank), plus costs of suit and attorneys' fees. The suit may be brought in federal or state court within one year after the occurrence of the violation. [Reg. CC § 229.21]

2. Deposit Availability Under the U.C.C.

If the above federal statute does not regulate the availability of funds (because, *e.g.*, the check is deposited during the first 30 days after the account is opened), Article 4 of the U.C.C. will do so. The U.C.C.'s gap-filling availability rules follow. It should be noted that nothing forbids the banks from *shortening* the time limits listed below should the bank decide to accommodate a request of its customer (the same is true under Regulation CC).

a. Money

A customer may draw against money deposited in an account on the next *"banking day"* (*see* p. 89). [U.C.C. § 4–215(f); Reg. CC § 229.10(a)]

Example: On the morning of April 10, Freda deposits $100 in her checking account (which contained only $5 at the time). That same afternoon, Freda writes a check to her landlord for $100, and the landlord proceeds straight to the bank and presents the check. Freda has no complaint if the bank elects to dishonor the check because it has until the next day to process it.

b. Checks

The length of time that a check must be deposited in an account before it must be made available for withdrawals under the U.C.C. varies according to how far the check must travel to reach the payor bank (the drawee). The *first* bank in which the check is deposited is the "depositary bank"; the depositary bank and all subsequent banks in the collection chain (except for the final "payor" bank) are also "collecting banks." [U.C.C. § 4–105]

(1) Where Depositary Bank and Payor Bank Are One and the Same

If the check drawer and the payee happen to have accounts at the same bank, that bank will be both the depositary and the payor bank. The bank will need some time to sort the item, examine the drawer's account, decide whether to pay the item, and make the appropriate entries. If the bank does not dishonor the item, the amount specified in the check becomes available for withdrawal by the payee at the opening of the *second* banking day after the day of deposit. [U.C.C. § 4–215(e)(2)] *But note:* If Regulation CC applies, it requires next business day availability for checks deposited in the same bank on which drawn (*see* p. 119), and, being federal law, it supersedes inconsistent state law (the U.C.C).

Example: Jack and Jill have separate accounts at Big Hill Bank. Jack writes a check to Jill, which she deposits in her account on Friday, the day after she opened the account. Jill may draw against this amount only if the check has not been dishonored by Tuesday (the second *banking* day, assuming neither Friday, Monday, nor Tuesday is a holiday and that Jill deposited the check on Friday *prior to* the bank's "cutoff" hour, if any; *see* p. 89). Of course, the bank may allow Jill to draw against the check at an earlier time.

(2) All Other Situations—"Final Settlement" Rule

If the check must travel within a city (usually through a local clearinghouse) or across the country (usually through Federal Reserve Banks, which have efficient check collection machinery), the depositary bank must be allowed sufficient time for the check to go to the payor bank and (if dishonored) to come back before being required to permit its depositor to draw against the amount involved. The U.C.C. allows the bank to withhold the uncollected amount until "final settlement" occurs and the bank has had reasonable time to learn of that fact. [U.C.C. § 4–215(e)(1)]

(a) Recap of "Midnight Deadline" Rules

As discussed previously (p. 88), the payor bank has until its *midnight deadline* to dishonor an item presented to it through banking channels. If it does not do so by that time, *"final payment"* occurs and there can be *no dishonor*. The payor bank is then accountable for the amount involved, even if no such drawer or account exists.

(b) "Final Settlement"

At the moment of "final payment," all provisional settlements made as bookkeeping entries by banks in the collection chain firm up and become "final settlements." Dishonor of the item is no longer possible, so that the banks (and, after a reasonable time, the original depositor) may treat the item as paid. [U.C.C. § 4–215(c), (d), (e)(1)]

1) Note

The banks eventually clear their balances by means of a remittance draft, but this does not affect the availability of the amount collected. [*See* U.C.C. § 4–213, Off. Com. 2]

e.g. **Example:** Bill moves to Chicago to join a law firm and his parents give him a check for $1,000 drawn on their bank in Dallas. Bill's Chicago bank tells him that he must wait *10 days* after depositing the check in his new account before he may draw against it. The bank believes it needs this time to see if the check will go to Dallas, be dishonored, and return. If the Chicago bank has heard nothing in 10 days, it will assume that the Dallas payor bank made final payment and Bill may draw against his deposit. [*See* **Rapp v. Dime Savings Bank**, 23 U.C.C. Rep. 404 (N.Y. 1978)—reasonableness of bank practice requiring depositor to wait 15 days on collection of out-of-town checks is question for trier of fact]

EXAM TIP   **GILBERT**

The importance of final payment is that it destroys the check as a cause of action. Therefore, all of the Article 3 obligations (see discussion on liability of the parties p. 74) end because they are conditioned upon the dishonor of the check. Once the drawee makes final payment, *dishonor is no longer possible,* and the drawer and indorsers may no longer be held liable.

---

(3) Right of "Charge Back"

Prior to final settlement, a depositary bank or any other collecting bank that learns that payment on the item will not be made may "charge back" (reverse) any provisional settlement given its customer for the item. [U.C.C. § 4–214]

(a) Prior Use of Credit

The depositary bank's right of charge back is not affected by the fact that it has already permitted its depositor to draw against the item returned; the *depositor must repay* the money. [U.C.C. § 4–214(d)(1)]

(b) Failure to Use Ordinary Care

All collecting banks must use ordinary care in collecting items. [U.C.C. § 4–202] Failure to do so makes the bank liable for the amount of the item (unless the use of ordinary care would not have realized that amount).

1) Limited Liability for Consequential Damages

However, a collecting bank is not liable for consequential damages caused by its negligence (*e.g.*, Other checks that bounce) unless it acted in *bad faith.* [U.C.C. § 4–103(e)]

2) Speed of Collection

A collecting bank usually must pass items (or notices of dishonor) along the chain before its midnight deadline or be found not to have exercised ordinary care. In effect, this gives each collecting bank two days in which to act. If a bank takes longer to act, it has the burden of establishing that the delay was reasonable. [U.C.C. §§ 4–202(b), 4–108; *and see* p. 91]

3) Collection Route

To avoid charges imposed by some banks, collecting banks have been known to send checks for collection by very circuitous routes. The U.C.C., however, requires collecting banks to use a "reasonably prompt method." [U.C.C. § 4–204(a)]

4) Right of Charge Back Not Affected by Negligence

The failure of a collecting bank to exercise ordinary care in its collection duties does *not* destroy the bank's right of charge back, even though the negligent bank may be liable for damages. [U.C.C. § 4–214(d)(2)]

(c) Effect of Final Settlement

The right of a depositary bank to charge back an uncollected check expires at the moment final settlement occurs—*i.e.*, at the moment the payor bank makes "final payment." [U.C.C. § 4–214(a)]

e.g. **Example:** Samson owes Delilah $100 and gives her a check drawn on Samson's Bank for that amount. Delilah deposits the check in Delilah's Bank, which presents the check for payment to Samson's Bank during the morning of November 10. On November 15, Samson's Bank decides not to honor the check and returns it to Delilah's Bank. Delilah's Bank has no right of charge back against Delilah's account, because Samson's Bank had no right to dishonor the check after its midnight deadline. Once Samson's Bank held the check past its midnight deadline, "final payment" occurred and all provisional settlements—including the temporary bookkeeping entry between Delilah and her bank—became "final." The remedy for Delilah's Bank is against Samson's Bank, which is "accountable" for the item. [U.C.C. § 4–302; **Boggs v. Citizens Bank & Trust Co.**, 20 U.C.C. Rep. 148 (Md. 1976)]

| | | WHEN WITHDRAWAL AVAILABLE | | |
TYPE OF DEPOSIT	DAY OF DEPOSIT	NEXT BANKING* DAY	2ND BANKING* DAY	AFTER FINAL SETTLEMENT
MONEY		✓		
CHECKS (IF DEPOSITARY AND PAYOR BANK ARE THE SAME)			✓	
CHECKS (IF DEPOSITARY AND PAYOR BANK ARE THE SAME *AND* REGULATION CC** APPLIES)		✓		
CHECKS (ALL OTHER SITUATIONS)				✓

* A "banking day" is the part of the day in which the bank is open to the public for carrying on substantially *all* banking functions (*see* p. 89).

** Regulation CC is federal law that supersedes inconsistent state law (the U.C.C.).

1) Warranty of Timely Return

In many cases the depositary bank will have no idea whether the payor bank missed its midnight deadline (so that final settlement occurred and the depositary bank lost its right of charge back against its customer's account). However, Regulation CC creates a warranty made by all banks returning checks that they have done so within the deadlines specified by both federal and state law, so that a payor bank returning a check impliedly warrants that it has done so before its midnight deadline expired. [Reg. CC § 229.34(a)]

(d) Notice of Charge Back

The depositary bank need not give notice to its customer that it is charging back the amount of a returned check *before* doing so, but it *must send notice* to the customer that charge back has occurred *before expiration of its midnight deadline* (*i.e.*, midnight of the banking day following the banking day on which it learned the check was being returned). The penalty for failing to send this notice is whatever harm the customer can prove because of the delay. [U.C.C. § 4–214(a); and see **Appliance Buyers Credit Corp. v. Prospect National Bank**, 708 F.2d 290 (7th Cir. 1983)]

3. Final Payment

Final payment occurs at the moment the payor bank becomes *accountable* for the amount of the item presented and the provisional bookkeeping entries firm up so that final settlement occurs throughout the collection chain. The basic rules for determining this precise moment are contained in U.C.C. section 4–215(a), as follows:

a. Payment in Cash

Once the payor bank hands over the money, final payment occurs and it is too late to dishonor the check. [U.C.C. § 4–215(a)(1)]

b. Settlement

Final payment occurs when a bank settles for an item and has no right to revoke the settlement. For example, the bank may pay a presented item by issuing a cashier's check. This would result in final payment of the check originally presented even if the cashier's check were later dishonored. [U.C.C. § 4–215(a)(2), (b), Off. Com. 4, 8]

c. Failure to Revoke Provisional Settlement

If the payor bank has already made a provisional (conditional) settlement for the item presented—as it does for items presented through the check collection system (*see* p. 88), the payor bank has until midnight of the banking day following the banking day of presentment in which to reverse the provisional settlement in favor of the presenting bank and send the item back. If it fails to do so, the provisional settlement becomes final and final payment occurs. [U.C.C. §§ 4–215(a)(3), 4–301, 4–302] This is the most common method of making final payment, simply letting the time limits for dishonor expire.

(1) Regulation CC and Midnight Deadline Rule

Regulation CC permits payor banks to miss their midnight deadlines and still avoid final payment in two situations:

(a) Day After Midnight Deadline Passes

The first situation is where the bank will be able to return the item to the depositary bank before the close of business on the next banking day (or, if the return is made to a Federal Reserve bank, before its cutoff hour). [Reg. CC § 229.30(c)(1)]

Example: Every day Octopus National Bank ("ONB") returns checks to the Federal Reserve Bank by putting them in its armored car and sending them back to the Federal Reserve Bank. The armored car makes its last run at 4 p.m. A check for $500,000 is presented by the Federal Reserve Bank on Monday morning. On Tuesday at 6 p.m., ONB decides to dishonor the check. Before the Regulation CC rule just mentioned, the bank would have to "send" it back before Tuesday midnight, and the U.C.C. defines "send" to include mailing [U.C.C. § 1–201(39)], so the bank would put it in the mail, thus complying with the letter of the law. Regulation CC allows the bank to wait for the next day's armored car run as long as the check will ordinarily be received by the Federal Reserve Bank before its cutoff hour on Wednesday, thus getting it back quicker than mailing would.

(b) Highly Expeditious Means of Transportation

Regulation CC also permits a payor bank to miss its midnight deadline as long as it uses a "highly expeditious means of transportation, even if this means of transportation would ordinarily result in delivery after the receiving bank's next banking day." [Reg. CC § 229.30(c)(1)]

Example: Octopus National Bank ("ONB"), located in California, received a check for $2 million on Monday morning. On Tuesday evening, ONB decides to dishonor the check. It phones the depositary bank, located in Miami, and gives that bank a notice of large check return (*see* p. 89). On Wednesday morning, ONB delivers the check to an air courier for transportation directly to Miami, instructing the air courier to take it immediately to the depositary bank. Even though ONB did not "send" the check back before its midnight deadline, its use of a highly expeditious means of transporting the check back to the depositary bank excuses its violation of the usual rule.

Remember that payment is final when the bank has: (i) paid the item in *cash;* (ii) *settled* for the item without having a right to revoke the settlement (*e.g.,* issued a cashier's check); or (iii) made a *provisional settlement* for the item and *failed to revoke* the settlement in the time and manner permitted (*e.g.,* let the midnight deadline expire).

---

d. Legal Effect of "Final Payment"

When final payment occurs under any of the three methods just discussed (p. 126), the bank is "accountable" for the amount of the item and usually has no way to avoid payment. [U.C.C. § 4–302]

(1) "Four Legals" No Longer Apply

Once either certification or final payment of an item has occurred, none of the following (referred to as the "four legals" by bankers) can stop the bank from paying the item [U.C.C. § 4–303(a)]:

(a) *Notice* of problems (*e.g.,* notice of the drawer's death, incompetence, or bankruptcy) [*see* Bankruptcy Code §§ 542(c), 549(a)];

(b) The bank's right of *setoff;*

(c) Service of *legal process* (such as a garnishment order); and/or

(d) A *stop payment order* from the drawer.

Example: On Friday morning, payor bank certifies Drawer's check for $40,000. At noon Friday, the local sheriff serves a writ garnishing Drawer's account. The writ comes too late to encompass the $40,000, because the certification makes the bank itself liable on the check (*see* p. 97). A similar result would be reached if the bank had taken any of the steps to complete final payment on the $40,000 check.

Compare: Had the writ arrived *prior to* certification or final payment, the garnishment writ would have had priority.

(2) Rights of Payor Bank After Final Payment

Once final payment has occurred, the payor bank must pay the item and cannot recover the payment made except in the following circumstances:

(a) Bad Faith of Presenter

The common law doctrine of restitution for payment made due to mistake or fraud will permit the payor bank to undo final payment where the equities favor the bank and the other party acted *in bad faith (e.g.,* where the presenter knows the drawer has no funds in the bank, or the presenter is using the check as part of a criminal scheme). [**Bartlett v. Bank of Carroll**, 237 S.E.2d 115 (Va. 1977); **Demos v. Lyons**, 376 A.2d 1352 (N.J. 1977); and see U.C.C. §§ 1–103, 1–203, 3–418]

(b) Presentment Warranties

Similarly, final payment does not deprive the payor bank of its right to sue for breach of a presentment warranty. *Rationale:* Such a suit is "off the instrument" and thereby survives final payment. [U.C.C. § 4–208]

UNDOING FINAL PAYMENT	**GILBERT**
EVENTS THAT CANNOT UNDO FINAL PAYMENT	**EVENTS THAT CAN UNDO FINAL PAYMENT**
• *Notice* of problems • Bank's right of *setoff* • Service of *legal process* • *Stop payment order*	• *Bad faith* of the presenter • *Breach of a presentment warranty* • *Restitution* against wrongdoer

4. Check Encoding

When a check is deposited for collection, it must be magnetically encoded so that it can be read by automatic check processing machinery. The encoding is done with special "magnetic ink character recognition" ("MICR") symbols. The payor bank will issue the check with such encoding already on it for the number of the payor bank and the account number of the drawer, but it is the duty of the depositary bank (or whoever initiates the check collection) to encode the check with MICR symbols showing the *amount* of the check (this is done in the lower right hand corner). Following the lead of the few common law decisions on point, the Code creates a *warranty* that the check has been properly encoded, and the warrantor is liable for losses suffered as a result of the breach of this warranty. [U.C.C. § 4–209(a)]

5. Check Retention

In so-called check truncation systems, the banks avoid the necessity of passing around tons of paper each day by photocopying the check at the depositary bank end and then destroying it. All that is passed on through the bank collection process is a description of the check, and this is all that the payor bank receives. The effect of check truncation on the law was unclear until Regulation CC encouraged it and the Revision presented some rules of law about it. Under the U.C.C., anyone who retains an item pursuant to a check truncation system makes a *warranty* to subsequent banks that the warrantor has complied with the terms of the check truncation agreement, and the warrantor is liable for losses suffered as a result of the breach of this warranty. [U.C.C. § 4–209(b)] The entity retaining the items is required to maintain legible copies thereof for seven years. [U.C.C. § 4–406(b)] The information that travels through the system in lieu of the check itself is called a presentment notice. [U.C.C. § 4–110]

6. Check Collection in the 21st Century ("Check 21")

The original bank collection procedures required the physical movement of tons of checks around the world each day. As we progress into the 21st century, it occurred to bankers that this could all be avoided by simply photographing the checks and then sending the resulting images from bank to bank as computer files. This is an expensive change, but was made imperative by the tragic events of September 11, 2001, which had as a collateral effect the freezing of bank collections as planes sat on the ground for days. As a result, Congress put into place a statute, *"Check Collection in the 21st Century"* ("Check 21"), which creates the following check imaging system.

a. Check Images and Substitute Checks

Under the statute, banks have the right (not duty) to create an ***image*** of the check and pass it on if the receiving bank or person agrees to that. If not, the bank can then create a paper version of the check from the image, and this is called a ***"substitute check."*** [Check 21 § 3(16)] Some banks have created an app that allows their customers to create the image by photographing the front and back of the check, sending the image to the bank, and then retaining the original check after marking it "VOID." If the bank that allows the customer to create the image fails to take steps to make sure the original check cannot remain in circulation then it must pay damages to any entity that is harmed by the continued existence of the original check; 12 C.F.R. § 229.34(a)(i).

Example: When Paul Payee received a check for $4000 he used his cell phone to make an image of the check, and then electronically deposited the image into his bank, Depositary Bank, which allowed its customers to do this. Paul had an agreement with Depositary Bank that in this situation he would write the word "VOID" in large letters across the original check, but he did not do this with the $4000 check. Instead he used it to open a new bank account at Big Bank, which allowed him to withdraw $2000 of the deposited amount immediately. At the same time he withdrew the entire $4000 from his account with Depositary Bank. He then left town quickly. Depositary Bank presented the image of the check to the drawee bank and was paid the $4000. Later that same day Big Bank presented the original check to the drawee bank and it was dishonored. You are the lawyer for Big Bank. How can it recover the $2000 it allowed Paul Payee to withdraw? The answer is that Depositary Bank must pay damages to any entity that is hurt by the continued existence of the original check once the image was created. It could do this by making sure Paul Payee had written "VOID" on the original and then photographed the original check so marked. It didn't take steps to make sure the original wasn't still in circulation so it must pay Big Bank the damages it suffered.

(1) Truncating Bank

The bank that creates the image and preserves the original check is called a ***truncating*** bank. [Reg. CC § 229.2(eee)]

(2) Reconverting Bank

The bank that prints out the substitute check is called the ***reconverting*** bank. [Reg. CC § 229.2(zz)] When the reconverting bank creates the substitute check, it must add to it all the ***indorsements*** that would have been placed on a physical check passing through the bank collection system, so that there is a clear map of the route taken by the imaged check. [Reg. CC § 229.51(b)]

b. Legal Equivalence of Substitute Check

No one can refuse to take the substitute check, which is legally the same for all purposes (state and federal, including criminal prosecution and tax collection), as the original. Customers cannot insist on getting the original back. If the parties agree to imaging without a paper copy being created, the image also has the same legal effect as the original. These rules greatly speed up check collection, though there are some downsides to loss of the original (no fingerprints, *e.g.*, which can be important in criminal prosecutions).

(1) Mandatory Language on Substitute Checks

Before a substitute check qualifies as the legal equivalent of the original check it must accurately represent all of the information on the front and back of the original check and bear this legend: "This is a legal copy of your check. You can use it the same way you would use the original check." [Check 21 § 4(b)]

EXAMPLE OF CHECK CLEARING UNDER CHECK 21

1001101001010110
010110010101001

Step 1: Drawer writes check drawn on Bank C to Payee.

Step 2: Payee deposits check into her account at Bank A.

Includes *mandatory language*

Step 3: Bank A *(truncating bank)* creates an electronic *image* of the front and back of the check and the magnetic ink character recognition ("MICR") symbols, electronically indorses it, and sends it to Bank B.

Bank B

Step 4: Bank B *(reconverting bank)* creates a *substitute check* (because Bank C does not accept electronic images), indorses it, and presents it to Bank C for payment.

Step 5: Bank C processes the check, pays it, and may send a copy back to its customer (Drawer) in her monthly statement.

*The mandatory language is: "This is a legal copy of your check. You can use it the same way you would use the original check."

c. Warranties Under Check 21

Parties passing on the image/substitute check make both transfer and presentment warranties that the substitute check meets all of the requirements for legal equivalence and that there is no other substitute check floating around that will cause problems for other parties. [Check 21 § 5]

d. Expedited Recredit of Consumer Accounts

The statute allows *consumers* (but not nonconsumer customers) to get an expedited recredit to their account in certain circumstances when the consumer disputes the validity of the charge to the account (say, *e.g.*, the image is blurry and the bank charges the check to the wrong account). In that case, the consumer must report the problem within 40 days, and may demand an immediate recredit. The bank may investigate for 10 business days, or if it recredits the account while it investigates, for 45 calendar days. [Check 21 § 7] In turn, banks passing the check back to the truncating bank have a similar procedure for expedited recrediting of their various accounts. [Check 21 § 8]

(1) Safeguard Exceptions

Section 7(d) of the statute has "safeguard exceptions" (copied almost word for word from the same safeguard exceptions to funds availability in Regulation CC, *see* p. 120), describing situations where the bank need not recredit the account in accordance with the usual time limits.

e. Indemnity Actions

In addition to warranty liability, the statute creates *indemnity* liability against banks transferring either the image or the substitute check if doing so causes damages that could have been prevented by use of the original check. For example, if the image was blurry and this caused the wrong account to be tapped, the truncating bank would have to respond to an indemnity claim because if the original check had been transferred, the right account would have been debited. [Check 21 § 6]

f. Lawsuits

As a practical matter, this means that the original check must be preserved so that it can be found in the event of trouble and produced to help resolve the difficulty. All claims must be made within 120 days after the transaction that gives rise to the claim [*see* Regulation CC § 299.55(b)(1)] so that is the relevant period for preserving the original check. Lawsuits under Check 21 must be brought within one year after the transaction. [Reg. CC § 229.56(c)] *Notice of claims* must be given within 30 days after a claimant discovers the grounds for the claim or the amount of any recovery is reduced by the amount that such prompt notice would have provided. [Reg. CC § 229.56(d)] Suit may be brought in either federal or state courts.

g. Damages

If the warranty breach results in damages, they are measured by the amount of any loss (including interest, costs, reasonable attorney's fees, and other expenses of representation) proximately caused by the warranty breach. [Reg. CC § 229.53(b)(1)(i)] If the claim is one for indemnity, however, the measure of damages is slightly different. The claim is the amount of any resulting loss, *up to the amount of the substitute check,* plus interest and expenses (including costs and reasonable attorney's fees and other expenses of representation) related to the substitute check. [Reg. CC § 229.53(b)(1)(ii)] If more than one of the parties to the lawsuit has been negligent, Regulation CC creates a comparative negligence test so that the loss is apportioned among them according to their degree of fault. [Reg. CC § 229.53(b)(2)] For examples of comparative negligence, *see* the next chapter of this Summary.

Chapter Eight

Forgery or Alteration of Negotiable Instruments

Chapter Approach

Many of the lawsuits brought in connection with negotiable instruments deal with the aftermath of criminal activities such as forgery or alteration of the instrument. Because the criminal is rarely a promising defendant even when available, other parties to the instrument scramble to pass the loss on to others.

Various rules governing the forgery or alteration of commercial paper have been referred to previously in connection with "holder" status (*see* p. 26), warranties (*see* p. 101), and conversion (*see* p. 107). For unauthorized signatures, the main rule to remember is that an unauthorized signature will not be deemed that of the person whose name is signed *unless that person is precluded from denying it.* A similar rule applies to alterations. This chapter focuses on those circumstances under which a person *will be precluded from denying* what appears on the instrument. In all such cases, the person being precluded has acted "negligently" in a way that contributes to the loss, making that person the most responsible for the loss among the other innocent parties to the instrument. Examples include:

(i) *Issuing an instrument* in the name of a payee *to someone posing as the payee* or to a payee whom the maker or drawer intends to have no interest in the instrument;

(ii) *Leaving blank spaces* on the instrument or *failing properly to guard a name facsimile machine;* and

(iii) *Failing to notify the bank* of problems with the bank statement (particularly forgeries) which causes the bank further loss.

Thus, when confronted with a problem of forgery or alteration on an instrument, before you hold the bank liable for the loss, examine whether some other party should bear the responsibility because of negligence.

A. Common Law Principles

1. In General

The following two basic common law rules applicable to forgery and alteration have survived enactment of the U.C.C. and may affect the outcome of forgery suits.

2. Payment to Agent

Under the common law, delivery of a negotiable instrument to an *authorized* agent of the payee is the same as delivery to the payee. Thereafter, the *payee* assumes the risk that the agent may forge the payee's name to the instrument and appropriate the proceeds. If this happens, the debt is discharged as between the payee and the person delivering the instrument to the agent. [**Hutzler v. Hertz Corp.**, 39 N.Y.2d 209 (1976)]

3. "No Damages" Defense

No matter what happens to a negotiable instrument (forgery, alteration, etc.), it is a defense at common law that the proceeds reached the person entitled to them. If this occurs, there can be no successful lawsuit because (usually) there will be no damages. [*See, e.g.,* **Yeager & Sullivan, Inc. v. Farmers Bank**, 317 N.E.2d 792 (Ind. 1974)]

Example: Demitri Drawer gives Persephone Payee a check drawn to Payee's order, after which the check is stolen and Payee's indorsement forged thereon. The forger then obtains payment directly from Drawee ("payor") bank. Payee sues the bank in conversion and wins because the bank paid on a forged indorsement. [U.C.C. § 3–420] Once the bank has paid Payee, Drawer has no suit against the bank even though the bank originally made payment to the wrong person in breach of the "properly payable" rule because the money has now reached Payee and Drawer has no damages.

B. Validation of Forgery or Alteration

1. Introduction

The basic U.C.C. forgery rule is contained in § 3–403 and provides that an unauthorized signature will not be deemed to be that of the person whose name is signed unless that person is **precluded** (estopped) from denying it. The U.C.C. specifies a number of circumstances in which a forgery will be validated because the person whose name is used has done something to preclude him from raising the forgery issue. (Certain of these rules also apply to alterations of the instrument.)

2. Impostor Rule

The carelessness of the drawer or maker in **issuing** an instrument may make it very likely that the payee's name will be forged. In such cases, the U.C.C. treats the resulting forgery as **effective to pass good title** to later transferees, so that they qualify as "holders" of the instrument in spite of the forgery.

a. Issuance to an Impostor

An impostor is one who pretends to be someone else. The U.C.C. requires that drawers and makers be careful with whom they deal, and if they are duped into issuing an instrument to an impostor, the resulting forgery of the payee's name is nonetheless effective. [U.C.C. § 3–404(a)—note the spelling: the word ends in "or"]

Example: Larry Liar tells Jessie Jones that he is Milton Money, the town's wealthiest resident, and that he is collecting money for a new public library. Jones thereupon writes out a $50 check payable to "Milton Money." Liar's subsequent forgery of that name to the instrument is effective to pass good title to his transferees. If Jones finds out the truth, she has no complaint to her bank that the check was not "properly payable" due to forgery of the payee's name. (*See* p. 115)

(1) Impostor Need Not Communicate Face to Face

The common law impostor rule was sometimes limited to face-to-face encounters between the drawer and the impostor. However, the U.C.C. does *not* require face-to-face dealings, so the rule applies as well to misrepresentations through the mail or other forms of communication. [*See* U.C.C. § 3–404(a)]

(2) Identity of Actual Forger Irrelevant

Once the drawer or maker has issued an instrument to an impostor, the resulting "indorsement" of the payee is validated regardless of who actually forges it (*i.e.*, it need not be forged by the original impostor).

b. Issuance to Fictitious Payee or Payee Not Intended to Have Interest in Instrument

Section 3–404(b) provides rules where (i) the "person whose intent determines to whom an instrument is payable . . . does not intend the person identified as payee to have an interest in the instrument, or (ii) the person identified as payee of an instrument is a fictitious person. . . ." What does this convoluted mess mean? First, who is "a person whose intent determines to whom an instrument is payable"? According to § 3–110, that means the person who signs the instrument, or, if the instrument is signed by a machine, the person who furnished the payee's name. If that person does not intend the named payee to have any interest in the instrument *or*, regardless of what that person intended, if the named payee is a fictitious person (*i.e.*, a made-up name), the forgery of the *payee's name* is *effective* to negotiate the instrument.

Example: The corporate treasurer of Business Corporation added 50 extra names to the payroll, all names of former employees who had quit. He took the resulting checks, indorsed them by forging the ex-employees' names on the back, then signed his own name, and deposited the checks in his own personal account. Because he never intended the named payees to get the money, the forgeries are effective; his bank will become a "holder"; these checks will be properly payable from the corporate bank account even though they contain forgeries of the payees' names.

Example: Terry Thief submitted phony invoices to Business Corporation reflecting mythical sales of merchandise by "Sunrise Corporation," an entity that does not exist. Thinking these were real bills, the corporate treasurer gave Thief a check for the relevant amount made out to "Sunrise Corporation." Here, the corporate treasurer does not know what is going on and does intend the named payee to get the money, but because the named payee is fictitious, the result is the same as in the last example.

(1) Policy

Employers should watch their employees and know whom the company is dealing with. If employees are looting the corporation or are foolishly making out checks to nonexistent entities, the corporation, and not later innocent banks, should bear the risk.

c. Employer's Responsibility for Fraudulent Indorsements by Employee

An employer must bear the brunt of all employee misbehavior in connection with forgeries if the employee is entrusted with "responsibility" with respect to the instrument. "Responsibility" is defined in § 3–405(a)(3) to include any significant employee dealings with the instrument, including its preparation, mailing, bookkeeping duties, and check reconciliation (but not mere access to the instrument). Section 3–405 validates two types of forged indorsements: those of payees on checks issued *by* the employer, and the employer's name as payee on checks issued *to* the employer.

Example: Teresa Treasurer was responsible for signing checks on behalf of Business Corporation. She wrote a corporate check to "Supplies, Inc.," and then opened an account in that name at a bank and deposited the check there, after forging "Supplies, Inc." to the back of the check. This forgery is validated by § 3–405(b), and, unlike the original version of § 3–405, it does not matter whether or not Business Corporation owes a real debt to Supplies, Inc. [U.C.C. § 3–405, Off. Com. 3, Case #5]

Example: Teresa Treasurer was also responsible for depositing checks payable to the corporation into the corporate account. One day the corporation received a check for $300,000, and Teresa signed the corporate name to the back of the check, and then deposited it in her own bank account. Section 3–405 applies here also, and the corporation may not sue nonnegligent parties in conversion under § 3–420(a).

Compare: Calvin Cleaner, the janitor for Business Corporation, found a $300,000 check payable to Business Corporation behind a file cabinet as he was cleaning the file room. He forged the corporate name to the back of the check, signed his own name, and then deposited the check into his bank account at Big Bank, which collected the check from the payor bank. § 3–405 does not operate to validate the forgery here because Cleaner is not an employee entrusted with "responsibility" for the handling of the check. [U.C.C. § 3–405, Off. Com. 3, Case #1]

EXAM TIP   GILBERT

On an exam, recall that an employer is responsible for fraudulent indorsements made by employees *entrusted with responsibility for an instrument.* Thus, when an indorsement is forged by someone who is *not* entrusted with such responsibility, the general rule applies and the indorsement is *ineffective* as the signature of the person (or entity) whose name was signed.

---

d. Effect of Negligence by Subsequent Parties

The original 1962 version of the impostor rule did not say what was the effect of negligence by later parties (typically the depositary bank) taking the check with the forged indorsement thereon, and the courts reached different results. Some courts said that such negligence was irrelevant and applied the impostor rule anyway, while others refused to validate the forgery of the payee's name in favor of negligent takers of the check. The 1990 Revision settled the issue by using *comparative negligence* to allocate the loss where subsequent parties do not observe ordinary care in taking or dealing with the instrument after the payee's name is forged. [U.C.C. §§ 3–404(d), 3–405(b)]

Example: Flavia Fingers, bookkeeper of Business Corporation, stole a $100,000 check made payable to her employer, and forged "Business Corporation" on the back of the check. She then signed her own name, and deposited the check into her bank account at Octopus National Bank. Business Corporation is forbidden by the employer responsibility rule of § 3–405 from suing most innocent parties, but it has a *claim* against Octopus National Bank because it was negligent in allowing such a large corporate check to be deposited into an individual account, a highly suspicious circumstance. A jury will assign blame to the two parties and divide the loss between them accordingly.

3. Negligence Rule

Negligence can also validate forgeries or alterations. Section 3–406(a) provides:

A person whose failure to exercise ordinary care substantially contributes to an alteration of an instrument or to the making of a forged signature on an instrument is precluded from asserting the alteration or the forgery against a person who, in good faith, pays the instrument or takes it for value or for collection.

The Code has only the most limited definition of "ordinary care" [U.C.C. § 3–103(a)(7)], but the Official Comments to § 3–406 and the case law provide numerous examples:

a. Leaving Blanks or Spaces on Instrument

Filling in a blank or space without authority is an alteration, but if the maker or drawer carelessly leaves such blanks available to the wrongdoer, the maker or drawer should not be able to complain. [U.C.C. § 3–406, Off. Com. 3, Case #3]

If you come across a fact pattern where a drawer leaves a blank space after the figure (*e.g.*, "$10_____") and the word (*e.g.*, "Ten_____"), and the payee of the check fills in the blank space with a different amount (*e.g.*, "$10,000" and "Ten thousand"), remember that the drawee bank will **not be liable** for debiting its customer's account for the greater amount when the check is presented for payment. To avoid this outcome, the drawer should not have left the extra space blank (*e.g.*, she should have written "$10.00" and "Ten------").

b. Mailing an Instrument to Someone with Same or Similar Name of Payee

If the issuer of the instrument carelessly sends it to someone who will have no trouble cashing it because she has the same or similar name as the intended payee, that violates the standard of ordinary care. [**Park State Bank v. Arena Auto Auction, Inc.**, 207 N.E.2d 158 (Ill. 1965)]

c. Failure to Follow Internal Procedures

If the issuer has created a system designed to avoid check forgeries, it is negligence not to follow that procedure. [**Thompson Maple Products, Inc. v. Citizens National Bank**, 234 A.2d 32 (Pa. 1967)]

d. Failure to Guard Signing Device

If the issuer's signature is placed on the instrument by a machine or rubber stamp, the issuer is negligent if the machine or stamp is not closely guarded and gets into the wrong hands. [U.C.C. § 3–406, Off. Com. 3, Case #1]

e. "Proximate Cause" Requirement

Some courts have held that the negligent actions must be the "proximate cause" (here meaning *sole* cause) of the forgery or alteration, or the negligence is irrelevant. Thus, negligence in the *issuance* of an instrument (*e.g.*, delivery to the wrong party) is sometimes excused because the intervening criminal act of forgery breaks the chain of causation.

Example: Ned Nebbish tells Sam Stockbroker that he is the agent of Stella Starlight, who owns stock held by Sam's firm. Sam sells the stock at Ned's instruction, making a check for the proceeds payable to Stella but delivering it to Ned. Sam's action violates his firm's own rules requiring that he confirm that Ned was Stella's agent (which he was not). Ned then forges Stella's name to the check and cashes it. A court might permit Sam to recover the proceeds from the drawee bank (under the "properly payable" rule) on the ground that Sam's negligence in failing to follow internal procedures was not the proximate cause of the forgery. [*See* **Bagby v. Merrill Lynch, Pierce, Fenner & Smith, Inc.**, 491 F.2d 192 (8th Cir. 1974)]

(1) Criticism

This approach has been widely criticized as permitting results not intended by the U.C.C. drafters because it may allow negligent parties to shift losses to relatively innocent parties. [*See, e.g.*, 53 N.C. L. Rev. 1] It also conflicts with the comparative negligence concept that is prevalent in Article 3's forgery sections.

f. Effect of Subsequent Negligence

As is true of all the validation provisions, if more than one party is negligent, all such parties must share the liability according to their comparative fault. Section 3–406(b) states:

> Under subsection (a), if the person asserting the preclusion fails to exercise ordinary care in paying or taking the instrument and that failure substantially contributes to loss, the loss is allocated between the person precluded and the person asserting the preclusion according to the extent to which the failure of each to exercise ordinary care contributed to the loss.

EXAM TIP GILBERT

Notice that later parties are not completely protected from a prior person's failure to exercise ordinary care. In fact, later parties may be held liable for their own failure to use ordinary care based on a ***comparative negligence*** theory. For example, if a depositary bank should have been alerted to possible fraud when it paid the instrument (*e.g.*, the teller saw the payee fill out the instrument), it may be held comparatively negligent.

WHAT CONSTITUTES NEGLIGENCE?  GILBERT

THE FOLLOWING ARE EXAMPLES OF NEGLIGENCE THAT CAN VALIDATE FORGERIES OR ALTERATIONS

- ☑ Leaving ***blanks or spaces*** on the instrument.
- ☑ Mailing the instrument to someone with the ***same or similar name*** as the payee.
- ☑ Failing to follow ***internal procedures*** designed to avoid forgeries.
- ☑ Failing to safeguard the ***signing device*** (*e.g.*, rubber stamp).

4. Bank Statement Rule

Once a month (typically), a bank will return canceled checks to its customers, along with a statement of account. Failure to examine this statement is a form of negligence that can preclude the defenses of forgery and alteration.

a. Customer's Duty to Examine Statement

After receiving a statement, the customer must promptly use reasonable care in examining it for two things: (i) an unauthorized signing of the customer's *own* name as drawer; and (ii) any alteration (*e.g.*, a change in amount) on any item. [U.C.C. § 4–406(c)]

(1) Check Truncation and Duty to Examine

If the bank, pursuant to an agreement with its customer, does not return checks (either because the checks were retained at the depositary bank or because the payor bank itself keeps them; *see* p. 128), the bank may send the customer a description of the checks in lieu of the checks themselves. Under what Official Comment 1 calls a "safe harbor rule," the statement at a minimum must describe the following with regard to each check: item number, amount, and date of payment (note that the date and the payee are *not* required—the reason is that these things are not magnetically encoded on the check and cannot be read by automated processing equipment). This minimal information should be enough to alert the customer to problems. If the statement reflects a check the customer has no record of writing, that fact should indicate the possibility of check forgery. If the statement indicates that the amount of the check was greater than the amount shown on the customer's records, that fact should indicate an alteration has been made. [U.C.C. § 4–406(a)]

(2) Customer's Right to Copies

If the bank does not return items to the customer, the customer has the right to request legible copies of them for seven years. [U.C.C. § 4–406(b)]

(3) Effect of Check 21

The adoption of Check 21 (*see* p. 129) and the amendments it caused to Regulation CC will have a major effect on all of this. These days banks and their customers typically return all checks as images delivered electronically, or as substitute checks. Where that occurs, many of the above problems disappear because the customer has access to the actual contents of all checks drawn against the account.

b. Effect of Failure to Examine

If the customer fails to report a forgery or alteration problem within a reasonable time, the customer is precluded (estopped) from complaining to the bank that the item in question was not "properly payable" under U.C.C. § 4–401(a) if the bank can prove a *further loss* (other than the original payment) caused by this delay. [U.C.C. § 4–406(d)(1)]

Example: Colleen Customer fails to examine her bank statement and therefore does not notice a forgery of her signature done by Crystal Crook. The bank demonstrates that, had there been a prompt report of Customer's forged signature, it could have caught Crook while she still had the money.

(1) No Further Loss

Where, however, the bank has only its original loss from the improper payment and cannot show further damages caused by the delay in reporting, the customer is *not* estopped from asserting the forgery or alteration.

(2) "Repeated Offender" Rule

Moreover, where the statement has been available to the customer for a reasonable period (not more than 30 days) and there is no complaint about an unauthorized signature or alteration, the customer is estopped from demanding recredit on any other items forged or altered by the same wrongdoer and subsequently paid by the bank (until the customer gives notice). [U.C.C. § 4–406(d)(2)]

(a) Rationale

If the first forgery or alteration problem had been reported promptly, the bank would not have paid the other items. This demonstrates that the failure to examine the first check caused these further losses.

Example: Ellen Evil forges her husband Ed's name to 42 of his checks. The first forged check is returned to Ed in January, but he does not reconcile his statement or catch the forgery problem until September. Ed is thereby estopped from complaining to his bank about the 41 checks negotiated between January and August. [*See* **Gennone v. Peoples National Bank & Trust Co.**, 9 U.C.C. Rep. 707 (Pa. 1971)]

c. Result Where Bank Is Also Negligent

If the bank itself fails to exercise ordinary care in paying a check—as where a forgery is sloppy or an alteration is obvious—the above rules *do not apply.* If both parties prove the other was negligent, the loss is allocated between them on a *comparative negligence* basis. But if the customer can prove that bank did not pay the item in *good faith,* the customer always wins, even where the customer completely failed to report problems with the statement. [U.C.C. § 4–406(e)]

d. Burden of Proof

Each side has the burden of establishing lack of care by the other party. To take advantage of a § 4–406 preclusion, the bank must therefore establish that the customer failed to use reasonable care in examining the statement. To spread the loss, the customer must show that the bank failed to use ordinary care in paying the item. [U.C.C. § 4–406(d), (e)]

e. Cutoff Period

No matter who was negligent, § 4–406(f) bars all customer complaints first made more than *one year* after the statement was made available to the customer. If the customer does complain within the one-year period and the bank fails to take appropriate action, the statute of limitations for all Article 4 matters is three years from the accrual of the cause of action. [U.C.C. § 4–111]

f. Banks Must Assert § 4–406 Defenses

If a customer complains to the bank about an unauthorized signature or alteration and the bank has a defense under the bank statement rule, the bank *must* raise that defense against its customer. If it does not do so (and simply replaces the money in the customer's account), the bank may not pass its loss on to prior parties through breach of warranty suits or otherwise. [U.C.C. § 4–406(f)]

(1) Rationale

In such a situation, the bank has effectively caused its own loss.

(2) Failure to Assert Other Validation Provisions

Similarly, if the forgery or alteration is validated under the other sections mentioned above (*i.e.*, the impostor rule, the employer responsibility rule, the negligence rule), the payor bank may not ignore these validations, but must raise them against its customer or be barred from trying to pass the loss back to innocent parties, such as collecting banks. [U.C.C. §§ 4–406(f), Off. Com. 5; 3–417(c); 4–208(c)]

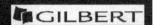

GENERAL RULE	Forged signatures are valid only as the signature of the *forger* and are invalid as the signature of the named payee.
EXCEPTIONS	Forgery will be valid as the name forged when:

- *Fictitious payee's signature forged*—issuance to impostor or a payee not intended to have an interest in the instrument.

- *Entrusted employee forges signature*—includes agents, not just employees.

- *Negligence contributed to forgery*—for example, leaving blank spaces or mailing to person with same name as payee.

- *Bank statement rule violated*—failure to discover forgeries or alterations within a reasonable time after receiving bank statement.

NOTE: If the taker fails to exercise ordinary care, the loss may be shared according to the negligence of each party.

C. Alteration

1. In General

As noted previously, the alteration of a negotiable instrument can result in breach of both transfer and presentment warranties, and negligence on the part of one connected with the transaction can preclude assertion of the alteration.

2. "Alteration" Defined

An alteration of the terms of a negotiable instrument occurs if it changes the instrument *in any way.* Changing the names or relations of the parties, changing the amount, or filling in blanks in an unauthorized fashion are examples of alterations. [U.C.C. § 3–407(a)]

3. Fraudulent Alteration

If a fraudulent alteration occurs, all prior nonnegligent parties are completely discharged from liability on the instrument (and, due to the merger rule, on the underlying obligation as well; *see* p. 73). [U.C.C. § 3–407(b)]

a. Effect of Negligence

However, if the alteration was caused by the negligence of a party, that party is *not* discharged—and is in fact liable on the instrument as it *now* reads, at least when sued by later good faith parties. [U.C.C. §§ 3–406, 3–407(b), (c); *and see* p. 139]

b. Discharge Is Personal Defense

Discharge is a personal (as opposed to real) defense (*see* p. 61). Thus, if an alteration causes parties to be discharged on the instrument, they are still liable according to the *original terms* of the instrument if the instrument is transferred to an HDC. [U.C.C. §§ 3–407(b), (c); 3–601(b)]

c. **Rights of Drawee Bank**

A drawee or payor bank may charge an altered instrument against the drawer's account according to its *original terms*. [U.C.C. §§ 3–407(c), 4–401(d)(1)]

d. **Incomplete Instruments**

The unauthorized completion of an incomplete instrument is an alteration, but an HDC and a drawee/payor bank may nevertheless enforce the instrument according to its terms *when completed.* [U.C.C. §§ 3–407(c), 4–401(d)(2); *and see* p. 115]

Example: Sonja Student signs a promissory note for $5,000 payable to Nightflyer Finance Company ("NFC") in return for a school loan. An interest rate is not provided, although the parties had agreed that interest would be at the rate of 9% per annum. The note is indorsed by Sonja's parents as accommodation indorsers. NFC's loan officer then changes the face amount to $6,000 and fills in the interest as 10%, whereupon the note is negotiated to a non-HDC. *Result:* The fraudulent alteration discharges Sonja and her parents from liability. The non-HDC has recourse only against NFC for breach of the transfer warranty against alteration. (*See* p. 101) If the note is transferred to an HDC, that party may enforce it against Sonja for $5,000 and 10% interest and against her parents for $5,000 and 9% interest. (If Sonja were found not to have been negligent in allowing the interest rate to remain blank, she would likewise owe only 9% interest.)

e. **Alteration of Certified Check**

The Revision contains a rule not found in the original version of Article 3. Section § 3–413(b) makes the acceptor of a certified check liable to a holder in due course for the *altered amount* unless the certification itself states the amount certified. The aim of the law here is to encourage banks certifying checks to state the amount thereof as part of the certification so as to prevent subsequent alterations. [U.C.C. § 3–413, Off. Com.]

EXAM TIP GILBERT

If on an exam you see a question where someone has fraudulently altered a negotiable instrument, first determine whether the party is *estopped* from asserting the alteration (as in the case of negligence). If not, then the fraudulent alteration discharges all parties from liability on the instrument. However, because discharge is a personal defense, a drawee/payor bank or an HDC may enforce the instrument against the discharged party: (i) according to its *original terms*; or (ii) in the case of unauthorized completion, according to its terms *as completed.*

D. Lost, Destroyed, or Stolen Instruments

1. General Rule

If an instrument is lost, destroyed, or stolen, its true owner (the payee or the payee's transferee) may still sue upon it, but must first *prove ownership and explain* the reasons for not producing the instrument. To protect the defendant from double liability in case the instrument should turn up in the hands of an HDC, the court may require the owner to post bond or give the defendant security against loss by reason of future claims. [U.C.C. § 3–309]

2. Lost Cashier's, Teller's, or Certified Checks

Some, but not all, jurisdictions adopting the Revision have also enacted § 3–312, which deals with lost, destroyed, or stolen cashier's checks, teller's checks, or certified checks. This is an alternative procedure to the one described in § 3–309.

a. Definitions

A "cashier's check" is a check drawn by the bank on itself (the issuing bank is both the drawer and the drawee); a "teller's check" is one drawn by one bank on another or that is payable through another bank; a "certified check" is an ordinary check that the drawee bank has signed ("accepted" is the technical term), thus exposing itself to primary liability. [U.C.C. §§ 3–104(g), (h); 3–409]

b. Declaration of Loss

According to the procedure specified in § 3–312, a customer who has lost such bank checks may come into the issuing bank and fill out a form called a "declaration of loss," describing the problem. If the bank check is presented within the 90-day period following the date of the check (or, for certified checks, the date of acceptance by the drawee), the bank will pay the presenter. If the check is not presented within the 90-day period, at the end of the period the bank pays the money to the customer who filled out the declaration of loss, and if the check later shows up, even in the hands of a holder in due course, the bank has no further liability, and the person in possession of the bank check will have to try and get the money from the customer.

E. Phony Cashiers Checks

A major scam is causing trouble across the globe using phony cashier checks and wire transfers. The victim can be anyone, but it is often a law firm! The scam typically goes like this:

Example: Lawyer Krista Major was contacted by phone by a man named Alexander Smith who asked her to represent him in drafting the settlement of a legal claim he has with his former employer, MidSize Corporation, who he accused of firing him illegally because he was an aging senior. He filed a lawsuit against them *pro se* and, since he had a lot of evidence (including a taped conversation in which upper management could be heard saying "let's dump this old geizer") the company now wants to settle for the amount of $100,000 plus any attorneys fees Smith has. Now he wants Krista Major to draft up the settlement agreement and get them to sign it, at which point the company will have its bank send her a cashiers check. He provides her with the complete file he has on the case, and she makes a call to the company, talks to the man in charge of the settlement agreement, and is assured that if she sends in the agreement the company will sign it and send her the cashiers check for $100,000 plus the amount of her fee. Satisfied, Krista Major drafts the agreement, gets it approved by her client, and sends it to MidSize Corporation along with her bill for $15,000. A cashiers check for $115,000, made out to her, promptly arrives in her mail. Alexander Smith asks her to deposit it at her bank and wire him $100,000 to his bank account in another city. Krista Major takes the check to her bank, Big Bank, and deposits it, asking the chief teller when it will be collected. The chief teller replies that since it is a cashiers check it is as "good as gold" and shows her that the bank's records already reflect that the check has "cleared." Delighted, she tells the bank to wire the $100,000 to her client's bank, and the bank does so immediately. But the very next afternoon her bank calls to tell her that the cashers check has been dishonored by the payor bank on which it was drawn ("no such account") and is a phony. Her bank wants her to return the $100,000. But that wire transfer went through almost instantly and the funds are gone. Further investigation shows that there is no such entities as Alexander Smith or Midsize Corporation. It was all an elaborate sting.

In this example the lawyer is in trouble. While the courts differ, many courts hold that the assurance the check has "cleared" doesn't stop the depositary bank from recovering the money if the check turns out to be a phony. The depositary bank also can argue she breached the transfer warranty of § 4–207(a)(2) that all signatures are authentic and here the drawer's signature was forged since the real bank named as drawer/drawee did not write this check. It was a complete phony. Compare **Valley Bank of Ronan v. Hughes**, 334 Mont. 335, 147 P.3d 185 (2006), with **Greenberg, Trager & Herbst, LLP v. HSBC Bank USA**, 17 N.Y.3d 565, 958 N.E.2d 77 (2011).

Best advice: Don't send the wire transfer until after the payor bank has made final payment on the cashiers check, and don't be dazzled just because it is a check written by a bank for a large amount with your name as payee.

And if you represent the depositary bank make sure it doesn't tell the depositing customer that the check has "cleared" until the bank is sure the payor bank has made final payment.

Chapter Nine

Electronic Banking

CONTENTS

Chapter Approach

Rather than move around tons of paper each day, bankers have taken steps to speed up and simplify the process of check collection by turning the paper instruments into electronic signals that can be read by automatic check processing equipment and/or computers. More and more of this will be done, and the law has had to adapt to the dramatic changes that electronic banking brings. As already discussed in Chapter Seven, Check 21 creates a federal system for the movement of checks as electronic images. Two other bodies of law deal more closely with the subject: *Article 4A* (Funds Transfers) of the Uniform Commercial Code and the *Electronic Fund Transfers Act,* a federal statute. Finally, the chapter concludes with a brief overview of the law of credit cards.

Anyone studying these laws must first confront the question of scope; *i.e.,* which, if either, of these statutes is relevant to the issue at hand. As explained below, they are *mutually exclusive.* One, but not both, may apply. Having resolved that issue, you should next ascertain what part of the relevant statute resolves the dispute, decide liability, and then explore whether liability can be passed on to another party. Finally, you should consult the remedial sections of the statute to determine the damages that must be paid.

A. Article 4A—Funds Transfers

1. Introduction

Most wire transfers in this country are carried out through the Federal Reserve banks, in which other banks throughout the United States (and other countries as well) maintain accounts through which electronic instructions can pass, and against which debits and credits can be entered. The federal government calls this system *Fedwire.* The Federal Reserve regulates the collection of checks and wire transfers through Regulation J [12 C.F.R. § 210], which has been amended so that its wire transfer rules are virtually identical to those of Article 4A of the Uniform Commercial Code.

2. Scope of Article 4A

Article 4A of the Uniform Commercial Code governs fund transfers in which payment orders are given to move money from one bank account to another.

a. Terminology

Understanding the terminology involved is important, so definition of the major terms follows.

(1) "Payment Order"

A payment order is the instruction made by a "sender" (*see* below) to a receiving bank—whether transmitted orally, electronically, or in writing—telling the bank to pay a fixed or determinable amount of money to a beneficiary. The payment order must not state any conditions to payment (other than time of payment), and the instruction must be transmitted directly by the sender to the receiving bank. [U.C.C. § 4A–103(a)(1)]

Example: Sam Sender phoned his bank, Octopus National Bank, and told it to transfer $500,000 immediately to Betty Beneficiary's account with Antitrust National Bank. Sam, the sender, has given a payment order, and Article 4A applies.

(a) Distinguish—Checks

A check does not qualify as a payment order because it is an instruction to pay that is *not transmitted directly to the receiving bank from the sender.* Instead, it is given to the payee by the drawer, and the payee must present the check in order to get money from the drawer's bank. Think of it this way: a check *pulls* money from the drawer's account, but a payment order *pushes* money out of the sender's account and into the account of the beneficiary.

(2) "Sender"

A sender is the person who gives a payment order to a receiving bank. [U.C.C. § 4A–103(a)(5)] Note that as a wire transfer moves from one entity to another, there can be many different senders.

(3) "Originator"

The *first sender* of a payment order is called the originator. Thus, in the example above, Sam was the originator. Sam was also a sender, but so was his bank, Octopus National Bank, when it passed his payment order along to Antitrust National Bank. Therefore, anyone giving a payment order is a sender, but *only the first person* doing so is the originator. [U.C.C. § 4A–104(c)]

(4) "Beneficiary"

The person who is the *final recipient* of a payment order is the beneficiary (*e.g.*, Betty in the last example).

(5) Bank Terminology

Payment orders can pass through a number of banks (with a Federal Reserve Bank typically being in the middle) before the money reaches the beneficiary. The first bank in the process is called the "originator's bank" and the last one is called the "beneficiary's bank." Any bank in between is called an "intermediary bank." Any bank giving a payment order to another bank is called a "sender" (*see* p. 151). Any bank to whom a payment order is given is called a "receiving bank." [U.C.C. §§ 4A–103(a)(3), (4); 4A–104(b), (d)]

PAYMENT ORDER	*Instruction* by a sender to a receiving bank *to pay a fixed or determinable amount of money* to a beneficiary.
SENDER	*Person who gives a payment order* to a receiving bank. (*Note*: There can be many senders as the wire transfer moves through the process.)
ORIGINATOR	*First sender*
BENEFICIARY	*Final recipient* of a payment order
ORIGINATOR'S BANK	*First bank* in the process
BENEFICIARY'S BANK	*Last bank* in the process
INTERMEDIARY BANK	*Any bank in between* the first and last banks
RECEIVING BANK	*Any bank* to whom *a payment order is given* (there can be many receiving banks in the process, including the beneficiary's bank).

b. Consumer Transaction Excluded

The Electronic Fund Transfers Act governs transfers into and out of *consumer* accounts. If the Electronic Fund Transfers Act (*see* p. 159) applies, Article 4A does not. [U.C.C. § 4A–108]

3. Acceptance and Rejection of Payment Orders

A key concept in Article 4A is the concept of "acceptance" of a payment order. Once a bank has "accepted" a payment order, it *must pay the funds* to the recipient of the order and has no right to change its mind and charge back the transaction on the books.

a. Acceptance Defined

The meaning of "acceptance" varies according to whether the bank making the acceptance is the beneficiary's bank.

(1) Acceptance by Receiving Bank Other than Beneficiary's Bank

A receiving bank that is *not* the beneficiary's bank accepts a payment order by *executing* it. Execution occurs when the receiving bank becomes a sender and passes on the payment order it received to the next receiving bank. [U.C.C. §§ 4A–209(a), 4A–301(a)]

(2) Acceptance by Beneficiary's Bank

The beneficiary's bank accepts a payment order if it does *any* of the following things, whichever happens first:

(a) Payment to Beneficiary

The beneficiary's bank accepts a payment order if the beneficiary's bank either (i) *pays* the beneficiary directly (by cash, check, etc.) or (ii) *credits* the account of the beneficiary or applies the money transferred to a debt owed by the beneficiary to the beneficiary's bank (*i.e.*, a setoff, *see* p. 118). *Payment does not occur until the beneficiary is **notified** that the money is available.* [U.C.C. §§ 4A–209(b)(1); 4A–405(a), (b); 4A–502]

(b) Notice of Availability

A beneficiary's bank also accepts a payment order if it **notifies** the beneficiary that the funds are **available for withdrawal** from the beneficiary's account. Of course, a notice that the funds may not be withdrawn until the beneficiary's bank actually receives the funds from the sender is not a notice of acceptance. [U.C.C. § 4A–209(b)(1)]

(c) Receipt of Funds by Beneficiary's Bank

Acceptance by the beneficiary's bank also occurs if the beneficiary's bank **receives full payment from the sender** of the payment order. Receipt typically occurs when the money is available for withdrawal from an account maintained with a Federal Reserve Bank or some other funds transfer system, or in an account that the beneficiary's bank maintains with the bank that is the sender. [U.C.C. §§ 4A–209(b)(2), 4A–403]

(d) Passage of Time

Acceptance of a payment order occurs if the beneficiary's bank **fails to reject** (*see* below) a payment order before any of the time limits mentioned below. Assuming there are sufficient funds in the sender's account to cover the payment order (or the sender otherwise makes full payment), the beneficiary's bank accepts a payment order if it fails to reject it before the **opening of its funds-transfer business day** (*i.e.*, that part of a day the bank is open to receive and process funds transfers [*see* U.C.C. § 4A–105(a)(4)]) or **within one hour** after that time. The beneficiary's bank may also reject the payment order if it does so **within one hour after the opening of the sender's business day following the payment date** (*see* below) stated in the payment order. [U.C.C. § 4A–209(b)(3), Off. Com. 7, 8]

(e) Payment Date

If the payment order states a payment date (and it is not required to do so), acceptance cannot occur before the payment date, and any credits to accounts before the payment date are subject to charge back and cancellation. [U.C.C. § 4A–209(d)]

BANK OTHER THAN BENEFICIARY'S BANK	BENEFICIARY'S BANK
• Upon *execution*—when bank (sender) passes payment order to next receiving bank.`	The first of: • Upon *direct payment* to beneficiary or *crediting* beneficiary's account. • Upon *notification* that funds are available for withdrawal. • Upon *receipt of full payment* from sender. • Upon *failing to reject* an order before the specified time.

b. Rejection of Payment Orders

The opposite of acceptance of a payment order is *rejection* thereof. Rejection is the receiving bank's announced intention not to accept a payment order. It requires *notice* (orally, electronically, or in writing) to the sender that the receiving bank will not accept the order or will not pay or execute it. No particular words are required. [U.C.C. § 4A–210(a)]

c. Bank May Accept or Reject, Not Both

If a bank accepts a payment order it may not later reject it. Conversely, if the bank rejects a payment order it may not later accept it unless a new payment order is sent. Thus, when the sender sends the payment order, the receiving bank is faced with a decision: It must accept or reject, but it cannot do both. [U.C.C. § 4A–210(d)]

d. Acceptance Not Required by U.C.C.

It is important to appreciate that Article 4A *never requires* a bank to accept a payment order. If a bank receives a payment order but has not yet received the funds described in the payment order, it is taking a risk if it goes ahead and accepts the payment order—*i.e.*, that the funds will never be received but that it will nonetheless have to pay the money to the beneficiary. This credit risk must be evaluated by the receiving bank. If the sender is, for example, an unstable, financially troubled bank, the receiving bank might be wise to delay acceptance of the payment order until it actually receives the funds. When in doubt, the receiving bank should reject the payment order and protect itself. [U.C.C. § 4A–209, Off. Com. 8]

(1) Acceptance Required by Contract

Even though the U.C.C. never requires a receiving bank to accept a payment order, the receiving bank might have made a *contract* with the sender or some other entity by which it is bound to accept a payment order. If so, its failure to accept would expose it to breach of contract remedies (*see* Contracts Summary).

e. Effect of Acceptance

Once the beneficiary's bank accepts a payment order, it must pay the funds to the beneficiary even if it does not receive them from the sender. [U.C.C. § 4A–404(a)]

(1) Time of Payment

Acceptance cannot occur prior to any payment date stated in the payment order (*see* p. 153). Once a beneficiary's bank has made its acceptance, the Expedited Funds Availability Act requires the beneficiary's bank to make the funds available to the beneficiary on the ***next business day*** (*see* p. 119).

(2) Notice to Beneficiary

Once acceptance occurs, the beneficiary's bank is required to notify the beneficiary of the funds availability before midnight of its next funds-transfer business day following the payment date. Notice may be given by any reasonable means, including mailing. [U.C.C. § 4A–404(b)]

(3) Damages for Failure to Pay

If the beneficiary's bank has made an acceptance and then fails to pay the funds to the beneficiary upon demand, it is liable for ***all damages,*** including consequential damages, of which it had *notice* at the time of its refusal. [U.C.C. § 4A–404(a)]

Example: Betty Beneficiary had the opportunity to buy a famous painting worth $500,000 for only $300,000 if she acted before May 1. On April 30, she borrowed the money from Sam Sender, her uncle, and he wired the money to her on that date. Her bank accepted the payment order but failed to allow her access to the money until after May 1. The bank is liable for her consequential loss of $200,000 only if she gave them notice of the possibility that the painting purchase would fall through if the money were not given to her on May 1. [U.C.C. § 4A–404, Off. Com. 2]

(a) Reasonable Doubt Defense

The bank can escape liability for consequential damages if it proves that it did not pay the money because the bank had a ***reasonable doubt*** concerning the right of the beneficiary to the payment. If, *e.g.*, the bank was reasonable in believing that Betty was not the Betty Beneficiary who had the account with the bank, it would not have to pay consequential damages. [U.C.C. § 4A–404(a), Off. Com. 3]

(4) Sender's Duty to Pay

Once a receiving bank accepts a payment order, the sender has a legal duty to pay the amount involved as of the payment date. [U.C.C. § 4A–402]

(a) Cancellation or Amendment of Payment Orders

A sender may cancel or amend a payment order by giving reasonable notice to a receiving bank ***before the receiving bank accepts*** the payment order. Once the payment order has been accepted, however, the sender loses this right and any stop payment order given by the sender to a receiving bank is ineffective and must be ignored by the receiving bank. [U.C.C. §§ 4A–211; 4A–404, Off. Com. 3]

(b) Bank Failure

If the sender or a receiving bank becomes insolvent after the acceptance of a payment order, the payment order is nonetheless effective, and whoever chose the sender or receiving bank must bear the loss. [U.C.C. § 4A–402(e)] Banks are encouraged to join associations that create loss-sharing rules, and such funds-transfer systems are permitted to adopt rules that vary the usual rules of Article 4A. [U.C.C. § 4A–501]

(c) Effect on Underlying Obligation

If the beneficiary agreed to accept payment by means of a funds transfer, acceptance by beneficiary's bank of the payment order results in the discharge of the underlying obligation, and this is true even if the beneficiary's bank becomes insolvent and fails to pay the money to the beneficiary. [U.C.C. § 4A–406]

Example: Sam Sender agreed to buy a painting from Betty Beneficiary by wiring her $100,000 on May 1. He ordered his bank to transfer that amount to Betty's account at Antitrust National Bank ("ANB") with a payment date of May 1, and his bank did so. ANB notified Betty that the money was in her account, but before she could withdraw it, ANB closed its doors forever and had no funds to pay its customers. Sam is entitled to the painting and Betty must try to recover the money from her bank.

EXAM TIP   GILBERT

Whenever an exam question involves a suit on the underlying obligation, pay attention to the *method of payment.* If payment is by means of a *funds transfer*, the bank's acceptance of the payment order *discharges* the underlying obligation, which is no longer available as a cause of action. However, if a *negotiable instrument* is accepted as conditional payment, a party can sue on the underlying obligation *after* the instrument has been *dishonored* (*see* p. 73).

---

1) Bank Charges

Banks impose a charge for handling wire transfers. They are allowed to take this amount out of the funds transferred (it is typically a very small charge). The reduction of the amount of the funds transferred by the amount of bank charges does *not* affect the above rule, so even if the bank informed Betty that the amount available to her was $100,000 minus the bank charge, the underlying debt between Sam and Betty is still paid, *unless* Sam fails upon demand by Betty to refund the bank charges to her. [U.C.C. § 4A–406(c), Off. Com. 5]

4. Misdescription of Beneficiary

Funds transfers frequently describe the beneficiary both by name and by an account number.

a. No Such Beneficiary

If the misdescription refers to a nonexistent or unidentifiable person or account, no one gets the rights of a beneficiary and a technical acceptance of the payment order cannot occur. [U.C.C. § 4A–207(a)]

Example: The payment order stated that $100,000 was to be transferred to Betty Beneficiary at Antitrust National Bank ("ANB"), account number 12345. Betty Beneficiary does not bank at ANB and has no such account there with that number. Acceptance of this payment order by ANB cannot occur and Betty Beneficiary has no right to any funds transferred to ANB.

When the beneficiary or account does not exist, the funds transfer cannot be completed. Therefore, **each sender in the transfer chain** is entitled **to get back the money it paid** on the payment order.

---

b. Wrong Account Number

Article 4A permits the banks to **ignore the name** of the beneficiary and deal **only in account numbers** (or other identifying numbers). The reason for this is that computer programs are doing much of the work and numbers are simply easier to understand and follow that names in most programs. If a mistake causes the beneficiary to be identified by the wrong account number, the beneficiary's bank is not liable if it put the money in the account listed in the payment order, and it has no duty to check to see if the name and number are correct. In this case, whoever made the mistake (with some exceptions, described below) must bear the loss. [U.C.C. § 4A–207(b)]

Example: Sam Sender told his bank, Octopus National Bank ("ONB"), to send $200,000 to Betty Beneficiary's account with Antitrust National Bank ("ANB"), account number 12345. ONB sent a payment order to ANB instructing it to credit $200,000 to the account of "Betty Beneficiary, account number 12346." Account number 12346 belonged to Iggy Innocent. ANB credited $200,000 to Iggy's account and notified him of its availability. Delighted, Iggy withdrew the money and left the state. In this case, ANB is not liable to Sam. Sam is not required to pay the amount of the payment order and may demand that ONB recredit his account because ONB made the mistake.

(1) Mistake by Originator

If the mistake was made by the originator (Sam), the originator's bank must still bear the loss **unless** the originator's bank gave **notice** to the originator that payment would be made on the basis of number alone even if different from the account of the named beneficiary. If the originator's bank gives such a notice to the originator, it is effective for all subsequent payment orders the originator gives to that bank. [U.C.C. § 4A–207(c)(2)]

Example: If, in the example above, Sam Sender had told ONB to wire $200,000 to Betty Beneficiary, but Sam told his bank the wrong account number, Sam would still not have to pay the amount of the payment order and ONB would bear the loss, **unless** ONB had warned Sam of the necessity of being careful because transfers would be made on the basis of number alone even if different from that of the named beneficiary.

(a) Rationale

Originators are not likely to know that banks do not check to make sure that the name of the beneficiary is the same as that listed as the account holder. But once the originators are warned of this practice, it is their responsibility to make sure that the number is correct.

(2) Where Beneficiary's Bank Is Aware of the Problem

If, prior to payment, the beneficiary's bank discovers a discrepancy between the beneficiary named in the payment order and the name on the identified account, the beneficiary's bank must investigate and clear up the problem, and if it pays the wrong person, must bear the loss itself. [U.C.C. §§ 4A–207(b)(1), (2), Off. Com. 2]

(3) Restitution from Recipient of Funds

Whoever ends up bearing the loss from the wrongful payment in the above situation may go after the person who received the funds but had no right to them. The cause of action is common law restitution ("money had and received"; *see* Contracts Summary). [U.C.C. § 4A–207(d)]

5. Erroneous Payment Orders

If an error is made during the transmission process (duplicate order, wrong amount, wrong beneficiary, etc.), the entity that makes the mistake must bear the loss and the responsibility of recovering the funds in a restitution action against the recipient wrongfully holding the funds (*see* p. 158). [U.C.C. §§ 4A–303, 4A–402]

a. Money-Back Guarantee

In such a case, the sender is not required to pay the amount represented by the original payment order. This is commonly called the money-back guarantee. [U.C.C. § 4A–402, Off. Com. 2]

b. Sender's Duty to Report

The sender must report the problem within a reasonable time (not exceeding 90 days) after the sender gets notification of the problem or the sender loses the right to interest on the money. [U.C.C. § 4A–304]

6. Criminal Fraud and Security Procedures

Wire transfers of the kind covered by Article 4A are frequently of fantastic amounts, very tempting to criminals. The U.C.C. encourages banks to develop security procedures designed to thwart criminal interference with funds transfers and to follow the procedures carefully. [U.C.C. §§ 4A–201, 4A–202]

a. Bank's Failure to Follow Security Procedure

If the bank fails to follow the security procedure and this leads to a loss, the bank must bear the loss. [U.C.C. § 4A–202(b)]

b. Criminal Activity in Spite of Security Procedure

If the customer and the bank have agreed to a security procedure and in spite of compliance therewith by both parties a fraudulent funds transfer occurs, the following rules apply:

(1) Breach of Customer's System

If the criminal gained access through a breach of the customer's system (whether or not the customer was negligent), the customer must bear the loss. [U.C.C. § 4A–202, 4A–203]

(2) Breach of Bank's System

If the customer was in no way responsible for the criminal's gaining access to the security procedure and instead the bank's system was breached, the receiving bank must bear the loss. [U.C.C. § 4A–202, 4A–203 (Official Comment to § 203 contains a good discussion and examples)]

 Example: Big Department Store paid all of its corporate debts by wire transfers to its major suppliers. Each payment was required to be verified by a coded instruction given to Big Department Store's bank along with each payment order. The code was kept in duplicate books at the offices of Big Department Store and its bank. A thief broke into the offices of Big Department Store one night, found the code book, and used it to send a phony payment order of $100,000 to an account the thief maintained at another bank. Big Department Store is required to pay the payment order. Big Department Store must bear the loss unless it can recover it from the thief.

Compare: If, in the above example, the thief had stolen the code book from the bank, the bank would have to bear the loss.

(3) Contrary Agreements Prohibited

The bank is not allowed to vary the above rules by agreement so that the customer would have to bear a greater responsibility for criminal activity. [U.C.C. § 4A–202(f)]

B. Consumer Transfers— Electronic Fund Transfers Act

1. In General

Article 4A does not apply to consumer fund transfers. Instead a federal statute, the Electronic Fund Transfers Act ("EFTA"), and its Regulation E govern any transaction in which a *consumer* uses electronic means to tap his/her bank account. [15 U.S.C. § 1693 *et seq.*; Regulation E, 12 C.F.R. 1005] The Consumer Financial Protection Bureau has jurisdiction over the statute and Regulation E.

2. Definitions

The most common transaction covered by the federal statute is use of a *debit card* in an *automated teller machine* ("ATM") to withdraw money from a bank account, but the Act and Regulation apply to any *electronic fund transfer.*

a. Electronic Fund Transfer

A transfer of funds not initiated by paper instruction (such as a check), initiated through an electronic terminal (*i.e.*, an ATM), telephone, or computer that authorizes a financial institution to credit or debit a consumer bank account is an electronic fund transfer ("EFT"). The term also includes all transactions initiated by a debit card (*see* below). [Reg. E § 1005.2(g)]

b. Debit Card

A debit card is an access device used by a consumer to transfer money out of a bank account. A debit card is different from a *credit* card; use of a credit card does *not* affect the consumer's bank account, but simply results in the accumulation of a debt owed to the issuer of the credit card. Federal law governs both (credit cards are regulated by the Truth in Lending Act [15 U.S.C. § 1601] and its Regulation Z [12 C.F.R. 1026]), but the rules are more favorable to debit card users than credit card users because Congress thought it a more serious matter for consumers to lose money from their bank accounts than merely to pile up debt.

c. Automated Teller Machine

An ATM is an electronic terminal into which a consumer inserts a debit card to work an EFT from or to a bank account.

d. Personal Identification Number

A personal identification number ("PIN") is the number that the consumer must punch into the ATM to gain access to the bank account.

3. Documentation

At various points in the relationship between the consumer and the bank wishing to allow the consumer to make electronic fund transfers, the bank must give the consumer certain disclosures of the consumer's rights. These include the basic initial contract between the parties, the bank statement, the slip that must be dispensed by the ATMs, and an annual statement of the consumer's liability for unauthorized EFTs. [Reg. E §§ 1005.7, 1005.8, 1005.9] The Federal Reserve Board has promulgated model forms for these purposes, and use of such forms without change completely insulates the financial institution from liability for documentation requirements under the Act and Regulation. [EFTA § 915(d)(2)]

4. Issuance of Debit Cards or Other Access Devices

For an EFT system to be profitable, the debit cards (or other access devices) must get into the hands of a lot of people who are then encouraged to use them. Banks are forbidden to mail out unsolicited *credit cards* [T.I.L. § 132], but are allowed to mail out unsolicited *debit cards* as long as the card is not in a *validated* condition. A card is "validated" if it can immediately be used to work an EFT; it is not validated if the consumer must first take some step (typically application for a PIN) before the card can be used.

e.g. **Example:** Big Bank mailed all of its consumer customers debit cards without asking them beforehand if they wanted the cards. The letter accompanying the cards informed the customers that if they wanted to be able to use the cards in ATMs, they had to write the bank and have it issue them PINs (*see* p. 160). The bank has not violated the law because the debit cards could not be used as mailed, and hence were not Validated. But if the letter accompanying the cards had informed the consumers what their PINs were, the bank would have violated the law.

5. Preauthorized Transfers

The consumer and bank may agree to automatic transfers into or out of the consumer's account for various purposes (*e.g.,* receipt of paycheck, payment of routine bills, etc.). The bank must either tell the consumer each time such a preauthorized transfer was scheduled to occur that it did or did not occur, or (what all banks actually do) give the consumer a telephone number the consumer can call to ascertain whether the EFT occurred. The consumer has the right to *stop payment* of the preauthorized transfer by giving the bank notice to do so anytime up to three business days before the scheduled date thereof. The bank may require oral stop payment orders to be confirmed in writing, and if it does so, oral stop payment orders cease to be effective 14 days after they are given unless so confirmed. [Reg. E § 1005.11]

6. Error Resolution

The law permits the bank to send out bank statements that report both checks and EFT activity in the consumer's bank account. The U.C.C. requires the consumer to report certain problems reflected by the statement (*see* p. 141). If the consumer wants to complain about difficulties with EFTs, the following rules apply:

a. Reporting Requirements

The consumer must give the bank *oral or written notice* of any supposed errors so that the notice is received by the financial institution *within 60 days* after the financial institution first sent the consumer the bank statement. The consumer must supply all information available to the consumer that is necessary to resolve the problem (*e.g.,* consumer's name, account number, why the consumer believes there to be an error, etc.). The bank may require oral complaints to be confirmed in writing within 10 days thereof. [Reg. E § 1005.11(b)]

b. Bank's Duties

The bank must promptly investigate the alleged error and must do so in good faith. It may not simply assume that no error was made. It must mail out its findings promptly and if the consumer was right in complaining about an error, the bank must make the necessary correction (and pay interest if the account bore interest). [Reg. E § 1005.11(c), (d)]

(1) Time Periods for Investigation

The bank has a free ride period of *10 business days* in which to investigate the error without having to recredit the account. If the bank wants a longer period of time, it can have up to *45 calendar days* if it recredits the account in the amount of the alleged error before the 10 business day period expires. [Reg. E § 1005.11(c)]

e.g. **Example:** Connie Consumer received her bank statement on September 1. It reflected a $200 EFT from her account that she had no record of having made. She phoned the bank on that date and demanded an investigation, and that same day filled out a written complaint. The bank need not recredit her account until 10 business days after September 1. If the bank cannot resolve the problem within that period, at the end of the 10 business days the bank must recredit her account, and on doing so has until October 15 in which to continue its investigation and resolve the dispute.

(a) Both Periods Run at Same Time

It is important to appreciate that *both* the 10 business day period and the 45 calendar day period start running at the moment the consumer complains. Thus, in the last example, when Connie complained on September 1, the bank had 10 business days from that date in which to investigate without putting the money back in her account. If it can resolve the problem within that period, well and good, but if not, and it wants whatever is left of the 45 calendar day period, at the end of the 10 business days it must recredit her account and give her access to the money. It would then have until October 15 to complete its investigation.

AN EXAMPLE OF EFT ERROR RESOLUTION

		JUne				
S	M	T	W	R	F	S
		1	2	3	4	5
6	7	8	9	10	11	12
13	14	15	16	17	18	19
20	21	22	23	24	25	26
27	28	29	30			

		JULY				
S	M	T	W	R	F	S
				1	2	3
4	5	6	7	8	9	10
11	12	13	14	15	16	17
18	19	20	21	22	23	24
25	26	27	28	29	30	31

		AUgust				
S	M	T	W	R	F	S
1	2	3	4	5	6	7
8	9	10	11	12	13	14
14	15	16	17	18	19	20
21	22	23	24	25	26	27
28	29	30	31			

		september				
S	M	T	W	R	F	S
		1	2	3	4	
5	6	7	8	9	10	11
12	13	14	15	16	17	18
19	20	21	22	23	24	25
26	27	28	29	30		

Tuesday, June 1 — 0

Saturday, July 31 — 60

Friday, August 13 — 73*

Tuesday, September 14 — 105

Tuesday, September 21 — 112

Customer discovers error (has *60 days* to report)

Customer reports; Bank begins its investigation

Bank must recredit Customer's account within *10 business days*)**

Bank's investigation ends (within *45 days*)**; if it finds no error, must give Customer *5 business days'* notice

Bank withdraws amount from Customer's account

* Includes nonbusiness (weekend) days.

** Remember that *both* the 10 business day period and the 45 day investigation period begin to run *at the same time* (when the customer reports the problem).

(2) Time Periods for Resolution

If the bank has recredited the account and then discovers there was *no error*, it must give the consumer five business days' warning before it withdraws the money from the consumer's account. The bank must furnish the consumer a written explanation of its findings and tell the consumer of the right to request the documents on which the bank relied in making its determination. [Reg. E § 1005.11(e)]

7. Unauthorized EFTs

If a criminal has somehow gained access to the consumer's debit card or other means of making an electronic fund transfer, who bears the loss?

a. "Unauthorized EFT" Defined

The term "unauthorized EFT" means any EFT from the consumer's account that was not authorized by the consumer and from which the consumer receives no benefit. [Reg. E § 1005.2(1)]

(1) Withdrawal of Agency Authority

The consumer is liable for all uses of a debit card that the consumer has given to another to use. However (unlike credit card law), the consumer can give the financial institution notice of withdrawal of authority and any transfers thereafter would be unauthorized (and, under the rules described below, the consumer would have no liability for them). [Reg. E § 1005.2(1)]

e.g. **Example:** Carl Consumer loaned his debit card to his sister Debbie and told her his PIN. She promised to take no more than $100 out of an ATM, but he was surprised to learn that she took out $200 each day for five days in a row. At the end of the fifth day, Carl phoned the bank and stated that Debbie should not be permitted to make further withdrawals. The next day Debbie used the card to withdraw another $200 from an ATM. Carl is liable for the first five transactions, but not the one following his phone call.

(2) Involuntary Transactions

The Federal Reserve Board's Official Commentary on the Act and Regulation (which has the force of law) provides that involuntary transactions are unauthorized EFTs. [Off. Staff Com. § 1005.2–Q2–27]

e.g. **Example:** Just as Connie Consumer stepped up to the ATM, the man in line behind her put a gun to her back and ordered her to withdraw the maximum amount the machine would give her. This is an unauthorized EFT, and Connie has only the $50 liability described below.

b. Consumer Liability for Unauthorized EFTs

The general rule is that a consumer is liable for only *$50 worth* of any unauthorized EFTs, and not even that amount if the consumer gives *notice* to the financial institution before that much is taken out. [Reg. E § 1005.6(b)] There are, however, two situations in which the consumer gets liability greater than $50, both of them reflecting consumer misconduct:

(1) Failure to Report Card Missing

If the consumer learns that the debit card is lost or stolen, and fails to report this to the financial institution within two business days thereafter, the consumer's liability for unauthorized EFTs increases to a *maximum of $500* for any unauthorized transfers taking place after the two business day period. However, the consumer is never liable for more than $500 in this situation. [Reg. E § 1005.6(b)(1)]

Example: Connie Consumer's brother George stole her debit card on a Monday. He knew her PIN because he had once watched her make a withdrawal from an ATM and had memorized the number when she punched it in. He took $200 from her account on Monday, and the same amount each day for the rest of the week. Connie knew George had stolen the card on Monday, but she did not want to report him to the bank or the police, so she tried to get the card back from him. He just laughed at her. On the following weekend, while he was asleep, she managed to recapture the card. When she received her bank statement she protested the withdrawals he had made. She is liable for $50 worth of the withdrawals he made on Monday and Tuesday, and for $450 of the withdrawals he made on subsequent days, for a total of $500. *Note:* The $50 from the first two days is *not* added to the $500 from the rest to get $550. Liability under the above rules never exceeds $500.

(2) Failure to Report Bank Statement Problems

The second situation in which the consumer is exposed to greater liability than $50 occurs where the bank sends the consumer a bank statement first reflecting unauthorized EFT activity. If the consumer does not report the problem within 60 days of the transmittal of the bank statement, the consumer has *unlimited liability* for unauthorized electronic fund transfers first occurring more than 60 days after the statement was sent out and up until the consumer does report the problem. This liability is *in addition to* that stated above. [Reg. E § 1005.6(b)(2)]

CONSUMER LIABILITY FOR UNAUTHORIZED EFTs	GILBERT
GENERAL RULE	Consumer is not liable for more than $50 of an unauthorized EFT.
EXCEPTIONS	Consumer may be liable for: (i) *Up to $500* if he fails to report a missing debit card within *two business days*; or (ii) An *unlimited amount* if he fails to report a bank statement problem within *60 days.* Note: A consumer's negligence does not alter the above rules.

(3) Negligence of Consumer

The Official Commentary on the Act and Regulation issued by the Federal Reserve Board states that consumer negligence in no way alters the above rules or exposes the consumer to greater liability. [Off. Staff Com. § 1005.6–Q6–6–5]

Example: Afraid he would forget his PIN, Carl Consumer wrote it on the debit card itself. When his wallet was stolen, Carl immediately phoned his bank and told them what had happened. Assuming no withdrawals have occurred before his phone call, Carl has no liability for any subsequent unauthorized EFTs.

8. Civil Liability of Bank

If the financial institution fails to follow the above rules, it is liable for all *actual damages* caused thereby, *punitive damages* between $100 and $1,000 (except in class actions where the maximum punitive damages are the lesser of $500,000 or 1% of the bank's net worth), *plus* costs and the consumer's attorney fees. If the consumer brings a baseless action for purposes of harassment, the prevailing financial institution may recover its attorneys' fees. These suits may be brought in any state or federal court having general jurisdiction within one year of the alleged violation. There is no amount in controversy limitation on federal or state jurisdiction.

EXAM TIP   🔲GILBERT

Keep in mind that Article 4A and the EFTA are *mutually exclusive*—only one can apply *Article 4A* applies to funds transfers involving money moving from bank to bank, while the *EFTA* applies to *consumer* funds transfers, *i.e.*, those where a consumer uses electronic means to make transfers to or from her bank account (*e.g.*, by debit card or ATM).

---

9. Foreign Remittances

a. The Basic Situation

Effective in February, 2013 and updated in 2020, the Consumer Financial Protection Bureau has promulgated an amendment to Regulation E that deals with foreign remittances. The term refers to transactions in which a consumer in the United States wires money to someone in a foreign country—for example someone who was born in a different part of the world may send periodic portions of his/her wages back to family in the country of origin. When there was no regulation of these electronic transfers a great deal of fraud and chicanery went on. [Reg. E § 1005, Subpart B]

b. Disclosures and Receipt Required

The regulation requires many things to be disclosed prior to the transfer taking place: the amount being transferred, all fees and taxes, the exchange rate, and the exact amount that will be received by the transferee. The sender must also be given a receipt (in English and in all relevant languages) containing these disclosures as well as other matters such as the name, telephone number(s), and website of the remittance transfer provider. [Reg. E § 1005.31]

c. Error Resolution and Cancellation of the Transfer

The Regulation contains a detailed procedure for resolving transmission errors (such as sending the wrong amount or non-receipt of the transfer, and provides various remedies if these problems arise. [Reg. E § 1005.33] There is also a right to cancel the transfer up until 30 minutes before it occurs. [Reg. E § 1005.34]

C. Consumer Transfers—Credit Cards

1. General Concepts

In 1970 the federal Truth In Lending Act was amended to add coverage of consumer credit card transactions. The statute is supplemented by Regulation Z, which is promulgated by the Consumer Financial Protection Board. [The Truth in Lending Act is formally called the "Consumer Credit Protection Act," 15 U.S.C.A. § 1601, and Regulation Z can be found at 12 C.P.R. Part 1026] The rules as to permissible disclosures prior to the issuance or use of the card (interest rates, terms of the card, etc.) are beyond the scope this Summary and are covered in the course in consumer law. This Summary restricts itself to the issuance of the card and the liability of the consumer for its use.

2. Issuance of the Credit Card

Unlike debit cards (*see* p. 160), credit cards may not be issued or distributed without the agreement of the consumer. [Reg. Z § 1026.12] A credit card that is sent to the consumer without his/her request is not validly issued and the consumer has no liability for charges made with such a card unless the consumer "accepts" the card by signing or using it (or authorizing another person to use it). [Reg. Z § 1026.12, Off. Staff Commentary 1026.12.2]

e.g. **Example:** Carl Consumer was surprised one day to receive a strange credit card in the mail. He'd not applied for it and didn't want it, so he threw it in the trash. It was subsequent used by someone unknown to charge hundreds of dollars. As long as Carl didn't sign the card, he has no liability for the charges.

3. Liability for Unauthorized Use

a. Giving the Card to Someone Else

If the consumer voluntarily allows someone else to use the card, the consumer is liable for all charges made thereon even if they exceed the amount the user promised to be limited to. Regulation Z does not answer this question, but the common law of agency does, saying that giving your card to another confers upon that person at least "apparent authority" to be your agent and bind you. **Steiger v. Chevy Chase Savings Bank**, 666 A.2d 479 (D.C. App. 1995).

e.g. **Example:** Betty loaned her credit card to her teenage daughter who promised to clear all charges with Betty before making them. The next day the daughter failed to mention the $1000 she charged on the card for new clothes. Betty is liable to the credit card company for the entire amount.

b. Unauthorized Use by Non-Agent

The consumer's liability for completely unauthorized use of an accepted credit card that is no more than $50 (or a lesser amount if the consumer notifies the card issuer before $50 is reached). [Reg. Z § 1026.12(b)] This upper limit is true even if the consumer does not notify the card issuer of the unauthorized use. Some card issuers, as a business decision, do not impose any liability for unauthorized use, but simply pass the loss back to the merchant who honored the card.

Example: A thief stepped from an alleyway and took Marvin's wallet at gun point. The next day the thief charged hundreds of dollars using the credit cards that were in the wallet, and the day after that hundreds more. Marvin has no liability beyond $50 even if he never notified the card issuer of the theft.

c. Asserting Defenses Against the Card Issuer

If there is something wrong with the product the consumer purchased using a credit card it is possible to have the credit card issuer reverse the charge. Reg. Z § 1026.12(c) allows the consumer to complain about the difficulty to the card issuer (tort claims are excluded) if the consumer has first tried to settle the problem with the merchant who honored the card. The Reg also requires that the amount involved must exceed $50 and have occurred in the consumer's home state or within 100 miles of the consumer's billing address, but the card issuers generally do not invoke these limitations, and will usually honor the consumer's request to reverse the charge without even inquiring into these two limitations. The card issuer then simply debits the account the merchant carries with it, leaving it up to the merchant to contact the consumer and try and work things out.

Example: When Roberto received the DVD he's ordered online from DVD World it was defective and wouldn't play at all. He contacted DVD World, but didn't get a response to his email of complaint. Roberto had charged the DVD to his credit card, so he contacted the bank that had issued him the card and explained this problem. The bank assured him it would be taken off of his bill, and then the bank debited this amount from the account that DVD World maintained with the bank. DVD World then contacted Roberto and agreed to accept the return of the defective DVD.

d. Billing Errors

If the consumer receives a bill from the credit card issuer and it contains a mistake (a charge not incurred, a product not shipped, an unknown transaction, etc., but not, as in the last example, a quality problem), Reg. Z § 1026.13 allows the consumer to complain of this billing error and require an investigation of the problem. The complaint must be made in writing within 60 days of the sending out of the bill first containing the error. The card issuer must acknowledge receipt of the complaint within 30 days and resolve it within two billing cycles (in no event longer than 90 days). In the investigation period the credit card issuer may not report the nonpayment as delinquent to credit reporting agencies.

Note that these two rights (asserting defenses and billing errors) are similar and in some situations would overlap. The consumer can try them both—in effect getting two bites at the apple. Use of one does not preclude the other if both are relevant.

Example: Helen failed to receive the product that she had ordered, but the charge appeared on her billing statement on January 15th. She failed to complain to the bank that had issued the credit card until April 1. The bank official who took her phone call explained to her that she needed to have made a written complaint of a billing error within 60 days of the mailing out of the first statement containing the error and now she was too late. She has missed the deadline for billing errors under Reg. Z § 1026.13, but can still exercise her right to assert her defense of nondelivery by the merchant per Reg. Z § 1026.12(c).

e. Penalties

The card issuer who does not comply with Reg. Z faces damages under § 130 of the statute, including actual damages, punitive damages and attorney fees. In addition, according to § 161(e) of the Truth in Lending Act, failure to follow the billing error rules leads to a forfeiture of up to $50 of the amount of the billing error, even if it turns out that the consumer was mistaken about the existence of the alleged error.

e.g. **Example:** If Helen in the last example had complained about the nondelivery in writing to her bank within the 60 day period, but the bank did not send her an acknowledgement within 30 days of receiving her complaint, the bank forfeits up to $50 of the amount of the transaction even if Helen was mistaken and she received the item she had ordered (this presumes she is in good faith in making this error).

Rationale: Congress wanted banks issuing credit cards to pay attention to consumer complaints. If banks could just ignore them and then report the consumer as delinquent when payment was not forthcoming, a consumer would have no real avenue of relief and would have an undeserved blot on his/her credit rating.

Exam Questions
and Answers

Question I

Antitrust National Bank ("ANB") tells Al that it will not loan him money for a new boat unless he can get someone to cosign a note for the proceeds. Al takes the note to his Uncle Rupert, who signs it on the back. The note shows Al as maker, with the face amount payable to the order of ANB.

One day before the note is to mature, Al tells ANB that he is without funds but should be able to repay the loan during the following year. The next day, Rupert arrives at ANB and tenders the amount due on the note. ANB (wishing to give Al more time to pay) refuses the money. Thirty days later, Al files a petition in bankruptcy, declaring that he has no assets.

Is Rupert liable for Al's debt to ANB? Discuss.

Question II

On Friday, Hector writes checks to all of his creditors. Although the amount in his checking account is less than the total amount of checks mailed that day, Hector knows that he will receive a payroll check the following Monday and plans to deposit it immediately to balance his account.

On Monday, Hector deposits his payroll check as planned, but the teller advises him that he cannot write checks against the amount deposited for six banking days. Despite Hector's protests and his statements about the prior checks, the bank dishonors certain of the creditors' checks presented to it on Wednesday.

Does Hector have a case against the bank for wrongful dishonor? Discuss.

Question III

Dr. Stretchem, a renowned plastic surgeon, hires Alice Smiles as his receptionist. Shortly after commencing work for Stretchem, Smiles begins a regular practice of stealing checks payable to Stretchem for medical services, forging Stretchem's indorsement on the back, signing her own name and depositing the checks in her account at Reliable State Bank ("RSB"). The checks are then collected from various payor banks throughout the country.

Stretchem discovers the scheme after an audit discloses that $48,000 is missing from his receivables, whereupon he fires Smiles and reports her activities to the police. His primary concern, however, is to recapture the $48,000 without filing numerous lawsuits against the payor banks involved.

Can Stretchem recover the money from RSB or from the patients whose checks were stolen? Discuss.

Question IV

Mr. and Mrs. Brown cosign a $10,000 promissory note for their nephew, Wastrel, the note representing a loan from Big National Bank ("BNB") to Wastrel to finance a sports bar. The note is to mature on June 30, but on that date Wastrel requests additional time to repay the loan and gives BNB a check for the amount due, postdated six months in the future. BNB agrees to the extension. When the bank attempts to cash Wastrel's check on December 31, however, the check bounces. BNB then writes to the Browns, demanding payment on the note.

The letter from BNB is the first the Browns have heard about Wastrel's note since they cosigned it. As their lawyer, what would you advise the Browns concerning their liability to BNB? Discuss.

Question V

Sandra Student and Honest John, a used car salesman, enter into the following agreement: Student gives John a check for $800, and John gives her the auto she has selected to drive for five days. If Student decides not to buy the car at the end of that period, she may return it and obtain her check. If she decides to keep the car, John may cash the check as payment therefor.

Student drives the car home, but on the following day it breaks down in the parking lot of her bank, College State Bank ("CSB"). Angered, Student enters the bank, fills out a stop payment order on her check, and arranges to have the car towed back to Honest John. The next morning, John brings Student's check to CSB and has it certified (at which point CSB transfers $800 from Student's account to the account used by the bank for certified checks). One hour after certifying the check, CSB discovers Student's stop payment order and it therefore refuses to cash the check when John presents it later that afternoon. John had rushed to cash the check after learning that the front end of the car had collapsed while being towed to his lot.

John sues both Student and CSB for the amount of the check. Discuss the liability of each defendant to John.

Question VI

Donna Desperate needs money for a trip to Europe, so she asks the "friendly people at Warmth Finance" to loan her $5,000. Warmth tells Donna that it will loan the money only if she will sign the following promissory note and get two financially responsible people to cosign with her:

I _____ promise to pay $5,000 plus 18% interest per annum on demand to BEARER; all indorsers and sureties waive rights to presentment and notice of dishonor. [There follow various clauses complying with the Truth in Lending Act, and a signature blank.]

Donna agrees and fills in her name on the first blank and at the bottom of the form. There are two blank lines below her name, and Warmth indicates it will pay the $5,000 as soon as she obtains the two cosignatures. Donna takes the note to her aging Aunt Martha and asks her to sign. Martha, who does not have her glasses, asks the amount of the note and Donna replies that it is for $200. Martha, who has always liked Donna, signs on the line indicated by her niece. That night, Donna takes the note with her to a concert starring Donny Dull, the new rock sensation. After the performance, Dull is mobbed by autograph seekers and screaming teenagers as he tries to leave the concert hall. In the confusion, Donna manages to get him to sign the second blank line below her name, but before she can leave, the note is ripped from her hand and trampled underfoot. Donna searches but cannot find the paper.

Two months later, Donna, Aunt Martha, and Donny Dull are sued by Ace Finance Company, a later holder of the note. Ace produces the soiled note, and a representative of the company testifies that Ace acquired the note as satisfaction for a $1,500 debt owed Ace by Rodney Respectable. Respectable told Ace that the note was dirty because he had accidentally dropped it in the mud. Respectable's blank indorsement is on the back of the note.

What is the liability of each of the defendants and Respectable in this situation? Discuss.

Question VII

Sammy, who is deeply in debt, tries to avoid his creditors but eventually is cornered by Muscle, who demands payment of a $5,000 debt owed to him. Muscle reputedly has close ties with organized crime, so Sammy promises to pay the full amount by check the following day. Muscle tells Sammy that his messenger will call for the check by noon that day.

The next day, Sammy writes a check for $5,000 on his account at Solvent State Bank ("SSB"), payable to Muscle. Shortly before noon, Sammy answers his doorbell to find a very large, sinister-looking gentleman on his porch. Fearing physical reprisals, Sammy thrusts the check into the man's hands, tells him to convey his apologies to Muscle, and bolts his door. The gentleman is in fact a building inspector, but he accepts the check, indorses it with Muscle's name, and deposits it in his own account at Reliable National Bank ("RNB"), which was $5,000 overdrawn. RNB credits the inspector's account, stamps its indorsement on the check, and sends it to SSB, which promptly pays the check.

One month later, Muscle arrives at Sammy's door and angrily insists that the $5,000 debt be paid immediately. Sammy shows Muscle the canceled check, but Muscle says that the signature is not his and that his messenger was ill on the day in question. Sammy reports the matter (including the mistaken delivery) to SSB and asks that his account be recredited with the $5,000. SSB does so, then sues RNB.

Does SSB have good causes of action against RNB?

Question VIII

Dizzy Dancer writes a check for $2,000 on his account with Rock Solid Bank ("RSB"), payable to Dizzy's creditor, Hilda Holiday. Hilda deposits the check in her account at Able National Bank ("ANB"), which presents the check through the usual collection channels to RSB on Monday, April 6, at 3 p.m. RSB has a 2 p.m. cutoff hour, technically ending its banking day at that time. On the morning of Friday, April 10, RSB discovers that Dancer has overdrawn his account, stamps the check "Drawn Against Insufficient Funds," and returns it to ANB. When ANB receives the check, Holiday has already withdrawn most of the $2,000 from her account at ANB.

What course of action can ANB pursue in this situation? Discuss.

Question IX

Max borrows $1,000 from his uncle, depositing $500 in his account with Octopus National Bank ("ONB") and $500 in his account with Antitrust State Bank ("ASB"). Max then writes a $500 check on each account payable to "Harvey Noone," a nonexistent person.

Max takes the first check (drawn on ONB) to Gullible Hardware, where he purchases considerable merchandise, and takes the balance of the $500 check in cash after indorsing it as "Harvey Noone." Gullible, which requested no identification from Max, stamps the check with its name and presents it to ONB on the following day. ONB promptly pays Gullible $500, which Gullible deposits in its own account at ONB.

Meanwhile, Max takes the second check (drawn on ASB) to Ralph's Haberdashery, where he again negotiates the check for merchandise and cash. Ralph likewise fails to request identification, but asks that Max indorse the check to him (Ralph Smith). Max obligingly writes, "Pay to Ralph Smith /signed/ Harvey Noone." That night a thief steals the check from Ralph's cash box, subsequently indorses it "Ralph Smith," and cashes it at ASB.

Two weeks later, Max receives his canceled checks and immediately informs both banks that the "Harvey Noone" signatures are forgeries. Max also claims to each bank that he was forced to pay the real Harvey Noone $500 cash when Noone did not receive the original check and demands that the bank replace $500 in his account. Upon Max's return of the checks, each bank credits his account with $500, which Max then uses to repay the loan from his uncle. Neither bank is aware of Max's dealings with the other, and neither investigates the accuracy of Max's statements concerning the checks.

A. Does ONB have an action against Gullible Hardware? Discuss.

B. What rights do ASB and Ralph Smith have with respect to Max's second check? Discuss.

Question X

Douglas Debtor borrows $4,000 from Nightflyer Loan Company ("NLC") and signs the following note:

> I hereby promise to pay $4,000 plus 10% per annum interest to the order of Nightflyer Loan Company on December 1, 2008.

> /s/ Douglas Debtor

After Debtor leaves the NLC office, the loan officer cleverly changes the amount shown on the note to $8,000. The note is then sold by NLC at a slight discount to Big Bank, which buys such commercial paper from time to time. Big Bank had no basis for suspecting that the face amount of the note had been changed by an NLC employee.

At maturity, the note is presented to Debtor, who refuses to pay. Big Bank then sues both Debtor and NLC. Can Bank collect from either defendant? Discuss.

Question XI

Mei Ling instructed Octopus National Bank ("ONB") to wire $8,000 from her account to Anastasia's account #12345 at Antitrust National Bank ("ANB") in order to close a business deal. By mistake ONB wired $8,000 to ANB account #12445, which belonged to Nigel. Informed by ANB of the credit to his account Nigel withdrew the money. When the business deal fell through because Anastasia had failed to receive payment, Mei Ling sued both ANB and ONB for $8,000 plus her consequential damages. Who should bear what loss?

Question XII

When Ahmed Jamal became ill and was unable to work he defaulted on his mortgage payments and knew it was only a matter of time before a foreclosure action would be filed. He had taken out the mortgage and signed a promissory note payable to the order of Local State Bank, the lender, when he had originally purchased the house three years ago. The mortgage deed was filed in the local county real estate records. The entity that brought the foreclosure action against Ahmed was not Local State Bank, but Octopus National Bank [ONB] which had acquired the mortgage contract through a series of assignments. ONB attached a copy of the original promissory note to the Complaint it filed, and asserted that the mortgage contract had been assigned to it. The copy of the promissory note shows that there are no indorsements of any kind on the note, which is still payable to the order of Local State Bank. When asked by the judge, ONB says it does not have possession of the original promissory note, and does not know what happened to it, but can prove that the mortgage contract was properly assigned by a series of transfers to it. Should the judge allows the foreclosure to go forward?

ANSWER TO QUESTION I

Rupert's tender of payment to ANB relieves him of liability for future interest on the debt, but it does not excuse his liability on the note. [U.C.C. § 3–603(c)] Normally, accommodation indorsers are entitled to have presentment made to the person primarily liable (here, Al, as maker of the note). However, Al had already dishonored the note by his anticipatory repudiation, and that excuses presentment by ANB. An indorser is never entitled to have presentment made to *himself,* so Rupert's liability under his indorser's obligation was fixed by notice of Al's failure to pay (which he apparently received). [U.C.C. § 3–415]

ANSWER TO QUESTION II

Hector probably has a case for wrongful dishonor. Though many banks *permit* their depositors to draw against uncollected checks, they generally are not required to do so. Under the Expedited Funds Availability Act, when funds must be made available from deposited checks largely depends on the nature of the check, but in any case $100 may be withdrawn on the day after deposit. Funds from government checks, bank checks, certified checks, and the like must be made available in whole on the business day after deposit. Other local checks must be made available for withdrawal by checks to third parties (such as the checks here) within two business days after deposit. Funds from nonlocal checks must be made available for withdrawal no later than five business days after deposit. Here, we are not told the nature of Hector's payroll check, but unless the check was not local, his bank would have to make funds beyond $100 available for withdrawal by checks to third parties on Wednesday, two days after the day of deposit. Therefore, Hector has a case against the bank for wrongful dishonor, and the bank is also liable to him for damages pursuant to § 611 of the Expedited Funds Availability Act.

ANSWER TO QUESTION III

Stretchem would have a good cause of action against RSB for *conversion* because this depositary bank paid checks owned by Stretchem containing his forged indorsement. [U.C.C. § 3–420(a)] However, Stretchem could not sue the patients involved for the medical services he performed. By delivering the checks to him, the patients transferred to Stretchem the risk that his name might be forged by his agents or employees. Hence, Stretchem's only recourse would be to sue RSB.

ANSWER TO QUESTION IV

According to § 3–605(c) of the Uniform Commercial Code, an extension of time given to the accommodated party (Wastrel) without the consent of the sureties and indorsers discharges them to the extent that they can prove loss caused by the extension, and they have the burden of doing so. [*See* U.C.C. § 3–605, Off. Com. 4 (and its illustrations)] If, for example, Wastrel had money at the time of the extension, so that he could have paid the bank then, but now he has no assets and is in bankruptcy, the Browns might escape having to pay some or all of the debt. As a practical matter this argument rarely works because the original promissory note will likely contain a consent to any and all extensions, and this will waive the discharge that would otherwise occur. [U.C.C. § 3–605(i)] The result is the same under the 2002 revision of Article 3. [U.C.C. (2002) § 3–605(b), (h)]

ANSWER TO QUESTION V

John v. Student

Student cannot be held liable to John on the check for two reasons: First, John knew of the auto's defects, so he is subject to a defense of breach of warranty. [U.C.C. § 3–305(a)(2)] Second, the drawer's obligation is discharged by certification of the check. [U.C.C. § 3–414(c)]

John v. CSB

CSB improperly certified Student's check (and debited her account) because a stop order had been placed on the check. Because the check was not "properly payable" once the stop order had been entered, CSB must recredit Student's account. [U.C.C. § 4–401(a)] A bank may not refuse to pay a certified check. [U.C.C. § 3–411] However, CSB has a valid counterclaim against John for breach of John's sales warranties to Student. This cause of action belongs to CSB because, on payment of the check, it was *subrogated* to Student's claims against the payee (John). [U.C.C. § 4–407]

ANSWER TO QUESTION VI

Ace v. Donna

Donna will undoubtedly assert a *personal* defense of failure of consideration on the note because she never received the loan from Warmth. However, this defense will not prevail against Ace if it is an HDC. To establish HDC status, Ace must persuade the trier of fact that neither the soiled condition of the note nor the large discount thereon ($1,500 for a face value of $5,000) gave it *notice* of suspicious circumstances.

Ace v. Martha

Martha will probably plead a *real* defense of fraud in the factum, on the ground that the amount of the note had been misrepresented to her. This defense is not likely to prevail because Martha was careless in protecting herself (*i.e.*, by failing to get her glasses and read what she was signing). At best, Martha has a *personal* defense of fraud, which could not be asserted against an HDC.

Ace v. Dull

Dull appears to have a good defense of real fraud (applicable even against an HDC) because he signed the note without having a proper chance to know that it was a legal instrument. [U.C.C. § 3–305(a)(1)(iii)]

Ace v. Respectable

If Ace loses its suit against Donna, Martha, and Dull, it can sue Respectable on his indorser's obligation. [U.C.C. § 3–415] If Respectable indorsed "without recourse," he has no contract liability, but he would still be liable to Ace for breach of transfer warranties that the instrument was not subject to any defense. Theft of the instrument is such a defense, and because Respectable apparently stole the note, he could not argue lack of knowledge. [U.C.C. § 3–416(a)(4)]

ANSWER TO QUESTION VII

Sammy appears to have been clearly negligent in handing his check to the building inspector, but whether such negligence meets the requirements of U.C.C. § 3–406 is arguable. If Sammy was not negligent, the inspector's forgery of Muscle's name (as payee) means that the check was not properly negotiated to the depositary bank ("RNB"), and that RNB consequently breached its presentment warranty in presenting the check to SSB for payment. [U.C.C. § 4–208(a)] Before SSB can sue on this warranty, however, it must show that it has not been overly generous to Sammy by recrediting his account and thereby waiving the U.C.C. § 3–406 defense of negligence. [U.C.C. § 4–208(c)]

ANSWER TO QUESTION VIII

ANB can sue RSB on the theory that, as payor bank, RSB became "accountable" for Dancer's check when it did not dishonor the item prior to its midnight deadline. [U.C.C. § 4–302] RSB had an established 2 p.m. closure of its banking day, which is permissible under U.C.C. § 4–107(1). As a result, Dancer's check was constructively received by RSB on Tuesday, April 7, and RSB had until midnight of the following banking day (April 8) to dishonor (Regulation CC would extend this until close of business on April 9). At that moment, RSB is deemed to have made final payment on the check. Consequently, its attempts on April 10 to dishonor the check are ineffective. The provisional credit given to Holiday was by then a *final settlement,* which would prevent ANB from charging the check back against her account. [U.C.C. § 4–214(a)]

RSB also violated its Regulation CC warranty of timely return. [Reg. CC § 229.34]

ANSWER TO QUESTION IX

A.   Because the checks written by Max involve a fictitious payee who was intended to have no interest therein, the resulting forgery of a "Harvey Noone" indorsement is effective to negotiate the checks. [U.C.C. § 3–404(b)] As to the first check, therefore, ONB's only action is against Max for fraud in seeking "recredit" of his account. Gullible Hardware breached no presentment warranties in seeking payment from ONB, and is not liable to the bank.

B.   ASB has no action against Ralph Smith on the second check because Smith did not indorse the check (which would create an indorser's obligation) and did not present or transfer it (which would create warranties). Due to Max's special indorsement to Smith, however, Ralph's signature was necessary to negotiation of the instrument. Hence, the thief breached a presentment warranty in forging Smith's signature and cashing the check at ASB, and the bank has a cause of action against the thief for breach of a presentment warranty. [U.C.C. § 4–208(a)(1)]

Ralph has a cause of action against ASB for *conversion* because the bank paid a check belonging to him upon a forged indorsement of his name. [U.C.C. § 3–420(a)]

ANSWER TO QUESTION X

Big Bank has a good cause of action against NLC for breach of its **transfer warranty** that no alteration in the note has occurred. [U.C.C. § 3–416(a)(3)] However, Bank has no action against Debtor because the fraudulent alteration by a holder ("NLC") discharges him as a party whose contract has been changed. [U.C.C. § 3–407(b)]

If Big Bank were an HDC, it could enforce the note for the original amount of $4,000. However, the instrument is not negotiable (in that it lacks order or bearer language), and HDC status is therefore not possible.

ANSWER TO QUESTION XI

ONB will certainly be liable to Mei Ling for $8,000 (the "money-back guarantee" applicable when a receiving bank fails to properly execute a payment order). Article 4A places the loss on the entity that made the mistake. ANB has no liability as long as it did not notice the discrepancy between the name of the beneficiary and the account number on the payment order. [U.C.C. § 4A–207] ONB has a restitution action against Nigel. [U.C.C. § 4A–207(d)]

As for the consequential damages, ONB is also liable for lost interest on the $8,000. [U.C.C. § 4A–204(a)]

ANSWER TO QUESTION XII

The judge should not allow the foreclosure to proceed. Ahmed's obligation as a maker of the note runs to a "person entitled to enforce" [PETE] the instrument. Strangely enough, if ONB had the original promissory note in its possession it would meet this definition in spite of the lack of the payee's indorsement because the *shelter rule* gives the payee's rights to all subsequent possessors of the note (see the definition of PETE in 3–301). But that won't help the bank here because it doesn't have possession of the note. Nor is a copy sufficient. There might be a hundred copies of the note, but a hundred entities would not be allowed to foreclose. Instead Ahmed's obligation runs to whoever possesses the original note. If it cannot be found ONB might use the lost instrument rules of 3–309 to persuade the court to recreate it, but might have trouble with the requirement that it prove it "was entitled to enforce the instrument when loss of possession occurred." In any event, the judge should at least make the bank post bond to protect Ahmed from liability in the event the note does turn up in the hands of some other entity (*see* 3–309(b)). If the judge throws out the foreclosure action on the grounds that ONB doesn't have standing since it isn't the real party in interest, ONB should pass the loss back to whoever sold it the note for breach of the contractual warranty that the assignment was valid.

Review Questions
and Answers

Review Questions

NEGOTIABILITY

1. "I promise to pay John Jones $10,000 on June 1, 2021. /s/ Molly Maker." Is this a negotiable instrument?

2. Brown Fashions is a sole proprietorship owned by Mary Brown. To secure a bank loan for the business, Mary signs a promissory note: "Brown Fashions." Is Mary personally liable on the note?

3. Triton Motor Parts, Inc. is sued on a promissory note signed "Triton Motor Parts, Inc. by Harry Schwartz, Secretary." The corporation pleads as a defense that Schwartz was never authorized to sign the note. At the time of the trial, will it be rebuttably *presumed* that Schwartz had such authority?

4. "I promise to pay to the order of Ajax Auto Sales, Inc. on or before September 15, 2021, *as per terms* of auto purchase contract signed this date (dated and signed)." Is the instrument negotiable?

5. "I promise to pay to the order of Sarah Smith the sum of $10,000 on or before February 15, 2021, *as down payment* on the purchase of my new home (signed)." Is the note negotiable?

6. "I promise to pay to the order of Virginia Washington the sum of $10,000 (signed)." Is the instrument negotiable although *no time for payment* is shown?

7. "I promise to pay to the order of Virginia Washington the sum of $10,000, 30 days after_____ (signed)." Is the instrument negotiable with the *date left blank*?

8. Is a postdated check negotiable before the date shown?

9. A note provides that payment is to be made "within 90 days following the date of this note, *or sooner upon completion* of my new house." Would the note be negotiable?

   a. Assume the note provided that payment was to be made "within 90 days from date hereof, except that if my new house is not finished by that date, time for payment *shall be extended* for five years." Would the note be negotiable?

NEGOTIATION

10. Drawer draws a check "pay to the order of Able *or* Baker." Baker alone indorses the check and cashes it at Bank. Is Bank a "holder" of the check?

11. Drawer draws a check "pay to the order of Able **and** Baker." Able indorses the check and cashes it at Bank, which inadvertently overlooks the fact that Baker's indorsement is **missing.** Is Bank a "holder" of the check? _____

12. Drawer draws a check payable to the order of Don. Don indorses the check, "Pay to Ed **only.**" Ed thereupon indorses the check and delivers it to Frank. Is Frank a "holder" of the check? _____

HOLDERS IN DUE COURSE

13. Al hires Bob to paint his house, and as payment in advance he delivers to Bob a negotiable promissory note for $5,000 (the amount of the painting contract). Bob indorses this note to Supplier as security for payment of a large outstanding balance owed for paint supplied on other projects. Bob later defaults on his painting contract with Al. Can Supplier enforce Al's note? _____

    a. Would the result be the same if Supplier accepted the instrument as security for the paint **to be supplied** for Bob's contract with Al (rather than as security for past balances due)? _____

14. Al executes a one-year negotiable note to Bob, calling for monthly interest payments. Al fails to make any of the interest payments. Bob transfers the note to Charles for value before maturity. Can Charles qualify as an HDC if he is **aware** that Al has not made the interest payments? _____

15. Al executes a one-year negotiable note to Bob, calling for monthly payments of **principal** and interest. Al is in arrears on one payment. Bob transfers the note to Charles for value before maturity. Can Charles qualify as an HDC if he is **aware** that Al is in arrears on one payment? _____

16. Amy gives Betty a check for $1,000. The check is dated. Six months later, Betty transfers the check to Charles for value. Can Charles qualify as an HDC? _____

17. Amy gives Betty a check for $1,000 and dates the check six months hence. On the date the check is due, Betty transfers it to Charles for value. If Charles is aware that the check was postdated, can he qualify as an HDC? _____

18. Maker executes a negotiable promissory note for $5,000 as down payment on the purchase of land from Seller. Seller transfers the note for value before maturity to Hilda, who is aware that the note arises out of a sale which has yet to be consummated. Can Hilda qualify as an HDC? _____

19. Art executes a negotiable promissory note to Bill for $10,000. One day before maturity, Bill sells the note to Clem for $5,000. Based on these facts alone, can Clem qualify as an HDC? _____

    a. Would the result be the same if Bill told Clem there might be "some trouble" with the note and suggested that Clem satisfy himself as to its collectibility, but Clem deliberately chose not to make further inquiry? _____

20. "Once an instrument has come into the hands of an HDC, any subsequent transferee is entitled to enforce it as if he himself were an HDC." True or false? _____

21. Arnold executes a negotiable note to Barb. Before maturity, Barb indorses and delivers the note to Charles. Arnold fails to pay the note when due. Charles brings suit against Arnold and attaches a copy of the note to his complaint. Arnold files an answer that asserts that Barb was guilty of fraud in procuring the note. In this situation, the burden of proof is on Arnold to prove not only Barb's fraud, but also that Charles is not an HDC. True or false? _____

CLAIMS AND DEFENSES ON NEGOTIABLE INSTRUMENTS

22. A real defense can be asserted only against an HDC, whereas personal defenses can be asserted against HDCs or non-HDCs. True or false? _____

23. Junior Jarvis, age 15, signs a promissory note on a stereo system purchased from Loud Sounds, Inc. Loud Sounds subsequently sells the note to Fearless Finance, an HDC. Junior fails to pay the note and is sued by Fearless. Can Junior assert infancy as a defense? _____

24. Edna Elderly signs a promissory note after she has been adjudged incompetent. Harold Holder later sues Elderly for payment of the note. Under state contract law, the note is voidable at the option of Elderly. Does it matter whether Harold is an HDC? _____

25. Sammy Smooth, a door-to-door salesman, tells Horace Homeowner that he will give him a free set of encyclopedias if he will sign a "letter of indorsement" for the books to be used in an advertising campaign. Horace signs the "letter," which is in fact a promissory note for $600 in payment for the encyclopedias. Smooth sells the note to Susan Saintly, an HDC. Horace learns the true nature of the document when Susan sues him on the note. May Horace assert fraud as a defense? _____

26. Wilbur acquires a promissory note on which his friend Orville is listed as a prior indorser. Orville asks Wilbur if he will agree not to sue him on the note "for old times' sake," whereupon Wilbur draws a line through Orville's name. Wilbur then sells the note to Lindberg, an HDC. Does Orville have a defense if Lindberg sues him on the note? _____

    a. Suppose instead that Orville gives Wilbur $50 in return for a signed agreement discharging Orville's liability on the note. Can this be asserted as a defense against Lindberg if he sues Orville on the note? _____

27. Forgery of any signature on a negotiable instrument will prevent any subsequent taker from being an HDC. True or false? _____

28. Only where the instrument in question was obtained by theft may the "jus tertii" of a third person be raised as a defense. True or false? _____

LIABILITY OF THE PARTIES

29. Albert purchases a painting from Ralph for $2,000, paying for it with a personal check for $500 and a promissory note on the balance due 60 days in the future. Ralph tries to cash the check, but it bounces. May Ralph sue immediately for the full amount due on the painting? _____

30. Ed owes Ivy College $2,500 for monies borrowed on his tuition. When this loan is due, he pays Reliable State Bank $2,500 and obtains a certified check payable to Ivy College. When Ivy attempts to cash the check, it is dishonored. May Ivy sue Ed on the $2,500 debt? _____

    a. Would the result be different if the certified check were payable to Ed but indorsed over to the College? _____

31. Betty obtains a loan of $200 from Gouge Finance Company and signs a note calling for repayment of the principal in 90 days plus interest in an amount left blank. Gouge later fills in "10%" in this blank space. Is Betty obligated to pay this interest? _____

32. Wilbur gives Orville a check in payment of a debt, which Orville indorses to Amelia to pay for a pair of skis. When Amelia attempts to cash the check, it is dishonored by Wilbur's bank. Can Amelia sue Orville on the check? _____

33. Zelda executes a promissory note that is indorsed in turn by Alex, Bess, and Carl. Carl conveys the note to Diane, who presents it to Zelda for payment at maturity. If Zelda dishonors the note, may Diane recover the full amount of the note from Bess? _____

34. The common law rights previously afforded to sureties on negotiable instruments have been superseded by the U.C.C. True or false? _____

35. An accommodation maker of a note has greater rights than the maker of the note. True or false? _____

36. Although a surety is usually not liable to her principal, liability exists if the surety signs the instrument prior to the principal. True or false? _____

37. Susan borrows $5,000 from Able Finance Company, signing a promissory note and giving Able an original Picasso sketch as collateral. Susan's cousin Bert cosigns the note as accommodation maker. Shortly thereafter, the sketch is destroyed by a fire at Able. Is Bert discharged on any portion of the note? _____

    a. Suppose instead that Able has the sketch appraised and it is found to be a reproduction. Would the result be the same? _____

38. Richard's promissory note to Large Bank has been cosigned by Bill and matures on October 1. At maturity, Richard asks for and receives a 30-day extension to pay on the note. Bank makes no reference to Bill in the extension. Is Bill discharged from liability on the note? _____

39. If a surety has guaranteed collection of a negotiable instrument, the holder may seek payment directly from the surety without first pursuing the maker or acceptor. True or false? _____

40. The "midnight deadline" rule requires action by midnight on the day the item is acquired. True or false? _____

41. The period within which notice of dishonor must be given varies between banks and nonbanks. True or false? _____

42. Protest is rarely used in cases other than drafts drawn or payable outside the United States, its territories, or possessions. True or false? _____

43. Indira sends a check to Big Oil Company to pay her gasoline credit card bill. The check is lost in the mail and does not reach Big Oil for eight months, at which time it is presented to Indira's bank for payment. May the bank dishonor the check? _____

44. While some circumstances may extend the time within which banks are required to give notice of dishonor, only a waiver can excuse compliance altogether. True or false? _____

45. Eunice is the drawee on a draft for the sale of widgets to her by Edgar. When the holder, Big Bank, presents the draft to her, Eunice refuses to accept unless the time period specified is changed from 30 to 60 days. May Big Bank proceed against prior indorsers on the draft? _____

    a. Suppose Big Bank agrees to the change. When the draft is presented in 60 days, Eunice refuses to accept. May Big Bank proceed against Edgar? _____

46. Big Bank is the drawee on a check drawn by Jeff. The holder of the check fails to present it to the bank for one year. Is Jeff discharged on the check? _____

47. Smith signs a promissory note with the name "William Jones," telling the payee, Brown, that he is Jones's agent. In fact, Smith was not authorized to act for Jones. Does Brown have any recourse on the note? _____

    a. Suppose Smith was in fact authorized to sign for Jones, and signs the note "R. Smith" after informing Brown that Jones is his principal. Jones subsequently declares bankruptcy. Does Brown have any recourse against Smith on the note? _____

48. If the transferor of a negotiable instrument has received consideration, all later transferees are covered by the transfer warranties provided in U.C.C. Article 3. True or false? _____

49. Elton loses a blank check, which is discovered by John. John fills out the check for $200 payable to his friend Bernie, signing Elton's name. Bernie indorses the check and deposits it at Reliable State Bank, which in turn presents it to Drawee Bank for collection. Does Drawee have a warranty action against Reliable if Drawee pays on the check? _____

50. The payor on a negotiable instrument has an action for breach of presentment warranties, but only against the party who physically receives payment or acceptance. True or false? _____

51. U.C.C. Article 3 governs actions for conversion of negotiable instruments and preempts common law actions on this ground. True or false? _____

52. Able writes a check for $1,000 to Baker. Baker indorses the check "For deposit only" and signs his name. The check is then stolen by Charlie, who indorses it and deposits it in his bank, which forwards it to Abie's bank for payment. Is Abie's bank liable for conversion if it pays the check? _____

      a.   Is Charlie's bank liable for conversion?   _____

53. Will writes a check payable to Zoey. The check is stolen from Zoey by Xavier, who forges Zoey's indorsement and cashes the check at Your Town Bank. Your Town presents the check to Valley Bank, the drawer's bank, for collection. If Valley pays on the check, can Zoey successfully sue Valley for conversion?   _____

BANK DEPOSITS AND COLLECTIONS

54. In cases of wrongful dishonor, the drawer must prove actual damages in order to recover against the defendant bank. True or false?   _____

55. Marco purchases a cashier's check from City Bank made payable to Sean as a down payment on a car. Marco finds the car defective and rescinds the sale, giving notice to City Bank before the cashier's check is presented for payment. Can Sean enforce payment?   _____

56. Willard gives a check to Steven, who cashes it at his bank. Steven's bank presents it to Willard's bank, which pays it in spite of a stop payment order Willard gave his bank before the presentment. Must Willar's bank recredit Willard's account?   _____

57. Sarah deposits a $100 check payable to her in her account at Big Bank. The check is drawn on Little Bank, located in the same city. If the item is not dishonored by Little Bank, is Sarah entitled to draw on the amount deposited on the banking day after deposit?   _____

58. Once final payment occurs, the payor bank is accountable for the amount of the check in question and has no recourse in its liability on the instrument. True or false?   _____

FORGERY OR ALTERATION OF NEGOTIABLE INSTRUMENTS

59. Fred Fleece stops Melissa Malleable on the street and tells her that he is the Guru Mundi, an eminent spiritualist collecting funds for a meditation center in New Mexico. Melissa gives Fred a check for $10, which Fred "indorses" with Mundi's name and subsequently uses to purchase wine at Larry's Liquors. Larry's cashes the check at Melissa's bank. Does Melissa have recourse against the bank for payment on a forged instrument?   _____

      a.   Would the result be the same if Fred had called Melissa and induced her to send the check by mail?   _____

      b.   Would the result be the same if Fred had lost the check and it was subsequently picked up and "indorsed" with Mundi's name by Chuck Cheatem?   _____

      c.   Does Melissa have any recourse against Larry's Liquors on the check if she can show lack of due care in checking Fred's identity?   _____

60. Under the "negligence rule," lack of due care by a person that substantially contributes to a forgery or alteration estops that person from asserting the forgery or alteration against any later transferee. True or false?   _____

61. Reliable State Bank sends Herbert his monthly statement, enclosing canceled checks paid on Herbert's account. One of the checks has been altered to increase the amount from $100 to $1,000. Herbert scans the checks, fails to catch this alteration, and files the statement away. Six months later, Herbert balances his checkbook and discovers the alteration. Is he entitled to a $900 credit to his account at Reliable? _____

    a. Would the result be different if the alteration consisted of a line through the original amount and the insertion of "$1,000" above the line? _____

62. Unauthorized completion of a note with blanks left by the original parties is an alteration and prevents enforcement of the note as completed. True or false? _____

ELECTRONIC BANKING

63. At the end of each day, Big Department Store orders its bank to withdraw electronically all of the day's deposits from the accounts its branch stores maintain throughout the country. Article 4A applies to these wire transfers. True or false? _____

64. A computer hacker broke the security code between Big Department Store and its bank and transferred $2 million to the account of the hacker. Big Department Store may require its bank to recredit the account. True or false? _____

65. Bahar signed an agreement telling her bank to pay her mortgage automatically each month. One month she phoned the bank one week before the date of transfer and told the bank not to make the payment. The bank may ignore her request because it is not in writing. True or false? _____

66. Robert's debit card was stolen from him by a thief. Because Robert had written his PIN on the card, the thief was able to take $200 from an ATM on the day of the theft. That evening Robert realized the card was gone and phoned his bank to tell it so. The next day the thief withdrew another $200. Robert is responsible for all of these withdrawals. True or false? _____

67. Fatima lost her credit card when her purse was snatched at a mall. She failed to notify the credit card issuer that it had been stolen, and the thief used the card to make charges of $3385 before the credit card issuer became aware of the problem and took the necessary steps to cancel the card. Fatima is liable for this amount. True or false? _____

Answers to Review Questions

1.	**NO**	It lacks words of negotiability. [p. 9, p. 17]
2.	**YES**	Use of a trade name by a sole proprietor binds the proprietor as if her own name had been signed. [p. 9]
3.	**YES**	The form of signature is sufficient to raise the presumption. [p. 10]
4.	**YES**	"As per" merely identifies transaction out of which instrument arises, and does not condition promise to pay. [p. 11]
5.	**YES**	Designation of the transaction or account to be credited with the payment does not condition the promise to pay. [p. 11]
6.	**YES**	It will be deemed payable on demand. [p. 15, p. 17]
7.	**NO**	If the date is left off the instrument and its maturity depends on a date being stated, the instrument is not enforceable until the date is filled in by someone with authority to do so. [p. 16]
8.	**YES**	Postdating does not affect its negotiability. [p. 17]
9.	**YES**	Acceleration clauses do not affect negotiability. [p. 16]
a.	**YES**	This extension clause does not affect negotiability because the time is certain. [p. 17]
10.	**YES**	An instrument drawn payable to either of several payees can be indorsed by any one of them. Indorsement and delivery constitute negotiation, so as to make Bank a "holder." [p. 29]
11.	**NO**	The restrictive indorsement ("pay to Ed *only*") did not affect the negotiability of the instrument. Ed's signature was a general indorsement and converted the check to bearer paper. Hence delivery to Frank made him a "holder." [p. 32, p. 34]
12.	**YES**	The interest attachés when "value" is given, and the commitment to make the loan is "value" under the U.C.C. [p. 42]
13.	**YES**	Supplier qualifies as an HDC and therefore cuts off personal defenses (default by Bob). Supplier has taken for "value" (as security for antecedent debt). The fact that the *instrument* was given for an executory promise is immaterial (*i.e.*, executory consideration is good consideration, even though it is not "value" for purposes of being an HDC). [p. 40]
a.	**NO**	Because here Supplier would be giving *executory* consideration, and that is *not* "value" for HDC purposes. [p. 40]
14.	**YES**	Knowledge of default in payment of *interest* does not defeat HDC status. [p. 44]

15. **NO**   Knowledge of default on *any* part of *principal* prevents HDC status. [p. 44]

16. **NO**   Checks become overdue 90 days after their date, and this would prevent HDC status. [p. 45]

17. **YES**   Mere knowledge that an instrument has been postdated is not enough to defeat HDC status. [p. 17]

18. **YES**   Knowledge that an instrument arises out of an executory agreement does *not* affect HDC status (unless there is knowledge of its breach). [pp. 45–51]

19. **PROBABLY**   Mere size of discount does not constitute notice of a defense to an instrument, although some courts have indicated that a very large discount might indicate bad faith. [p. 50]

a. **PROBABLY NOT**   This would appear to be a *purposeful* failure to make inquiry, constituting *bad* faith. [p. 46]

20. **FALSE**   While the statement is generally true, it is subject to an exception: A person who was a party to fraud or illegality affecting the instrument cannot become an HDC in this manner. [p. 54]

21. **FALSE**   Arnold need only prove his defense against Barb; the burden then shifts to Charles to prove his status as an HDC. [p. 55, p. 56]

22. **FALSE**   A real defense may be asserted against both HDCs and non-HDCs, but a personal defense can be asserted *only* against a non-HDC. [p. 60]

23. **DEPENDS**   If state law makes the contracts of infants either void or voidable, infancy is a real defense assertable against the HDC, Fearless. [p. 61]

24. **YES**   Where the contract of an incompetent is merely voidable (rather than void), incompetency is a *personal* defense and cannot be asserted against an HDC. [p. 61]

25. **NO**   Only fraud in the factum can be asserted against an HDC. Here, even though Horace did not realize he was signing a negotiable instrument, there is no fraud in the factum unless he had no reasonable opportunity to read the note or understand it. [p. 62]

26. **YES**   Wilbur's action in drawing a line through Orville's name created a discharge on the face of the instrument, and Orville thus has a real defense assertable against Lindberg. [p. 64]

a. **DEPENDS**   Unless the discharge of a prior party is apparent from the face of the instrument, or the HDC knows of the discharge, discharge is a *personal* defense and therefore not assertable against an HDC. [p. 65]

27. **FALSE**   If the forgery concerns a name not necessary to negotiation—*i.e.*, anyone other than the payee or a special indorsee—HDC status is still possible. However, the forgery may be a *real defense* assertable against the HDC by the person whose name is forged. [p. 66]

28. FALSE   Violation of a restrictive indorsement is likewise a permissible defense, even though a jus tertii. [p. 69]

29. NO   Under the merger rule, Ralph cannot sue on the part of the obligation represented by the promissory note until the instrument is presented for payment and dishonored. However, he *can* sue Albert on the $500 portion represented by the bad check. [p. 73]

30. NO   The certified check made Reliable State Bank the party liable thereon, and canceled Ed's underlying obligation to the college. Ivy must seek recourse against the bank. [p. 73]

a. YES   Here, Ed's indorsement gives Ivy a suit against him *on* the instrument. [p. 73, p. 78]

31. YES   Because she signed the incomplete note, Betty has an obligation as maker to pay interest at the rate subsequently filled in by Gouge, although she would have a personal defense against Gouge if 10% was not the agreed-upon rate. [p. 75, p. 144]

32. DEPENDS   If Orville merely indorsed the check with his signature, Amelia can sue him on his indorser's obligation. But if Orville added the words "without recourse," Amelia could not proceed against him. [p. 78]

33. YES   As holder, Diane may sue *any* prior indorser for the full amount of the note, since each is jointly and severally liable thereon unless they signed as part of the same transaction, in which case they are co-sureties, liable pro rata to each other. [p. 78]

34. FALSE   While certain of these rights (*e.g.*, reimbursement) have been codified by the U.C.C., the surety still enjoys various common law rights. [p. 79]

35. TRUE   The accommodation maker (surety) has the rights of a maker *plus* the special U.C.C. and common law rights of surety. [p. 80]

36. FALSE   A surety is not liable to the principal (and may enforce the right to reimbursement) regardless of the order in which the instrument is signed. [p. 81]

37. DEPENDS   If the fire were attributable to carelessness or negligence on the part of Able, Bert (along with Susan) would be discharged on the note up to the value of the sketch. [p. 82]

a. NO   Although there is a loss in value of the collateral, it is not due to lack of care by Able. Hence Bert remains fully liable on the note. [p. 82]

38. NO   There is no discharge by a nonprejudicial extension, and Bill has the burden of showing prejudice. [p. 83]

39. FALSE   Where a surety guarantees collection (as opposed to payment), the holder must first pursue the maker to an unsatisfied judgment or show that this would be a useless act. [p. 85]

40. FALSE	Action is required by midnight on the banking day *after* the first banking day. [p. 88]	
41. TRUE	Banks must give notice before their midnight deadlines, while nonbanks have 30 days after dishonor (or receipt of notice) within which to act. [p. 89]	
42. FALSE	While protest is never required, it is still frequently used in other situations as presumptive evidence of dishonor. [p. 90]	
43. YES	A check presented more than six months after its date is considered "stale" and may be dishonored by the drawee bank. (The bank may also pay the check, if it acts in good faith.) [p. 90]	
44. FALSE	Impossibility and prior dishonor (among other circumstances) will completely excuse this procedural requirement. [pp. 93–94]	
45. YES	An acceptance conditioned upon an alteration in the terms of a draft may be treated by the holder as a dishonor, and, after giving notice of dishonor, it may proceed against prior parties. [p. 96]	
a. PROBABLY NOT	Unless Edgar consented to the modification in time period, he was discharged by the bank's prior agreement to that change. [p. 96]	
46. DEPENDS	Jeff (as drawer) is discharged only if the bank became insolvent during the delay in presentment. [p. 87, p. 90]	
47. YES	Brown can treat the signature as Smith's own and proceed against him as maker of the note. And, if Jones accepted the benefits of the note or otherwise acted to *ratify* the signature, Brown may proceed against Jones. [p. 98]	
a. NO	Smith has no liability as long as an HDC did not hold the note. [p. 100]	
48. FALSE	Subsequent transferees are covered by the Article 3 warranties only if the transferor *indorses* the instrument. [p. 102]	
49. NO	Reliable was a person entitled to enforce *John's* check, so the first presentment warranty is not breached. Thus, unless Reliable had knowledge that Elton's signature had been forged, Drawee has no warranty action. [p. 104]	
50. FALSE	The payor can sue anyone in the chain of transfer for breach because each such party is deemed to make the presentment warranties. [p. 105]	
51. FALSE	Article 3 generally preserves the common law of conversion. [p. 108]	
52. NO	Abie's bank (the *second* bank to see the check) is entitled to rely on the presumption that the restrictive indorsement has been complied with. [p. 108]	
a. YES	The *first* bank to which an item is transferred for collection is required to comply with a restrictive indorsement. [p. 108]	

53. YES Wrongful taking of a check constitutes conversion. Because Xavier's signature was ineffective, Valley Bank took the instrument wrongfully. As payee, Zoey would be a proper plaintiff in such an action for conversion. [p. 109]

54. TRUE Actual damages must be shown; where the dishonor is outrageous, some courts also allow punitive damages. [p. 113]

55. YES Payment cannot be stopped on a cashier's check. [p. 116]

56. NO Steven's bank, having given value for the check, is an HDC and if Willard's bank had dishonored the check (as it should have) Steven's bank could have enforced the check against Willard (assuming he does not have any real defenses) whose drawer's obligation runs to a holder of the check like Steven's bank. Willard's bank is *subrogated* to the HDC rights of Steven's bank and obtains its ability to ignore Willard's defenses. [p. 117]

57. YES Under the Expedited Funds Availability Act, $100 of the proceeds from deposited checks must be made available for withdrawal on the business day after the day of deposit. [p. 119]

58. TRUE The bank is accountable; but even after final payment it can recover the amount paid *off* the instrument if there is a showing of bad faith by the presenter or breach of presentment warranties. [p. 127]

59. PROBABLY NOT Melissa probably failed to exercise reasonable care to ascertain Fred's true identity. Under the "impostor rule," Fred's subsequent forgery is sufficient for negotiation to Larry's Liquors. Hence, the check was properly payable when presented to the bank. [p. 137]

a. YES Under the U.C.C., "face to face" dealings between the impostor and the drawer are not required. [p. 137]

b. YES The identity of the actual forger is irrelevant. [p. 137]

c. YES Where later parties are negligent, the Code uses comparative fault to resolve the problem. [p. 139]

60. DEPENDS If the later party failed to observe ordinary care, comparative fault principles will allocate the loss between them. [p. 141]

61. DEPENDS Herbert's negligence in failing to report the alteration within a reasonable time will result in an estoppel to claim that the altered check was not "properly payable" if the bank can establish that the delay caused it damages over and above the original mistaken payment (*i.e.*, it could have recovered the money from the wrongdoer but for the delay). [p. 142]

a. YES Here, the bank's negligence in failing to observe and check on an obvious alteration means that it has not observed ordinary care, and comparative fault principles will allocate the loss between the parties. [p. 143]

62. FALSE   It is an alteration, but both HDCs and the drawee/payor bank can enforce the note as completed. [p. 145]

63. FALSE   Big Department Store is not giving a payment order because it is the *payee*. [pp. 150–151]

64. TRUE   As long as the customer was in no way negligent in allowing the security procedure to be breached, the bank must bear the burden of recovering from the hacker. [p. 159]

65. FALSE   The Electronic Fund Transfer Act permits oral stop payment orders on preauthorized EFTs. [p. 160]

66. FALSE   Robert's negligence is irrelevant, and federal law makes him responsible for only $50 of the $200 withdrawn before his phone call and for none of the money withdrawn thereafter. [p. 163, p. 164]

67. FALSE   Fatima's maximum liability for unauthorized use of her credit card is no more than $50 per card, so that is her only exposure here. [pp. 166–168]

Table of Cases

Index